LEVERAGE YOUR LANGUAGE SERIES...

ITALIAN FLUENCY

TWIN WORDS
and
ESSENTIAL VOCABULARY

SUSAN ELIZABETH NUS

TO MOM AND DAD,
ALWAYS

A PAOLO,
AMORE MIO

CONTENTS

PART TWO – COGNATES,
THE "TWIN WORDS" OF LANGUAGE

COGNATES THROUGH GRAMMAR

PART TWO - CONTINUED

COGNATES THROUGH CATEGORIES

FALSE COGNATES – FALSE FRIENDS

PART THREE
ESSENTIAL VOCABULARY

THE THOUSAND ESSENTIAL ITALIAN VOCABULARY WORDS

INTRODUCTION

If you want to significantly improve your Italian, *Italian Fluency* will take you there. This unique book works on three levels.

First, *Italian Fluency* provides both the budding and seasoned linguist with a wealth of practical, everyday information on how to immerse yourself in the language, even if you can't get to Italy any time soon. The various aspects of the four modalities *(reading, writing, listening and speaking)* are explored. The Resources section in the back of the book provides a wealth of interesting ideas and practical methods, enabling you to dive into Italian and take off, wherever you are.

Second, *Italian Fluency* will show you thousands of words that you already know in English, but in Italian form. If you want to improve your Italian through vocabulary expansion, you'll be amazed at how many *cognates, or twin words,* exist between these two languages, and often, how very closely the Italian words resemble their English counterparts. These words are your springboard to fluency. You actually have a variation of thousands of Italian words in your head, and this book will show you those words clearly in Italian and English format. You'll find *Italian Fluency* to be a *treasure* of accessible Italian vocabulary. Many common, predictable spelling and suffix changes exist between Italian and English. Once you understand these ongoing differences between the two languages, vocabulary will multiply, comprehension will soar (both reading and auditory) and whole aspects of the language will open up to you.

Third, *Italian Fluency* will show you the most frequently used words in Italian. In order to speak this crazy, magically beautiful language, a facility with approximately one thousand words is key. Many of these words are cognates, however... many are not. You'll find hundreds of inspirational thoughts, proverbs, pithy quotes and zingers filled with wisdom, wit and humor to help you learn Italian. Sentences filled with high frequency vocabulary, used in context, assist in clarifying key vocabulary essential for fluent speech.

This is a companion book for the Italian learner who wants to focus on vocabulary expansion. There are dozens of "how to" Italian language grammar books on the shelves, and this is not one of them. This collection of accessible twin words and essential vocabulary, with its strong emphasis on vocabulary building, will complement your grammar study. With it you can unlock your language skills and bring this gorgeous language to life, by learning a multitude of words "that you knew, but didn't know you knew."

PART ONE

GOING FOR FLUENCY

IF YOU REALLY WANT TO LEARN ITALIAN...

AUTHOR'S NOTE...

The Italian language is considered by many to be the world's most beautiful language. "Distinctive, classy, rich, zesty, lusty and musical..." All these words have been used to describe this particular Romance language; the language of music, art, culture, food, fashion and love. If you're serious about learning Italian, approach it as a wonderful, lifelong pursuit. Your linguistic effort is well worth your time; it will benefit your travel exponentially. And for those interested in brain stimulation, studying a foreign language is an intellectual adventure, aiding significantly in brain health and quality-of-life issues:

> "Being bilingual, it turns out, makes you smarter. It can have a profound effect on your brain, improving cognitive skills not related to language and even shielding against dementia in old age... It forces the brain to resolve internal conflict, giving the mind a workout that strengthens its cognitive muscles... In a recent study, scientists found that individuals with a higher degree of bilingualism... were more resistant than others to the onset of dementia and other symptoms of Alzheimer's disease: the higher the degree of bilingualism, the later the age of onset."

And as for travel, needless to say, your trips to Italy will be richly blessed as a result of your efforts. Language skills can turn a trip into an adventure. If you yearn to experience the awe of true discovery, language ability is your key to a superior travel experience, (not to mention a really fun time...) You'll have the distinct advantage of being able to travel to the Motherland and visit those incredible, obscure medieval hill towns and rural areas where not a soul speaks English. Traveling off-the-beaten-path is perhaps the most exhilarating kind of travel, and all the more exciting and satisfying when you know the language. You can go where others fear to tread.

Italy is one of the *prime* global destination spots. Why? Italy is absolutely dripping with culture, even by European standards. Italy's got something for everyone, whether your interests are the most prestigious art or fashion on the planet, a breathtaking diversity of intense natural beauty or Italy's everyday *gioia di vivere/joie de vivre/joy of life* that no culture seems to top. It's the birthplace of the Renaissance... no small cultural blip. It's an utterly spectacular country with legendary cuisine, some of the best wine on the planet, a wildly disproportionate amount of quality art and architecture, jaw-dropping landscapes, tremendous geographical diversity and beauty, fantastic people, and, oh... a gorgeous language!

1. Yudhijit Bhattacharjee, Why Bilinguals are Smarter, The New York Times, Sunday Review, March 25, 2012

WAYS TO IMPROVE
YOUR ITALIAN

FUN ACTIVITIES

In order to become fluent, finding language activities that you enjoy is *essential*. Once you find these, you may be hooked for life. You will be successful with languages if you make learning the language your hobby, if you are motivated and if it's *FUN*. Reading in Italian (whether it's surfing Italian websites, reading newspapers online, Wikipedia, or the latest John Grisham translation) is a blast. Relying solely on your textbook probably won't cut it… textbooks have their place, but once you reach a critical mass of Italian grammar and vocabulary, it's time to move on to more authentic and engaging materials, (referring to your textbook as necessary, of course.) You could enjoy yourself more by reading your favorite author, who is probably translated into Italian. And in so doing, you'll be reinforcing both grammar and vocabulary. Love Michael Crichton? His entire body of work is translated into Italian and is reasonably easy reading if you have a decent knowledge of Italian and have already read the book in English.

THE INTERNET

The internet has opened up countless dimensions to language learning, including endless websites, blogs, YouTube, Wikipedia, etc. Melissa Muldoon, an American and unabashed Italophile, writes in her blog called "Diario di una Studentessa Matta:"

> "I do not live in Italy. I live 6,000 miles away in California. But I travel to Italy EVERYDAY simply by logging onto my favorite Italian blogs, websites and Facebook pages. There are so many amazing resources enabling me to connect with Italy. Through Twitter I exchange tweets with Italians in real time and on sites like LiveMocha, Impariamo, Skype & Facebook I can chat with friends, share photos, stay informed of current events and know and understand the country better. By using the internet I have found ways to stay connected to the country 24-7!"

DON'T STRESS ABOUT GRAMMAR

A major factor that enhances language learning is *not* worrying too much about grammatical correctness; you *will* make mistakes, just accept it, it's part of the process. This is a key point that can make or break a successful linguist. Some people just can't get the words out because of fear of mistakes, while others just glide along, and in so doing become fluent, improving steadily as they continue practicing, speaking and enjoying the language.

STEP INTO ANOTHER PERSONA

There's something to be said for being a bit of a mimic, "ham" or actor with the language. When you speak another language, notice how you slip into another persona, and it's *fun*. When speaking Italian, you may feel a bit more elegant, sophisticated and worldly. It definitely has parallels to acting. Italian has a theatrical, over-the-top quality that lends itself to this transformation, which in turn may make you a more convincing speaker. If you're willing to lose yourself a little bit to the language, and imitate the way Italians use their consonants, vowels, voice, tone, intonation and body gestures, you'll be a more successful speaker.

BE PATIENT WITH YOURSELF

A substantial aspect of learning a language is simply a matter of *exposure, exposure, exposure* to the four modalities (reading, writing, listening and speaking.) Find and stick with the different methods that are most enjoyable for you. The longer you stick with it, the easier, and more natural and gratifying the language will become. Modalities aside, nuts and bolts, when learning a foreign language, students initially need to study both grammar and vocabulary. With a basic knowledge, you can then take off into your favorite areas of interest to improve vocabulary, conversation and better language ability.

FIND YOUR MODALITY

In learning a language, it's instrumental to know that there are four "modalities," or methods of language acquisition. The more you do each of these daily, the faster the language will come together for you. These modalities are further developed in the following four sections (pgs. 20-28) and in the Resources section (pgs. 336-346.) The four modalities are:

READING
WRITING
LISTENING
SPEAKING

READING

If you enjoy reading Italian and are a visual learner, there are endless resources with today's books, internet, smartphone/tablet apps and more. You can read Italian newspapers online, pull up Wikipedia in Italian or google anything of interest that you'd normally research in English.

WRITING

A certain amount of writing is extremely helpful, particularly in learning your verbs. Even if you're not a kinesthetic learner, you'll benefit from the hand-brain connection. Realize that all those high frequency, irregular verbs that you need to get a handle on (*essere, avere, fare, andare, dovere, potere, volere*) are *essential* if you want to speak fluently. These verbs will gel much faster in your brain if you write them and test yourself, as this kinesthetic exercise helps to "cement" vocabulary in your brain. To optimize this activity, say the verbs aloud as you write. In this way, you are using three modalities simultaneously, which enhances the learning and memorization process.

LISTENING

If you enjoy learning through listening and are an auditory learner, listen to Italian language CDs, podcasts, radio or watch YouTube, Italian movies, news, cooking shows, sitcoms or the soaps. As you get more sophisticated, there are hundreds of Italian radio stations that you can listen to that cover a huge variety of topics including travel, culture, politics, religion, etc. Sources for listening and watching Italian are discussed in the Resources section in the back of the book.

SPEAKING

Also practice speaking to the extent that you can. If you live in the United States, you may find speaking opportunities to be the most elusive. Search out Continuing Education classes, Italian language groups, University Language Conversation tables, hire a tutor, get a Skype Language Pal, and when traveling, check out Italian neighborhoods (New York, Boston, Philadelphia, Chicago, Cleveland, and San Diego for starters.)

***

With practice, you'll identify your best modality. If you learn best through reading, capitalize on reading. If you enjoy one modality more than the others, you'll learn best through that modality. And while it's fine to concentrate on that particular learning method, don't forsake the others completely; they're all important. The practice of the four modalities will help synthesize the language for you.

You may wonder how or if you can manage to work these modalities into your life. I live in Texas, and despite the dramatic cultural expanse between Italy and Texas, given today's technology, I use Italian throughout the day. Every day I *read* Italian newspapers and do research online through Wikipedia and search engines. I *listen* to Italian music, podcasts, RAI radio and RAI TV. I *write* emails and text friends in Italian. And Skype makes it easy to *speak* with friends.

Concentrate on your favorite modality to absorb this beautiful language. The more you study and enjoy Italian, the sooner it will come together.

READING

You know what they say about real estate? It's a matter of *location, location, location*. Well, languages are a matter of *exposure, exposure, exposure*. And reading Italian on a daily basis is perhaps the most powerful and accessible way to initially get that exposure to ultimately make the language come together for you.   Reading helps tremendously to coalesce the language because you'll constantly and repetitively be reinforcing grammar and vocabulary. Reading books and articles is a natural and comprehensive method of absorbing grammar and vocabulary; it's a more organic (and fun) way of acquiring the language than through a text book; you'll be learning language through context. Reading in Italian is not hard if you choose reading materials well.

READ WIKIPEDIA

This free internet encyclopedia is one of the coolest resources for language development. Wikipedia has articles in English, Italian and several dozen other languages. Choose any topic of interest, read the English first if necessary for subject-matter orientation, and then read the same topic in Italian. You'll be oriented, and much of the information will make sense to you. (Be aware that the English vs. Italian articles may be compiled differently, depending on the topic, and are not strict translations, but separate articles.)

This point is key: read articles on whatever intrigues you. Wikipedia has thousands of articles on virtually anything you find engrossing: history, current events, the arts and sciences or some wacky media personality. Reading interesting articles consistently in Italian will consolidate grammar, vocabulary and improve comprehension skills significantly. And it's one über-fun way to learn the language.

READ BOOKS

Think about the most enjoyable books you've ever read. Chances are excellent that you can find those same books translated into Italian. You'll find a huge variety of favorite American and British authors translated into Italian. Case in point, you'll find essentially the complete works of Isaac Asimov, Mary Higgins Clark, Jackie Collins, Dan Brown, Michael Crichton, Ken Follett, John Grisham, Stephen King, Dean Koontz, Robert Ludlum, James Patterson, Harold Robbins, Danielle Steel and many more, translated into Italian for your reading pleasure. Or take in your favorite series; whether it's Twilight, Harry Potter, Eragon, Lord of the Rings, etc.; these and many more are widely translated in Italian and available in book form.

Reading books that you've previously read in English will not overwhelm you, since you'll already be oriented. Keep the English version handy, since you'll inevitably want to compare vocabulary and phrases. It may be necessary to read the Italian book paragraph by paragraph; first read the English paragraph, then the Italian. Or first read the English chapter in its entirety, then the Italian. As you get more proficient, you'll be able to read these books in Italian without needing the English version.

There will be words you don't know, but since you've already read the English version, context will help you figure out meaning. Avoid looking up every word, just concentrate on the broad meaning. Don't get bogged down on every unknown vocabulary word, just keep plugging along and enjoy the vocabulary you do know, and notice those grammatical aspects that you're familiar with. Highlighting interesting information is useful, since there is a cognitive process involved; once you've highlighted it, there is a certain sense that you "own" that information.

READ ITALIAN NEWSPAPERS

Read Italian newspapers online for free daily (La Stampa, Corriere della Sera, La Repubblica for starters.) Reading Italian newspapers is not as difficult as it sounds. Granted, reading about Italian politics can be difficult, even if you're grounded in the subject. However, if you're reading an article that you're already familiar with, such as a saturation-coverage event like 9/11, a catastrophic natural disaster or a big celebrity death, you'll be amazed how much you can understand. So, when a huge news event happens, that's definitely an excellent time to hit the Italian newspapers online.

Reading lighter topics is easier and will keep you engaged. You might not understand every word, but you'll learn a lot through context. Read the short little articles, read the sentences or paragraphs that accompany the photos in Photo Gallery, or watch the Video Gallery. Look at parts of the paper that interest you, whether it's the Home, Culture, Cinema, Sports or Health. See the Resources section for more information.

SURF THE INTERNET

Virtually anything that you would normally research in English on your search engine is available in Italian cyberspace. Just plug your desired topic into your search bar with the words in Italian and explore. Improve your Italian as you research new topics.

"SHOULD I USE ROSETTA STONE?"

People often ask if they should use Rosetta Stone. The various programs such as Pimsleur, Michele Thomas, Yabla, Living Language, etc., are a terrific complement to classroom or self-study and they can only help. Everyone can benefit from these programs but it's advantageous to choose the program that best suits your learning style. Bottom line, the more exposure you have to the language, the sooner it will come together for you. Most importantly, you'll learn a language better when you're exposed to it through a wide variety of contexts, with as much possible exposure to the four modalities.

WRITING

Writing Italian may not seem as attractive or important as the other modalities, but a certain amount of writing is quite beneficial. Writing and practicing the irregular (yet *essential*) verbs and mastering them can help you to get over the linguistic hump that leads to fluency.

WRITE AND PRACTICE YOUR VERBS
Verbs are the glue that holds a language together.
Trying to speak a language without knowing your verbs is like trying to live but breathing only intermittently. Doesn't work too well... If you want to speak this gorgeous language, quit hemming and hawing, 'cuz here goes... Study your verbs, write your verbs, test yourself, and rock on! Read 'em, write 'em, say 'em out loud until they come naturally. Those little buggers are *crucial* and the more you do this, the better you will communicate and more the language will make sense to you... *and to others!* Pay special attention to The Seven Verbs That You Can't Live Without (pgs. 198-99.)

WRITE NEW VOCABULARY
Log, collect and compile new vocabulary as you learn it. Keep a dedicated, running vocabulary list of all new words that you learn in a notebook. Equally important, highlight every vocabulary word that you look up in the dictionary. As you look up future words, those previously highlighted vocabulary words will pop up at you. Cool...

WRITE TO DO LISTS OR JOURNALS
Do you keep a To Do list? Keep it daily *in Italian*. Initially you'll find that you're constantly looking up words to devise your list, but soon, you'll have memorized many essential, high frequency words, which will be assimilated into your gray matter. Use full sentences or at least include verbs in entries whenever possible. As you advance, work toward keeping a journal in Italian.

WRITE AN ITALIAN PEN PAL
Being able to write in Italian strengthens your language ability and has its advantages down the road. Having an Italian pen pal is one method of improving your writing skills. There are numerous sites where you can find an Italian email pen pal, as Italians and foreigners in general want to improve their English. Just google "Italian pen pals" to pull up a variety of sites.

LISTENING

Listen to Italian *every day*. Comprehension is a key aspect of language ability. You may be able to listen for hours every day, whether commuting, exercising or relaxing. This daily consistency is very powerful; the more you listen to Italian, the less "foreign," the language will sound to you. The more time you spend listening and reading, the more it will come together, the more it will make sense, the more vocabulary you'll memorize, the more comfortable you'll be, and the more you will love this language.

Improving comprehension is an ongoing effort which takes time. Finding engaging auditory avenues to listen to is half the battle. You'll notice that the more you're oriented to the topic, the easier it is to understand. Check out the Resources section for specifics on this topic.

LISTEN/WATCH ITALIAN YOUTUBE

YouTube in Italian is a fantastic language tool. In terms of finding fun and interesting comprehension exercises, it's totally tubular. Indulge your interests and investigate what's out there. Whether your passions are food, travel, music, exercise, nature, science, alternative medicine or how-to/DIY, there is a wealth of appealing YouTube. While viewing the videos, you'll be improving not only your Italian but also your knowledge of the subject.

My favorite way to use YouTube is to see recipes in action. Watch a few cooking videos, expand your culinary repertoire, and in the meantime, figure out what to make for dinner. As an example, type in Italian a favorite food or ingredient, such as, *melanzana,* and see dozens of eggplant recipes appear. As you watch people showing you how to make authentic Italian recipes in their kitchen, you'll be learning through context and will be amazed how much you understand, as comprehension is facilitated by the set, ingredients and actions taking place in front of you. These videos are step-by-step, so much so, that you can often follow the recipe even without full comprehension of the language.

To watch YouTube in Italian, type in a broad category of interest such as *astromomia,* to see what's available or type something more specific such as *la Terra, galassie,* or *buchi neri, (Earth, galaxies,* or *black holes.)* Research *how-to* or *Do-it-yourself/DIY* activities, by typing, *come fare ... or fai da te...* followed by the subject of your choice. Take a simulated walk through Siena, (type *Siena.)* Or watch its famous horse race by typing *il palio.* Enjoy and explore YouTube; it's a treasure for the language learner.

LISTEN TO AUDIO BOOKS

There are several excellent Italian language audio CD systems available. But besides this obvious choice, there are *audio books/audio libri*. *Audio books/audio libri* are a *fantastic* language tool. Listen on your smartphone or in your car. It's quite a potent tool, not only for comprehension but also for vocabulary and reinforcing grammar. The technology is pretty new in Italy, and audio book choices are still somewhat limited, (that is to say that the market tends more toward Italian literary classics rather than contemporary literature.) But in terms of listening and working on your comprehension, audio books are an excellent way of staying connected to the language here in the US.

It's recommended that you choose a book available in both English and Italian. Read or listen first in English and then listen to the corresponding audio book translated into Italian. With this orientation, you could spend *months* listening to the chapters over and over again. Every time you listen, you'll pick up new words and phrases, all the while reinforcing vocabulary. You'll almost certainly find it helpful to buy the Italian translation of the book when you buy the audio. Though Italian audio books can be pricey, after all is said and done, this strategy is very cost effective. As you listen to it over and over again, you'll constantly be reinforcing grammar, vocabulary and comprehension. With every listen, you'll notice new words, phrases and grammatical points that you've previously studied. Absorb the story as the language continually makes more and more sense to you.

LISTEN TO ITALIAN MUSIC

Many foreigners learn English by listening to American and British Rock music. Conversely, in my 20's, I learned a tremendous amount of Italian by listening to Italian Rock and Pop (Lucio Dalla, Claudio Baglione, Pino Daniele, etc.,) and by reading the lyrics and translating them. Absorbing the language through music is an effortless and pleasurable method; it's enjoyable, repetitive and fun. The lyrics of many Italian songs can be found through your search engine. The English translation can be found on Italian music lyric websites. Do your own translation first, and compare translations. You'll reap linguistic benefits through the enjoyment factor.

LISTEN/WATCH ITALIAN MOVIES

Dozens of Italian classic and contemporary videos are available for viewing. Be aware, the first 10-15 minutes of watching an Italian film may feel like "shock and awe," but strangely, after that, the language won't sound quite so foreign, and you might find that, by the end of the film, you're really in the zone. Hint for excellent linguistic practice: watch the movie *twice*; the first time with the English subtitles *on*, and then watch it again with the subtitles *off*. The second time you listen to it, you'll be thoroughly oriented, and your comprehension and cognitive linguistic skills will really be clicking. Just *feel* those neural synapses connecting... See the Resources section for a list of popular titles.

LISTEN TO ITALIAN RADIO

Rai Radio is a personal favorite smartphone app, with numerous stations available, as well as an endless variety of podcasts ranging from current events, culture, food, sports, politics and more. It will keep you connected to the language, expand your vocabulary and improve your comprehension. Besides Radio Rai, there are hundreds of independent Italian radio stations available. Initially, comprehension may be a blur, but give it time; if you stick with it, you'll start to isolate words, then phrases, then themes.

SPEAKING

If you want to speak Italian, or any other language for that matter, this is the deal: *don't worry about making mistakes.* Making grammatical mistakes is a normal part of the process, so just focus on getting your point across. Italians really do appreciate foreigners who put forth the effort to speak their language. No one will fault your grammar. If you want to speak this beautiful language, you need to start *speaking,* and the more, the better. *Let the grammatical chips fall where they may!* Speakers who have a balanced disregard for grammatical correctness in favor of getting their point across enjoy the language more and advance in their goal. Bottom line, being nervous about making mistakes is simply going to sabotage your speaking ability and exacerbate the situation. Just *enjoy* speaking this crazy, beautiful language and *try speaking from your gut, not your brain.* It's more important to speak with flow rather than with grammatical accuracy. If you keep talking and practicing, fluency will come. But it will *never* come if you don't practice and utilize the language through fear of making mistakes.

THE LANGUAGE PROCESS

As you learn a language, you first learn to read and comprehend, but your speaking ability develops more slowly. This is natural. All that reading, writing and listening you've been doing are the preparatory elements necessary to get you to the speaking stage. Don't be frustrated if speaking comes slowly, as this is a latter stage in the acquisition process. Initially, you'll first think in English and then translate into Italian in your mind. As you become fluent, you'll no longer process from English to Italian. You'll just think in Italian as you speak the language.

Should you travel to Italy without being able to speak the language very well, your trip will benefit nonetheless from your study; you'll be able to comprehend much more, both in listening to the spoken language and your engagement of the written word; signs, advertisements and newspapers may become an engaging puzzle or spring to life as you decode them. Your journey will become a trip not only geographically or culturally, but also linguistically and will take on a whole new level of interest. Restaurant menus, overheard conversations and interactions with the locals will be interesting instead of confusing, and you won't feel like such an outsider. In short, the language will start, little by little, to make sense to you. (Not to mention that many of the Italians that you encounter will be delighted that you are trying to speak their language.)

ACCENTS IMPROVE WITH TIME

If you're not happy with your accent, just chill. With practice, your accent will improve. One thing to keep in mind is that mouth muscles need to be developed to make certain sounds correctly and this doesn't happen overnight. Improving your accent is a process which involves, among other things, cognition, muscle development and time.

OBSERVE AND IMITATE

Keep in mind that observation and imitation of native Italian speakers will transform your skills. Observe Italians and imitate. Tap into your inner actor and imitate the language and gestures, and lose yourself to the language for a while. For instance, Italians use their voices and intonation differently than English speakers. Their vowels are pronounced differently from English vowels. And they definitely use their hands and body differently than English speakers. Obviously, this is an intuitive process that is better learned by imitation than through a book. Observe, intuit, and have fun with the language.

WINE, THE GREAT FACILITATOR

If you enjoy the noble grape, raise your glass, because a little vino really helps the language flow... When you converse in Italian with the benefit of a moderate amount of vino, you'll be amazed how well it can facilitate conversation... at times it's almost magical. There have actually been quite a few very informal scientific studies to test this theory... You'll realize how much the Italian that you've studied has actually been "fermenting" in your brain. This new found confidence can really encourage your linguistic prowess, in experiencing the excitement of communicating in a different language.

SPEAK WITH AN ITALIAN SKYPE PAL

There are people all over Italy, (and all over the world, too) who want to talk with you on the phone in order to improve their language skills. Trade language practice time, make a friend and become more culturally aware. On the Skype Home Page, go to "Language Learning" to get started.

GOING TO ITALY...

Keep in mind that when in Italy, you'll be forced to use your Italian more in smaller towns than in big cities. Demographically, older Italians typically can't speak a word of English whereas a teenager may speak English pretty well. If practicing Italian is one of your primary goals while in Italy, you'll have much more opportunity in remote areas. Students have told me that after months or years of practice, it was difficult for them to practice their Italian in Rome or Florence, because so many people wanted to "practice their English on them." One student of mine, a Hispanic physician, got a double whammy: in Florence people wanted to practice both their English *and* Spanish on him... Bigger towns are full of people who speak English and will sabotage your efforts, however, in a village; you may well find that not a soul speaks English. So if you're going to Italy with the goal of using your hard-learned Italian, avoid the tourist horde and venture forth to those silent, soul-soothing medieval hill towns, and experience that sense of awe and wonder. The people in those little towns are wonderful, and you'll have a delightful and more authentic cultural experience where you'll really be appreciated by the locals.

Take advantage of your trip and buy books, dictionaries and audio books while you're there – go into bookstores and browse through your favorite topics, whether it's science, fashion or nature. If you find the books too arduous, look in the Children's section for those same topics. Also check out the various children's encyclopedias on the bookshelves, which cover a wide range of topics, including Animals, Nature, Science, History, Geography, the Arts, etc. There's definitely something for everyone.

TAKE A LANGUAGE COURSE IN ITALY

Italy is one of the primary meccas for food, wine, art and tourism worldwide, and consequently there are dozens of language schools and programs geared towards foreigners who want to learn Italian. These programs will give you the opportunity to settle into a town or city for a while and explore the region. There's also an economic advantage to taking a language course, as spending time studying the language can be less expensive than touring the country for that same amount of time and staying in hotels. Italian Language schools can assist you with finding housing during your stay, whether in a hotel, residence or with a family.

Large metropolitan centers such as Rome, Milan and Florence offer dozens of Italian Language schools. However, also consider, for above mentioned reasons, classes and programs in the beautiful and culturally rich mid-sized towns, such as Verona, Parma, Siena, Urbino, Perugia, etc. Your trip may prove to be less expensive, and if you choose to lodge with a family, your experience may be more engaging. When choosing a language school, location should inform your decision; you may prefer a big city over a smaller town, or you may want to be up north so you can travel to France, Switzerland, Austria, etc. on the weekends.

It can't be stressed enough that you'll profit immeasurably from your experience if you hang with Italians, and not people of your own culture... Many students naturally gravitate to people of their own background, (such as other Americans or Brits) and return home with a mere superficial knowledge of the language. While there, do what you can to assimilate into the culture: take advantage of cultural events, join groups, take classes, attend religious services, attend performances, (movies, concerts, opera) and hang out in the piazza or park and talk to people.

For further information and helpful research tips, go to:
http://italian.about.com/cs/languageschools/bb/register.htm?nl=1

TAKE A COOKING COURSE IN ITALY

Some of Europe's top cooking schools are in Italy, where you can vacation in luxury villas with breathtaking views, dine on utterly sumptuous food and drink and swim in heated pools, which is OK, if you like that sort of thing... Depending on your interests, the program and the season, you can participate in grape or olive harvests, go truffle hunting, attend wine tastings, or go to the spa. If a culinary vacation sounds like fun, start researching, because they're available in every region of Italy, and they will satisfy both the soul and *the stomach/lo stomaco*...

PART
TWO

COGNATES, THE
"TWIN WORDS"
OF LANGUAGE

COGNATES THROUGH GRAMMAR

WHAT'S A COGNATE?

A *cognate,* as it's known in linguistic circles, is a word that is the same or similar in two different languages. A *cognate* is a word that has a *twin word* in another language. The words *cognates* and *twin words* will be used interchangeably in this book.

People who are "good with languages," either instinctively, or through experience, take great advantage of the extraordinary amount of cognates at their disposal. In this book, we will explore many different groups of cognates; cognates that function as nouns, adjectives, adverbs and verbs, as well as categories (people, food, wine, health, etc.) making you increasingly more fluent with what many consider to be the world's most beautiful language.

One of the most powerful and easiest ways to learn a language is to build up a solid knowledge of grammar in conjunction with good sense of cognate use. Being aware of *cognates,* or *twin words,* and using them, makes speaking a language exponentially easier. These twin words are absolutely the most valuable and overlooked gift in language acquisition. Bottom line, cognates are the ultimate cheap trick if you want to learn a language.

In language acquisition, memorizing vocabulary often stymies the language student, since vocabulary words are almost by definition, "foreign." With the use of cognates, however, memorization is relatively effortless, since there's such a strong native language link.

The twin words in this book are geared toward practical and conversational vocabulary. The lists are not meant to be exhaustive. The various lists don't contain esoteric or extraneous words, but vocabulary, that with a basic grasp of grammar, will enable you to communicate on a wide variety of everyday topics much more articulately and easily than before.

TYPES OF COGNATES

OBVIOUS COGNATES

Some words are true *twin words*, or *cognates*, words so close in both languages that it's obvious that the two words are linked linguistically.

arrivare – to arrive
il movimento – movement
intelligente – intelligent

PARTIAL COGNATES

Then there are partial cognates, words that are linked linguistically, but not as closely; there are words in English to help you make the connection.

pensare – to think; think *pensive*
il dente – tooth; think dental
male – badly; think *malignant or malaise*

DISTANT COGNATES

Finally, there are distant cognates, where there is some distant word relative or some lost historic link that helps you make a word connection. Sometimes that's all you need for the word to make sense to you.

trovare – to find; think of *a treasure trove,* which is *a find/discovery*
la rabbia – anger; we call a *rabid* dog a "mad dog"
sinistra – left; in the Middle Ages, left-handed people
were thought to be *sinister*

SECOND LANGUAGE COGNATES

Even if you've never studied a foreign language, you actually have a huge stockpile of words percolating in your brain, ready to be transformed into corresponding Italian words. These words are often so close, that seeing them on paper is sometimes all it takes to make the connection in order to memorize them. (Work on that grammar and pronunciation, though!) And if you've studied another Romance language, you have yet another very significant stockpile of vocabulary available for use.

decidere – décider – decidir – decidir (Italian, French, Spanish, Portuguese)
il mare – la mer –el mar – o mar (Italian, French, Spanish, Portuguese)
ieri – hier – ayer (Italian, French, Spanish)

Cognates, twin words, similar words or parole simili, call them what you will, exist across the language spectrum. The Latin, Italian, Spanish, French, Portuguese, Catalan and Romanian languages are so closely linked and their cognates are so pervasive and similar that often the same word or a close variation exists in many of them. Here is an example:

MY GOOD FRIEND ALWAYS SINGS AND DANCES WELL.
Il mio buon amico sempre canta e balla bene. *Italian*
Mi buen amigo siempre canta y baila bien. *Spanish*
Meu bom amigo sempre canta e dança bem. *Portuguese*
Meu bon amic sempre canta i balla bé. *Catalan*
Mon bon ami toujours chante et danse bien. *French*

FALSE COGNATES

Also known as "false friends," be aware that a small percentage of words are unreliable as cognates, in that they don't always mean what they appear. For instance:

preservativo, yes, it means *preservative*,
but its more common meaning is *condom (!!)*
attualmente means *currently* and not *actually*, as you might expect
tastare – to touch or feel, not *to taste*

USING COGNATES TO YOUR ADVANTAGE

Cognates, also known as *twin words,* provide you a huge shortcut to learning Italian. They can assist you in making this foreign language seem much less foreign. Some variation in pronunciation and/or spelling will exist, but you generally know them when you read or hear them, so learn to trust your instincts. Examples are endless:

> *delizioso – delicious*
> *evidente – evident*
> *importante – important*
> *interessante – interesting*
> *necessario – necessary*
> *persona – person*
> *quantità – quantity*
> *qualità – quality*
> *(eccetera – et cetera!)*

These cognates are invaluable linguistic tools that allow you to expand your vocabulary easily, tapping into languages you already know. Since there's already a strong link in your own language, memorization of its Italian counterpart comes particularly easily. And once you get a feel for using cognates, you'll have literally thousands more Italian words at your disposal.

And if you know another Romance language, you'll have a huge linguistic advantage, because you'll have countless cognates from that language as well. The only difference between *casa (house)* in Spanish and *casa* in Italian is a slight difference in pronunciation. Some examples of Spanish verbs that are very similar or the same (give or take minor spelling changes) in both languages are: *amar/amare, cambiar/cambiare, conocer/conoscere, dar/dare, esperar/sperare, encontrar/incontrare, pasar/passare, pensar/pensare, recordar/ricordare, saber/sapere, seguir/seguire, suceder/succedere, vivir/vivere* and *usar/usare.* In some cases, just slap a final *e* to the Spanish infinitive, check the spelling, and boom, you've got the Italian verb.

The French connection likewise has multiple cognates with the Italian language: *arriver/arrivare, commencer/cominciare, dire/dire, finir/finire, manger/mangiare, mettre/mettere, parler/parlare, partir/partire, sentir/sentire, and tenir/tenire* to name a few verbs.

Many words are cognates across the board between Italian, French and Spanish, with minute variations. Here are just a few examples:

dormire – dormir – dormir (to sleep)
venire – venir – venir (to come)
difficile – difficile – difícil (difficult)
interessante – intéressant – interesante (interesting)
intelligente – intelligent – inteligente (intelligent)
l'edificio – l'édifice – el edificio (the building)
(Italian, French, Spanish)

Some cognates *sound* the same in two languages, such as the Italian word *bagno* and the Spanish word *baño, (bathroom)* but are spelled differently. Conversely, some words are *spelled* the same in both languages, such as the Italian and Spanish word *edificio (building)* but are pronounced differently.

Italian is a direct offshoot of Latin. English, to a lesser but nonetheless substantial degree, also evolved from Latin. English and Italian sound very different, but linguistically, in the grand scheme of things, are actually quite similar (grammatically, syntactically, structurally, etc.) in many ways. So similar, in fact, that Italian is a relatively simple language to acquire for English speakers, particularly given the endless cognates available between the two languages. Once you get a feel for using these twin words, you'll be able to tap in to literally thousands of words that you "already know." Here are some descriptive adjectives of people that require no translation:

comico, decisivo, difficile, differente, famoso, impaziente, misterioso, modesto, morale, nervoso, popolare, religioso, serio, speciale, strano, studioso, stupido, timido, virile

NOUN COGNATES

nouns - nomi

This section contains many suffix-based cognate lists which will give you insight into the ongoing differences between Italian and English and how the language works through the use of widely used suffixes and spelling changes. Both active language (speaking ability) and receptive language (comprehension) will improve as whole aspects of the language open up to you. Additionally, memorization will be facilitated due to the repetition found in the suffix groups. Once you're familiar with the vast wealth of *cognates, or twin words*, shared between Italian and English, you'll be more at home with Italian. You'll need to keep plugging along with grammar and get a handle on pronunciation, but the vocabulary aspect of language learning will be vastly facilitated if you tap into the wealth of pre-existing, transparent vocabulary readily available to you.

This section will also help with pronunciation, in that if you know where to put the stress, the word just flows and is easier to pronounce. The suffix lists provide a uniformity of stress placement, e.g., the stress will always go on the same syllable per list, no matter how long the word. As you gain clarity on where to place stress, pronunciation in general improves. Read each list out loud to increase both vocabulary and pronunciation.

Regarding the nouns listed in this chapter and book, note that the Italian definite article is included in the Italian column, but the English definite article is not listed. There are various reasons for this. The Italian definite article is listed due to its wide variability (there are seven different ways to say *the* in Italian.) In addition, the definite article is used more in Italian than in English. The English definite article is omitted so you can focus on the cognate nouns and their relationship to their Romance language twins.

THE –EZZA ENDING
-ezza = -ty, ity, -ness

It's a huge advantage to have all these twin words available to you when learning a language. Memorization is simple. Take advantage of these cognates, because you'll still need to memorize regular vocabulary, and there are many essential non-cognates that you must know to be fluent. When time comes to memorizing the non-cognates, you'll realize indeed what a gift cognates are…

The suffix *–ezza* primarily relates to our suffixes *–ty or –ity*. The emphasis goes on the first syllable of *-ezza*, which makes pronunciation easy. Read the list aloud several times; this will cement both pronunciation and memorization.

al – *TEZ* – za
cer – *TEZ* – za

l'altezza – height, altitude
la certezza – certainty
la franchezza – frankness, candor
la freschezza – freshness
la gaiezza – gaiety
la gentilezza – kindness ("gentleness")
l'incertezza – uncertainty
la purezza – purity
la ricchezza – richness, wealth
la sicurezza – security
la tenerezza – tenderness
la timidezza – timity, shyness

THE –MENTO ENDING
-mento = -ment, etc.

Here's an assortment *(un assortimento)* of nouns ending in *–mento*. Notice that all these words are masculine. Since they're so close to their English counterpart, they're a cinch to remember.

The emphasis always goes on the *–MENT* syllable, making pronunciation easy. Read through the list several times to solidify both pronunciation and comprehension.

as – sor – ti – *MEN* – to
ce – *MEN* – to

l'assortimento – assortment
il cemento – cement
il commento – comment
il complimento – compliment
l'elemento – element
l'incoraggiamento – encouragement
l'incremento – increment
l'investimento – investment
il lamento – lament, complaint
il momento – moment
il movimento – movement
il nutrimento – nutrient
il parlamento – parliament
il pigmento – pigment
il sacramento – sacrament
il sedimento – sediment
il segmento – segment
il sentimento – sentiment
lo strumento – instrument
il tormento – torment

THE –NTE ENDING
-ante = -ant
-ente = -ent
-onte = -ont

The following are common word endings, in both Italian and English. As nouns, their gender can be either feminine or masculine, although they're generally masculine. Since the nouns end in "e" and their gender isn't obvious, you'll need to remember the article.

As with most Italian words, accent is on the second to the last syllable, no matter how long the word.

in – gre – di – *EN* - te
or – ri – *ZON* – te

l'agente – agent
l'ambiente – ambiance, environment
l'assistente – assistant
il cliente – client
il consulente – consultant
il continente – continent
il dente – tooth (think dental)
il deterrente – deterrent
l'elefante – elephant
la fronte – front, forehead
il gigante – giant
l'infante – infant
l'ingrediente – ingredient
l'istante – instant
la mente – mind (think mental)
l'orizzonte – horizon
il proponente – proponent
il serpente – snake, serpent
lo studente – student

THE –NZA ENDING
-anza = -ance, etc.
-enza = -ence, etc.

These suffix endings are common in both Italian and English. *–anza* and *–enza* and their English counterparts refer to a "quality or state of" its corresponding root. As in English, there is no rule to determine whether the suffix starts with an "a" or an "e," so note that detail. Also note that all nouns in this category are feminine, adding to ease of use. As with the majority of Italian words, accent goes on the penultimate, or second to the last syllable.

a – do – le – *SCEN* - za
am – bu – *LAN* – za

l'adolescenza – adolescence
l'ambulanza – ambulance
l'apparenza – appearance
l'arroganza – arrogance
l'assistenza – assistance
la benevolenza – benevolence
la coincidenza – coincidence
la conferenza – conference
la convenienza – convenience
la corpulenza – corpulence, obesity
la coscienza – conscience
la demenza – dementia
la differenza – difference
la divergenza – divergence
l'eccellenza – excellence
l'eleganza – elegance
l'emergenza – emergence, emergency
l'esistenza – existence
l'esperienza – experience
l'essenza – essence
l'esuberanza – exuberance
l'evidenza – evidence
la flatulenza – flatulence

l'indipendenza – independence
l'ignoranza – ignorance
l'impazienza – impatience
l'importanza – importance
l'impotenza – impotence
l'imprudenza – imprudence
l'indifferenza – indifference
l'indulgenza – indulgence
l'influenza – influence, flu
l'innocenza – innocence
l'insistenza – insistence
l'insolenza – insolence
l'intelligenza – intelligence
l'intransigenza – intransigence
l'obbedienza – obedience
l'opulenza – opulence
la partenza – departure
la pazienza – patience
la potenza – power, strength (think potent)
la precedenza – precedence
la preferenza – preference
la presenza – presence
la prudenza – prudence
la resistenza – resistence
la ripugnanza – repugnance
la sentenza – sentence (verdict)
la sofferenza – suffering
la sufficienza – sufficiency
la temperanza – temperance
la tendenza – tendency
la vacanza – vacation
la vigilanza – vigilance
la violenza – violence

THE –TÀ ENDING
-tà, -ità = -ity

This category of cognates is always feminine and the noun itself has the distinction of not changing in the plural. Notice that the related definite articles, verbs and adjectives change to reflect the plurality of the noun, but the noun itself is invariable.

La città americana è molto grande.
Le città americane sono molto grandi.

C'è un'università qui in questa zona.
Ci sono due università qui in questa zona.

The accent mark on the last syllable tells you
that you must stress the last syllable.

a – bil – li – *TÀ*
a – gi – li – *TÀ*

l'abilità – ability
l'agilità – agility
l'atrocità – atrocity
l'autorità – authority
la banalità – banality
la brevità – brevity
la brutalità – brutality
la capacità – capacity
la città – city
la civiltà – civility
la crudeltà – cruelty
la dignità – dignity
la dualità – duality
la durabilità – durability
l'enormità – enormity
l'entità – entity
la fatalità – fatality
la felicità – felicity, joy
la generosità – generosity

la legalità – legality
la maggiorità – majority
la maturità – maturity
la minorità – minority
la modernità – modernity
la moralità – morality
la musicalità – musicality
la nazionalità – nationality
la nudità – nudity
la nobiltà – nobility
l'onestà – honesty
l'ospitalità – hospitality
la popolarità – popularity
la povertà – povery
la principalità – principality
la profanità – profanity
la pubertà – puberty
la publicità – publicity
la purità – purity
la qualità – quality
la quantità – quantity
la rarità – rarity
la sessualità – sexuality
la severità – severity
la sincerità – sincerity
la similarità – similarity
la società – society, firm, club
la spiritualità – spirituality
la stupidità – stupidity
l'umanità – humanity
l'umiltà – humility
l'uniformità – uniformity
l'unità – unity
l'università – university
la vanità – vanity
la varietà – variety
la virilità – virility
la verginità – virginity
la volgarità – vulgarity

THE –ZIA/-ZIO ENDING
-zia = -cy, ce
-zio = -ce

Stress on this list varies; accent on the second to the last syllable for political categories (autocraZIa, burocraZIa, democraZIa, diplomaZIa, teocraZIa...) However, accent falls on the third to the last syllable for other words (giustIZia, etc.)

l'au – to – cra – *ZI* - a

l'autocrazia – autocracy
la burocrazia – bureaucracy
la democrazia – democracy
la diplomazia – diplomacy
la teocrazia – theocracy

di – *VOR* – zi - o

il divorzio – divorce
la giustizia – justice
l'infanzia – infancy
la malizia – malice
la notizia – news (think notice)
lo spazio – space

THE –ZIONE ENDING
-zione = -tion

The Italian noun ending *-zione* relates to our *-tion* ending. Many of these cognates exist among words in both Italian and English. All Italian nouns ending in *–zione* are feminine. Remember, if the noun starts with a vowel, you need to elide the vowel with an apostrophe, as in *l'educazione*. This is a large suffix category. Many examples are presented here but the list is by no means exhaustive. Hundreds more exist in their technically specific areas and more can be found in the *Cognates through Categories* section.

No matter how long these words are, pronunciation is a snap.
Accent always goes on the penultimate syllable:

am – mi – ni – stra – zi - *O* - ne
co – mu – ni - ca – zi - *O* – ne

l'amministrazione – administration
l'attenzione – attention
l'attrazione – attraction
l'automazione – automation
l'azione – action
la cancellazione – cancellation
la collezione – collection
la competizione – competition
la comunicazione – communication
la concezione – conception
la condizione – condition
la contraddizione – contradiction
la convinzione – conviction, belief (not the legal sentence)
la coordinazione – coordination
la correzione – correction
la corruzione – corruption
la costruzione – construction
la creazione – creation
la definizione – definition
la destinazione – destination
la determinazione – determination

la direzione – direction
l'eccezione – exception
l'educazione – education, upbringing, manners
l'elevazione – elevation
l'elezione – election
l'emozione – emotion
l'eruzione – eruption
l'evaporazione – evaporation
la frazione – fraction
la frizione – friction
la funzione – function
la giustificazione – justification
l'inflazione – inflation
l'intenzione – intention
l'intuizione – intuition
l'investigazione – investigation
la navigazione – navigation
la nazione – nation
l'obiezione – objection
l'occupazione – occupation
l'operazione – operation
la partecipazione – participation
la penetrazione – penetration
la persuasione – persuasion
la popolazione – population
la porzione – portion
la posizione – position
la produzione – production
la realizzazione – realization
la reazione – reaction
la respirazione – respiration, breathing
la ricognizione – recognition
la ricreazione – recreation
la semplificazione – simplification
la sensazione – sensation
la separazione – separation
la situazione – situation
la soddisfazione – satisfaction
la soluzione – solution
la stazione – station
la tradizione – tradition
la trasformazione – transformation

ADJECTIVAL COGNATES
adjectives - aggetivi

THE –BILE ENDING
-abile = -able, ible
-ibile = -able, ible

The *–abile* and *–ibile* word endings indicate *possibility or potential.* In Italian, accent generally falls on the penultimate syllable. In this category, no matter how long the word, accent always goes on the third to the last syllable, that is, the first vowel of the *–abile* or *–ibile* sequence: *A* – bi - le or *I* – bi - le.

me – mo – *RA* – bi - le
pos – *SI* – bi – le

abile – able
accessibile – accessible
accettabile – acceptable
addattabile – adaptable
adorabile – adorable
affabile – affable
agile – agile
ammirabile – admirable
applicabile – applicable
comparabile – comparable
compatibile – compatible
corruttibile – corruptible
deplorabile – deplorable
desiderabile – desirable
flessibile – flexible
formidabile – formidable
immaginabile – imaginable
impeccabile – impeccable
impossibile – impossible
inescusabile – inexcusable
inseparabile – inseparable

inesplicabile – inexplicable
intelligibile – intelligible
invisibile – invisible
irritabile – irritable
leggibile – legible
memorabile – memorable
orribile – horrible
osservabile – observable
possibile – possible
potabile – potable, drinkable
presentabile – presentable
responsabile – responsible
revocabile –revocable
scusabile – excusable
separabile –separable
stabile – stable
suscettibile – susceptible
terribile – terrible
vulnerabile – vulnerable

THE –EVOLE ENDING
-evole = -able

The –*evole* ending, like the –*abile* and –ibile word ending, indicates *possibility or potential*. In Italian, stress generally falls on the penultimate syllable. In this category, however, as with the previous ending, stress goes on the third to the last syllable, (that is, the first vowel of –*evole*) no matter how long the word is:

am – mir – RE – vo - le
con – for – TE – vo - le

abominevole – abominable
ammirevole – admirable
confortevole – comfortable
considerevole – considerable
desiderevole – desirable
disonorevole – dishonorable
durevole – durable
favorevole – favorable
meritevole – of merit, worthy
notevole – notable, substantial
onorevole – honorable
sfavorevole – unfavorable
socievole – sociable

THE –IVO ENDING
-ivo = -ive, -al

The Italian *–ivo* ending relates to the English *–ive* ending. Accent always goes on the second to the last syllable, no matter how long the word.

ac – cu – sa – TI - vo
of – fen – SI – vo

abortivo – abortive
abusivo – abusive
accusativo – accusative
conclusivo – conclusive
creativo – creative
curativo – curative
decisivo – decisive
effettivo – effective
educativo – educational
estensivo – extensive
emotivo – emotional
furtivo – furtive
impulsivo – impulsive
invasivo – invasive
lucrativo – lucrative
negativo – negative
offensivo – offensive
positivo – positive
primitivo – primitive
radioattivo –radioactive
selettivo – selective

THE –OSO ENDING
-oso = -ous
also -ate, -ive, -izing, etc.

The *–oso* ending indicates an *availability or abundance* of something. No matter how long the word is, the accent always goes on the first "o" of the suffix, the penultimate syllable. For more *–oso* adjectives, specific to people, see pages 81-85 in the Cognates through Categories section.

in- du-stri – O – so
scan – da – LO – so

ambizioso – ambitious
appetitoso – appetizing
affettuoso – affectionate
avventuroso – adventurous
clamoroso – clamorous
comatoso – comatose
delizioso – delicious
difettoso – defective
difficile, difficoltoso – difficult
disastroso – disastrous
disgustoso – disgusting
famoso – famous
favoloso – fabulous
furioso – furious
geloso – jealous
generoso – generous
giudizioso – judicious
glorioso – glorious
grandioso – grandiose
industrioso – industrious
indecoroso – indecorous
invidioso – envious
laborioso – hard working, industrious

litigioso – litigious
luminoso – luminous
malizioso – malicious
meraviglioso – marvelous
meticoloso – meticulous
miracoloso – miraculous
misterioso – mysterious
montagnoso – mountainous
mostruoso – monstrous
muscoloso – muscular
nervoso – nervous
numeroso – numerous
odoroso – odorous, smelly
pomposo – pompous
precipitoso – precipitous
pretenzioso – pretentious
prezioso – precious, valuable
prodigioso – prodigious
prosperoso – prosperous
religioso – religious
rigoroso – rigorous
rischioso – risky
scandaloso – scandalous
silenzioso – silent
sospettoso – suspicious
spazioso – spacious
studioso – studious
superstizioso – superstitious
tedioso – tedious
tempestoso – tempestuous
toruoso – tortuous, winding
vertiginoso – dizzying (vertigo)
vittorioso – victorious
voluminoso – voluminous

THE –NTE ENDING
-ante = -ant
-ente = -ent
also -ing, -ive, -ing, -ial, -ory

You will find *–ante* and *–ente* on the end of both Italian adjectives
and nouns.   As with the majority of Italian words,
stress falls on the penultimate syllable.

ab – bon – DAN - te
ac – co – mo – DAN - te

abbondante – abundant
accomodante – accommodating
adolescente – adolescent
aggravante – aggravating
agitante – agitating
ambulante – ambulatory
arrogante – arrogant
allarmante – alarming
assorbente –absorbent
assistente – assistant
astringente – astringent
attraente – attractive
benevolente – benevolent
conveniente – convenient
congruente – congruent
deficiente – deficient
devastante – devastating
diligente – diligent
dipendente – dependent
eccellente – excellent
eccitante – exciting
efficiente – efficient
elegante – elegant
eloquente – eloquent

emergente – emerging
esuberante – exuberant
flagrante – flagrant
frequente – frequent
ignorante – ignorant
imminente – imminent
impaziente – impatient
importante – important
impotente – impotent
incessante – incessant
incipiente – incipient
inclemente – inclement
indulgente – indulgent
influente – influential
infuriante – infuriating
ispirante – inspiring
intelligente – intelligent
interessante – interesting
irritante – irritating
ispirante – inspiring
negligente – negligent
obbediente, ubbidiente – obedient
osservante – observant
paziente – patient
pertinente – pertinent
prominente – prominent
repellente – repellant
recente – recent
riluttante – reluctant
rivoltante – revolting
seducente – seductive
stimolante – stimulating
sufficiente – sufficient
transiente – transient
urgente – urgent

ADVERBIAL COGNATES
adverbs - avverbi

The –MENTE ENDING
-mente = -ly

This group of *adverbs, or avverbi,* is easy to memorize and pronounce. You'll enhance your Italian by using these descriptive words. Pronunciation is a breeze; all words have their emphasis on the -*MENT* syllable. Read through the list aloud, stressing the penultimate syllable and you'll find your Italian to be more nuanced and refined with the addition of this user-friendly vocabulary.

as – so – lu – ta – MEN - te
be – ne – vol – MEN - te
cer – ta – MEN - te

artisticamente – artistically
assolutamente – absolutely
banalmente – banally
benevolmente – benevolently
certamente – certainly
completamente – completely
correttamente – correctly
curiosamente – curiously
divinamente – divinely
elegantemente – elegantly
eternamente – eternally
evidentemente – evidently
fatalmente – fatally
formalmente – formally
fortunatamente – fortunately
francamente – frankly
frequentemente – frequently
frugalmente – frugally
generalmente – generally

gentilmente – kindly
gioiosamente – joyously
gradualmente – gradually
indubbiamente – indubitably
maliziosamente – maliciously
medicalmente – medically
naturalmente – naturally
necessariamente – necessarily
normalmente – normally
ovviamente – obviously
paradossalmente – paradoxically
particolarmente – particularly
praticamente – practically, essentially
precisamente – precisely
pretenziosamente – pretentiously
probabilmente – probably
radicalmente – radically
rapidamente – rapidly
regolarmente – regularly
seriamente – seriously
sicuramente – surely, certainly, securely
sinceramente – sincerely
specialmente – specially, especially
tecnologicamente – technologically
tediosamente – tediously
telepaticamente – telepathically
tragicamente – tragically
trivialmente – trivially
ufficialmente – officially
vagamente – vaguely
velocemente – quickly (velocity)
verticalmente – vertically
violentemente – violently

VERBAL COGNATES

"Verbs are the glue that holds a language together."

Yes, verbs are the glue that holds a language together. Without verbs, you're talkin' "Caveman..." If you want to master a language, verbs are your path to linguistic enlightenment.

Verbs are such a crucial aspect of language, therefore this chapter has two verb lists. Below is a list of high frequency verbs, which are essential for basic language fluency. The longer list includes a wealth of verbal cognates that will enable you to navigate Italian with increased fluency, especially if you have a good handle on the modal verbs *(potere, volere, dovere;* see page 199.) These infinitives can be used with modal verbs, and can also be converted into past participles, (to be used with Passato Prossimo) and can be used as adjectives, enriching your Italian exponentially. These lists are not exhaustive, and many more cognate verbs exist, if you are so inclined.

HIGH FREQUENCY VERBS

accompagnare – to accompany
avere – to have
In your mind, place an "h" in front of the verb.
See the word "have" in the word; "__have__re"
arrivare – to arrive
cominciare – to start, commence
completare – to complete
comunicare – to communicate
considerare – to consider
consistere – to consist
continuare – to continue
costare – to cost
credere – to believe (think creed, credence)
decidere – to decide
desiderare – to desire
dimenticare – to forget (think dementia)
discutere – to discuss
dividere – to divide
dormire – to sleep (think dormitory)
esistere – to exist
essere – to be (think essence)
entrare – to enter

finire – to finish
frequentare – to frequent, attend
giocare – to play (think to joke, jocular)
girare – to turn, gyrate
guardare – to watch, look (a guard watches)
incontrare – to meet (think to encounter)
includere – to include
introdurre – to introduce
inventare – to invent
invitare – to invite
lavare – to wash (think lavatory)
lavorare – to work, labor
leggere – to read (think legible)
mantenere – to maintain
menzionare – to mention
muovere – to move
occupare – to occupy
offrire – to offer
osservare – to observe
pagare – to pay
partire – to leave (think to de<u>part</u>)
passare – to pass
pensare – to think (think pensive)
permettere – to permit
portare – to take, bring, get, carry (porters bring things)
possedere – to possess
preferire – to prefer
preparare – to prepare
presentare – to present, introduce
produrre – to produce
ricevere – to receive
ricordare – to remember (to record in your brain)
ridurre – to reduce
rimanere – to remain
rispondere – to respond
ritornare – to return
scrivere – to write (think to scribble, scribes write)
servire – to serve
soddisfare – to satisfy
spendere – to spend
studiare – to study
telefonare – to telephone
trovare – to find (<u>find </u>that treasure <u>trove</u>)
unire – to unite
usare – to use
vendere – to sell (vendors sell)
visitare – to visit

VERBS – VERBI

abbandonare – to abandon
abbreviare – to abbreviate
abdicare – to abdicate
abusare – to abuse
accelerare – to accelerate
accettare – to accept
accompagnare – to accompany
accusare – to accuse
acquistare – to acquire
adattare – to adapt
adorare – to adore
adulare – to flatter (adulation)
aggiustare – to adjust, fix
ammirare – to admire
amputare – to amputate
annunciare – to announce
applicare – to apply
approvare – to approve
archiviare – to file, archive
assemblare – to assemble
associare – to associate
assumere – to assume
attivare – to activate
aumentare – to augment, increase

ballare – to dance (ballerinas dance)
basare – to base
bloccare – to block

calcolare – to calcolate
calibrare – to calibrate
calmare – to calm
cancellare – to cancel, erase
categorizzare – to categorize
catturare – to capture
causare – to cause
celebrare – to celebrate
certificare – to certify

civilizzare – to civilize
classificare – to classify
comandare – to command
combattere – to fight, combat
commentare – to comment
compensare – to compensate
competere – to compete
completare – to complete
computere – to compute
comunicare – to communicate
concentrare – to concentrate
condensare – to condense
confermare – to confirm
confessare – to confess
confiscare – to confiscate
conformare – to conform
connettere – to connect
conservare – to conserve
considerare – to consider
consistere – to consist
consolare – to console
consolidare – to consolidate
consultare – to consult
consumare – to consume
contaminare – to contaminate
contare – to count
contattare – to contact
contemplare – to contemplate
contenere – to contain
contentare – to make content, please, satisfy
contestare – to contest
continuare – to continue
contrarre – to contract
contrastare – to contrast
contribuire – to contribute
controllare – to control
convergere – to converge
conversare – to converse
convertire – to convert
convincere – to convince
cooperare – to cooperate
coordinare – to coordinate
copiare – to copy

correlare – to correlate
corrodere – to corrode
cospirare – to conspire, plot
costare – to cost
creare – to create
criticare – to criticize
curare – to cure
curvare – to curve

danzare – to dance
datare – to date (something, not someone)
debilitare – to debilitate
decifrare – to decipher
declinare – to decline
dedicare – to dedicate
definire – to define
deformare – to deform
degenerare – to degenerate
deliberare – to deliberate
demolire – to demolish
desiderare – to desire
descrivere – to describe
detestare – to detest
dialogare – to dialogue, converse
dibattere – to debate
difendere – to defend
differenziare – to differentiate
dimostrare – to demonstrate
dipendere – to depend
disciplinare – to discipline
disconnettere – to disconnect
discriminare – to discriminate
disinfettare – to disinfect
dislocare – to dislocate
disorientare – to disorient
dispensare – to dispense
disputare – to dispute
disseminare – to scatter
dissolvere – to dissolve
dissuadere – to dissuade
distribuire – to distribute
distinguere – to distinguish
distruggere – to destroy

disturbare – to disturb
divergere – to diverge
diversificare – to diversify
dividere – to divide
divorziare – to divorce
divulgare – to divulge
documentare – to document
drammatizzare – to dramatize
drogare – to drug
duplicare – to duplicate

eccedere – exceed
eccellere – excel
eccitare – to excite
economizzare – to economize
educare – to educate
effettuare – to effect, implement
elaborare – to elaborate
eliminare – to eliminate
eludere – to elude
emanare – to emanate
emergere – to emerge
emettere – to emit
emigrare – to emigrate
entrare – to enter
enumerare – to enumerate
enunciare – to enunciate
esagerare – to exaggerate
esaminare – to examine
esasperare – to exasperate
esclamare – to exclaim
escludere – to exclude
esercitare – to exercise
esibire – to exhibit
esitare – to hesitate
espandere – to expand
esplodere – to explode
esportare – to export
esprimere – to express
estendere – to extend
estinguere – to extinguish
evacuare – to evacuate
evadere – to evade
evocare – to evoke
esistere – to exist

65

fabbricare – to manufacture, fabricate
facilitare – to facilitate
falsificare – to falsify
familiarizzare – familiarize
favorire – to favor
fermentare - ferment
fertilizzare – to fertilize
figurare – to figure
filmare – to film
finalizzare – to finalize
finanziare – to finance
flirtare – to flirt, romance
fluttare – to fluctuate
focalizzare – to focus
formalizzare – to formalize
formare – to form
formulare – to formulate
fortificare – to fortify
forzare – to force
fotografare – to photograph
frammentare – to fragment
fratturare – to fracture
frequentare – to attend, frequent
frustrare – to frustrate
funzionare – to work

garantire – to guarantee
generalizzare – to generalize
generare – to generate
gesticolare – to gesture
giocare – to play (think *to joke*)
girare – to turn, gyrate
giudicare – to judge
giustificare – to justify
governare – to govern
gratificare – to gratify

identificare – to identify
idratare – to hydrate
ignorare – to ignore
illuminare – to illuminate
illustrare – to illustrate
imbarcare – to embark
imitare – to imitate
immaginare – to imagine
immigrare – immigrate
implementare – to implement
implicare – to imply, implicate
importare – to import
impressionare – to make an impression
imprigionare – to imprison
improvvisare – to improvise
incitare – to incite
inclinare – to tilt, incline
includere – to include
incoraggiare – to encourage
incorporare – to incorporate
incorrere – to incur
incrementare – to increment, increase
incriminare – to incriminate, imply
indicare – to indicate
infestare – to infest
infiammare – to inflame
influenzare – to influence
informare – to inform
infuriare – to infuriate
iniziare – to initiate
inserire – to insert
insinuare – to insinuate
installare – to install
insultare – to insult
intensificare – to intensify
interpretare – to interpret
interrogare – to interrogate
interrompere – to interrupt
intersecare – to intersect
intervenire – to intervene
intimidire – to intimidate
intitolare – to entitle
introdurre – to introduce

invadere – to invade
inventare – to invent
invertire – to invert
investigare – to investigate
investire – to invest
invidiare – to envy
invitare – to invite
irritare – irritate
isolare – to isolate
ispezionare – to inspect

lacerare – to tear, lacerate
lamentare – to lament
laminare – to laminate
lanciare – to launch
liquidare – to liquidate
litigare – to argue, fight, litigate
localizzare – to localize
lubrificare – to lubricate

manipolare – to manipulate
mantenere – to maintain
massimizzare – to maximize
maturare – to mature
meccanizzare – mechanize
mediare – to mediate
meditare – to meditate
menzionare – to mention
militarizzare – to militarize
minimizzare – to minimize
misurare – to measure
mitigare – to mitigate
mobilizzare – to mobilize
modellare – to model
moderare – moderate
modernizzare – to modernize
modificare – to modify
monopolizzare – to monopolize
motivare – to motivate
muovere – to move

narrare – to narrate
negoziare – to negotiate
notificare – to notify
nutrire – to nourish

obbedire – to obey
obbligare – obligate
obiettare – to object
obliterare – to obliterate
occupare – to occupy
odiare – to hate (think odious)
odorare – to smell
offendere – to offend
offrire – to offer
onorare – to honor
operare – to operate
ordinare – to order
organizzare – to organize
orientare – to orient
osservare – to observe
ottenere – to obtain

pagare – to pay
parcheggiare – to park
passare – to pass
permettere – to permit
persuadere – to persuade
possedere – to possess
praticare – to practice
preparare – to prepare
produrre – to produce
promettere – to promise
proteggere – to protect

rendere – to render
ridurre – to reduce
rinnovare – to renovate
rispondere – to respond
ritornare – to return
rivelare – to reveal

salvare – to save
scappare – to escape
scendere – to descend
sciare – to ski
scusare – to excuse
sedurre – to seduce
servire – to serve, be useful
sistemare – to fix, arrange, organize
soddisfare – to satisfy
soffrire – to suffer
sorprendere – to surprise
spendere – to spend
stabilire – to establish
stimolare – to stimulate
stressare – to stress
studiare – to study
suggerire – to suggest

telefonare – to telephone
terminare – to terminate, finish
tormentare – to torment
tornare – to return
trasferire – to transfer
trasmettere – to transmit

umiliare – to humiliate
unificare – to unify
unire – to unite
utilizzare – to utilize

vacillare – to vacillate
visitare – to visit
votare – to vote

zigzagare – to zigzag

SPELLING CHANGES

Following are examples of some common spelling changes you'll find between Italian and English. Familiarity with these changes will enhance both oral comprehension and reading ability.

-cc = -xc

eccedere – to exceed
eccellente – excellent
eccessivo – excessive
l'eccesso – excess
eccetera – ectetera
eccetto – except
eccezionale – exceptional
l'eccezione – exception
eccitante – exciting

-i = -l

biondo – blond
la fiamma – flame
il fianco – flank, hip, side
il fiore – flower
l'infiammazione – inflammation
il pianeta – planet
il piano – plan
il pianoforte – piano
la pianta – plant
il piatto – plate
la piazza – plaza

dropped –n

costante – constant
la costruzione – construction
la difesa – defense
ispettore – inspector
l'istinto – instinct
l'istituto – institute
il mostro – monster
lo strumento – instrument
il trasporto – transport

-o = -ho

l'omicidio – homicide
l'onestà – honesty
onesto – honest
l'onore – honor
onorevole – honorable
orizzontale – horizontal
l'orizzonte – horizon
l'ormone – hormone
orrendo – horrendous
orribile – horrible
l'ospedale – hospital
l'ospitalità – hospitality
l'ostaggio – hostage
ostile – hostile

-s, -ss = -bs

assente – absent
assolutamente – absolutely
assoluto – absolute
assurdo – absurd
ostacolo – obstacle
osservare – to observe
l'ossessione – obsession

-s = -dis, -mis, -in, -un

scomodo – uncomfortable
scontento – discontent, unhappy
scorretto – incorrect
scortese – discourteous
sfortuna – misfortune
svantaggio – disadvantage
sventura – misadventure, mishap

-s, -ss = -x

esagerato – exaggerated
esattamente – exactly
esatto – exact
l'esistenza – existence
l'esperienza – experience
esperto – expert
esplodere – to explode
l'esplosione – explosion
esportare – to export
l'espressione – expression
estendere – to extend
esterno – external
estinguere – to extinguish
estremo – extreme
flessibile – flexible
la galassia – galaxy
il massimo – maximum
l'ossidazione – oxidation
il sesso – sex
sessuale – sexual
la sessualità – sexuality
(for verbs in this category, see page 65)

-tt, = -bt, -ct, -pt

accettabile – acceptable
accettare – to accept
l'accettazione – acceptance
l'architettura – architecture
l'aspetto – aspect, as in appearance
l'attività – activity
l'atto – act
l'attore – actor
il carattere – character
il condotto – conduct
il conflitto – conflict
compatto – compact
il contatto – contact
corretto – correct
direttamente – directly

diretto – direct
il direttore – director, manager
il dottore – doctor
l'effetto – effect
esattamente – exactly
esatto – exact
fatto – fact, done
l'impatto – impact
insetto – insect
intatto – intact
ispettore – inspector
ottagono – octagon
l'oggetto – object
ottare – to opt
l'ottava – octave
ottenere – to obtain
ottico – optic
ottimista – optimist
ottimo – optimal, great
ottobre – October
il patto – pact
perfetto – perfect
la pittura – picture
il progetto – project
scettico – skeptical
la struttura – structure
il trattore – tractor

-vv = -bv, -dv

l'avventura – adventure
avventuroso – adventurous
l'avverbio – adverb
ovviamente – obviously
ovvio – obvious

COGNATES THROUGH CATEGORIES

PEOPLE
LA GENTE

PEOPLE AND THEIR OCCUPATIONS
LA GENTE ED LE SUE OCCUPAZIONI

Lei/lui è... S/he is the...

l'agente – agent
l'agricoltore – farmer
l'annuciatore – announcer(masc.)
l'annuciatrice – announcer (fem.)
l'artista – artist
l'atleta – athlete
l'architetto – architect
l'assistente – assistant
l'attendente – attendant
l'attore – actor(masc.)
l'attrice – actress (fem.)
l'autore – author (masc.)
l'autrice – author (fem.)
la ballerina – dancer
il barbiere – barber
il barista – bartender
il consulente – consultant, counselor
la costumista – seamstress (costume maker)
il/la dentista – dentist
la disegnatrice – designer (fem.)
il disegnatore – designer (masc.)
il dottore – doctor (masc.)
la dottoressa – doctor (fem.)
l'elettricista – electrician
il/la farmacista – pharmacist
il/la fotografo – photographer
il/la giornalista – journalist
la guardia di sicurezza – security guard
il/la macchinista – machinist, technician
il meccanico – the mechanic
il medico – medical doctor
la modella – model

il/la musicista – musician
l'operatore – operator, worker
il pilota – pilot
il pittore – painter (masc.)
la pittrice – painter (fem.)
il poliziotto – police officer
il postino – the postman
lo scienzato – the scientist
lo scultore – sculptor
il soldato – soldier
il tassista – taxi diver
il tecnico – technician
la veterinaria – veternarian

VARIOUS NOUNS
NOMI VARI

l'adolescente – adolescent
il dissidente – dissident
l'emigrante – emigrant
l'immigrante –immigrant
l'infante – infant
la persona – person
lo studente – student
la studentessa – student
il terrorista – terrorist
il vagabondo – vagabond
la vittima – victim

QUALITIES AND FACTORS OF PEOPLE
LE QUALITÀ E FATTORI DELLA GENTE

l'abilità – ability
l'ambizione – ambition
l'apparenza – appearance, look
l'aspetto – appearance, look, aspect
la bellezza – beauty
la capacità – capacity
il carattere – character
la classe – class
la competenza – compentence
la competitività – competitiveness
la consistenza – consistency
la dignità – dignity
la diplomazia – diplomacy
l'efficienza – efficiency
l'emozione – emotion
l'entusiamo – enthusiasm
la femminilità – femininity
la generosità – generosity
la gentilezza – kindness (gentleness)
l'identità – identity
l'indipendenza – independence
l'intelligenza – intelligence
la lealtà – loyalty
la mascolinità – masculinity
la maturità – maturity
la moralità – morality
l'onestà – honesty
l'ottimismo – optimism
la pazienza – patience
la personalità – personality
la produttività – productivity
il senso dell'umorismo – sense of humor
la sensualità – sensuality
la sincerità – sincerity
l'umiltà – humility
l'umore – mood, temperment
l'umorismo – humor
la vanità – vanity
la voce – voice

NOUNS OF EMOTION
NOMI DEI EMOZIONI

Ho molto/a...   I have much...
Mi sento...   I feel...
(use definite or indefinite article as needed)

la confusione – confusion
la contentezza – happiness, contentment
la felicità – happiness, felicity
la gratitudine – gratitude
la gelosia – jealousy
la generosità – generosity
la gioia – joy
l'indifferenza – indifference
l'infelicità – unhappiness, misery
l'interesse – interest
la nostalgia – nostalgia, homesickness
la passione – passion
la preoccupazione – worry (think preoccupation)
la rabbia – anger (think rabies; mad dog)
la serenità – serenity
la soddisfazione – satisfaction
la timidezza – timidness, shyness

FAMILY AND FRIENDS
LA FAMIGLIA E GLI AMICI

Ecco...   Here is the...
("is" is understood in the Italian)

l'amico/a – friend (think amigo)
il/la bebè – baby
la collega – colleague (fem.)
il collega – colleague (masc.)
la compagna – companion (fem.)
il compagno – companion (masc.)
il fratello – brother (think fraternity)
la madre – mother
la mamma – mom, mommy
il padre – father

il papà – dad, daddy
il/la parente – relative
note: *il parente* = relative, NOT *parent;*
parent = *il genitore*, see pg. 189
la sorella – sister (think sorority)

NATIONALITIES - LE NAZIONALITÀ

The Italian language doesn't capitalize as much as the English language. For example, weekdays and months are not capitalized in Italian. Even acronyms only capitalize the first letter. Thus, note that the nationalities below are not capitalized. As always, make gender and number agreement, as necessary.

Il mio amico è ...   My friend is ...

africano – African
americano – Americano
asiatico – Asian
arabo – Arab
arabo saudito – Saudi Arabian
argentino – Argentinian
austriaco – Austrian
australiano – Australian
cinese – Chinese
francese – French
giapponese – Japanese
greco – Greek
indiano – Indian
israeliano – Israeli
marocchino – Moroccan
messicano – Mexican
polacco – Polish
russo – Russian
scozzese – Scotch
spagnolo – Spanish
turco – Turkish

Lui e' italiano. – He is Italian.
Lei e' greca. – She is Greek.
Gli uomini sono americani. – The men are American.
Le donne sono spagnole. – The women are Spanish.

DESCRIPTIVE ADJECTIVES OF PEOPLE
AGGETTIVI DESCRITTIVI DELLA GENTE

Italian adjectives agree in gender and number with the noun
they modify, so remember to make the agreement.

Il ragazzo é curioso. (masculine, singular)
La ragazza é curiosa. (feminine, singular)
I ragazzi sono curiosi. (masculine, plural)
Le ragazze sono curiose. (feminine, plural)

Lui è molto...   He is very...
Loro non sono molto...   They aren't very...
(make gender and number agreement as appropriate)

abile – able, capable
adorabile – adorable
affabile – affable
affettuoso – affectionate
aggressivo – aggressive
alcolizzato – alcoholic
alto – tall (think altitude)
altruista – altruistic
ambivalente – ambivalent
ambizioso – ambitious
annoiato – annoyed, bored
arrogante – arrogant
assurdo – absurd
ateo – atheist
atletico – athletic
attivo – active
austero – austere, dour
avventuroso – adventurous

basso – short (think base)
bizzarro – bizarre
brillante – brilliant
brutale – brutal

calmo – calm
capace – capable
civile – civil
comico – funny, comical
competente – competent
confuso – confused
contento – content, happy
coraggioso – courageous
cordiale – cordial
creativo – creative
crudele – cruel
curioso – curious

debole – weak (think debilitated)
decente – decent
decisivo – decisive
disabile – disabled
delizioso – delightful (think delicious)
deficiente – mentally challenged, stupid (deficient)
delicato – delicate, frail
difensivo – defensive
difficile – difficult
diffidente – diffident
diligente – diligent
dipendente – dependent
discreto – discreet
disciplinato – disciplined
disonesto – dishonest
distratto – distracted

eccentrico – eccentric
eccitante – exciting
eccitato – excited
educato – well bred
efficiente – efficient
egocentrico – egocentric, conceited
egoista – selfish, egocentric
eloquente – eloquent
emotivo, emozionale – emotional
energetico – energetic
entusiasta, entusiastico – enthusiastic
esperto – expert
estroverso – extroverted

famoso – famous
filantropico – philanthropic
fortunato – lucky (think fortuned)
fragile – fragile, frail
furioso – furious
furtivo – furtive

galante – gallant
geloso – jealous
generoso – generous
gentile – nice (think gentle)
(to say *gentle,* use *dolce* or *tenero*)

ignorante – ignorant
imbarazzante – embarassing
impaziente – impatient
impotente – impotente
impulsivo – impulsive
incapace – incapable
indipendente – independent
indulgente – indulgent
industrioso – industrious
inefficiente – inefficient
infantile – infantile
isterico – hysterical
innocente – innocent
innovativo – innovative
insistente – insistent
insofferente – insufferable
insolente – insolent
intelligente – intelligent
interessante – interesting
intollerabile – intolerable
intollerante – intolerant
introverso – introverted
invasivo – invasive
irritante – irritating
irritato – irritated
ispirante – inspiring

logico – logical
lunatico – moody, tempermental
(luna – moon; the moon reportedly affects mood)

meticoloso – meticulous
metodico – methodical
misterioso – mysterious
modesto – modest
morale – moral

negativo – negative
negligente – negligent
nervoso – nervous
nobile – noble
noioso – annoying, boring

obbediente/ubbediente – obedient
occupato – busy, occupied
odioso – odious, hateful
offensivo – offensive
onesto – honest
osservante – observant
ossessionato – obsessed
ostile – hostile
ottimista – optimistic

paziente – patient
perplesso – perplexed
perverso – perverse, perverted
pomposo – pompous
popolare – popular
positivo – positive
possessivo – possesive
povero – poor (think poverty)
preciso – precise
preoccupato – worried (stronger than preoccupied)
presuntuoso – presumptous
pretenzioso – pretentious
provocante – provocative

qualificato – qualified

raffinato – refined
razionale – rational
religioso – religious
resiliente – resilient
reverente – reverent
ricco – rich
rispettoso – respectful

scrupoloso – scrupulous
seducente – seductive
selettivo – selective
semplice – simple
senile – senile
sereno – serene
serio – serious
sicuro – secure, confident
sicuro di sé – self-assured (sure of oneself)
silenzioso – silent, quiet
sincero – sincere
sistematico – systematic
sofisticato – sophisticated
sospettoso – suspicious
speciale – special
spirituale – spiritual
strano – strange
studioso – studious
stupido – stupid
superstizioso – superstitious

tempestoso – tempestuous
timido – timid, shy
tollerante – tolerant
tranquillo – calm, tranquil

ubbediente/obbediente – obedient

vanitoso – conceited (think vain, vanity)
vigoroso – vigorous, robust
violento – violent
virile – virile
vulnerabile – vulnerable

FOOD
IL CIBO

WORLD CUISINE
LA CUCINA DEL MONDO

La cucina. a noun, has two separate meanings; *cuisine and kitchen.* In the sense below, it means *cuisine.*

Mi piace molto ...   I really like....
Non mi piace...   I don't like....

la cucina americana – American cuisine
la cucina cinese – Chinese cuisine
la cucina etnica – ethnic cuisine
la cucina francese – French cuisine
la cucina giapponese – Japanese cuisine
la cucina inglese – English cuisine
la cucina italiana – Italian cuisine
la cucina libanese – Lebanese cuisine
la cucina messicana – Mexican cuisine
la cucina spagnola – Spanish cuisine
la cucina vegetariana – vegetarian cuisine

FOOD NOUNS - NOMI DI CIBO

Io adoro...   I adore....

gli asparagi – asparagus
l'avocado – avocado

la banana – banana
il basilico – basil
i biscotti – cookies (think biscuits)

la bistecca – steak
i broccoli – broccoli
il budino – pudding
il burro – butter

il caffè – coffee
il calamaro – calamari, squid
le carote – carrots
il cereale – cereal
la cioccolata – chocolate *
il cioccolato – chocolate *
la barretta di cioccolata – chocolate bar
la tavoletta di cioccolata – chocolate bar
la tazza di cioccolata calda – cup of hot chocolate *
(* la cioccolata and il cioccolata are generally interchangeable)
la coca – cola, soda

le erbe aromatiche – aromatic herbs

il filetto – fillet
la frutta – fruit
la frutta fresca – fresh fruit
il frutto della passione – passion fruit
i funghi – mushrooms (think fungus !)

l'hamburger – hamburger

l'ingrediente – ingredient
l'insalata – salad

il kiwi – kiwi

la limonata – lemonade
il limone – lemon
le lenticchie – lentils

la maionese – mayonnaise
la margarina – margarine
la marmellata – marmalade, jam
il melone – melon
la menta – mint
la mostarda – mustard

l'olio – oil
l'oliva – olive
l'olio d'oliva – olive oil
l'origano – oregon

la pasta – pasta, pastry, dough
la pasta dolce – pastry
il pepe – pepper
la pera – pear
il pezzo – piece
la porzione – portion

il riso – rice
il rosmarino – rosemary

il sale – salt
il salmone – salmon
la salsa – sauce
la sardina – sardina
la spezia – spice
gli spinaci – spinach
il sidro – cider
la spina – bone (think spine)

il tè – tea
il timo – thyme
il tonno – tuna
la trota – trout

la verdura – vegetables (verdant; green - think greens)

lo yogurt – yogurt

THE TABLE - IL TAVOLO

il bicchiere – glass (think beaker)
la bottiglia – bottle
la forchetta – fork
il menu del giorno – menu of the day
il menu fisso – fixed, set menu
il menu turistico – tourist menu
l'ordine – order
il piatto – plate
il prezzo – price
il tavolo – the table
la tavola – the table

CONTAINERS, QUANTITIES, ETC.
I CONTENITORI, QUANTITÀ, ECC.

il bicchiere – glass (think beaker)
la bottiglia – bottle
la capacità – capacity
il cartone – carton
il chilo – kilo
il contenitore – container, crate, vessel, bin, box
il gallone – gallon
il litro – liter
la misura – size, measure
il pacco – package
il pacchetto – packet, pack
la parte – part
il pezzo - piece
la pinta – pint
la porzione – portion
il recipiente – container (think recipient)
il sacco – sack
il sacchetto – bag
il volume – volume
il tubo – tube

FOOD VERBS
VERBI DI CIBO

Devo... I must...
Voglio... I want...
Non posso... I can't...

bollire – to boil
friggere – to fry
marinare – to marinate
masticare – to chew (masticate)
nutrire – to nourish, feed
pelare – to peel
preparare – to prepare
salare – to salt
tostare – toast

FOOD ADJECTIVES
AGGETTIVI DI CIBO

Questo cibo è... This food is...
Vorrei qualcosa... I'd like something...

appetitoso – appetizing
arrosto – roasted
biologico – organic
brasato – braised
crudo – raw (crude, uncooked)
delizioso – delicious
fresco – fresh
fritto – fried
alla griglia – grilled
incluso – included
marinato – marinated
maturo – ripe (mature)
misto – mixed
potabile – potable
salato – salted
in salsa – in a sauce
squisito – delicious, exquisite
tiepedo – tepid, lukewarm
tenero – tender

WINE
IL VINO

OK, let's talk. Italy produces some of the BEST wine on the planet. If you doubt that, you haven't done enough, um… research… and you need to start. Italy's wine is globally recognized and drinking its vino is a delightful aspect of *The Italian Experience*. And in honor of the noble grape, certain enotological words will be listed that are not cognates.

Regarding the wine-language link, it's undisputed that a little vino can enhance language fluency. Moderate consumption can deliver significant linguistic benefits, and not just in the short term. Some people just need a little shot in the arm, (or in the mouth, so to speak) to see that they really can hold a conversation, thereby gaining some confidence that can enable them to turn a corner linguistically. Fortified by just a bit of wine, you may start to have conversations (however linguistically wobbly they may be,) and be inspired, invigorated and excited by the thrill that comes from communicating in a foreign language.

Vorrei… I would like…

una birra – beer
una bottiglia – bottle
un bicchiere – glass (think beaker)
un bicchiere di champagne – a glass of champagne
un bicchiere di vino – a glass of wine
un cocktail – cocktail
la lista dei vini – wine list
un liquore – liquor
il novello – new wine
(Similar to French Beaujoulais Nouveau. Should be drunk very young.)
un passito – passed
(Rich dessert wine. The grapes, typically moscato,
are left to dry before being pressed, which increases sugar content.
Even if you dislike sweet wine, this is delicious stuff.)
una riserva – reserve
(A higher quality version of the wine, often aged longer.)
un rosato – rosé
un rosso – red

uno spumante – a fully sparkling wine
(Produced in the strict manner known as spumante metodo classico,
similar to the French méthode champenoise.)
uno spumante naturale – a sparkling wine
(The bubbles are a result of fermentation, rather than added carbon dioxide.)
un superiore – superior
(Often categorized between standard and riserva.)
un tappo – cork (think tap)
la vendemmia – grape harvest
la vendemmia tardiva – late harvest
un vino vivace – a lively wine (think vivacious)
(A sparkling wine, less sparking than frizzante.)

WINE ADJECTIVES
AGGETTIVI DEL VINO

Vorrei qualcosa...   I'd like something...

alcolico – alcoholic
bianco – white
corposo – full-bodied (think corpulent)
fermentato – fermented
frizzante – semi-sparkling, fizzy
liquoroso – liqueur-like
locale – local
normale – normal, standard
regionale – regional
rosso – red
tranquillo/fermo – still, tranquil;
(Tranquil, as opposed to a sparkling wine.)

LEISURE
IL TEMPO LIBERO

NOUNS - NOMI

l'arte – art
l'associazione – association, club, membership
l'avventura – adventure
l'attività – activity
la banda musicale – band
la bicicletta – bike
le carte – cards
la chitarra – guitar
il ciclismo – cycling
il cinema – cinema, movie theater
la collezione – collection
il concerto – concert
la fotografia – photography
la galleria d'arte – art gallery
il giardino – garden
il giardino zoologico – zoo (zoologic garden)
l'hobby – hobby
l'interesse – interest
l'itinerario – itinerary
la macchina fotografica – camera (photo machine)
il mercato – market
il mercato dell'antiquariato – antiques market
il museo – museum
la musica – music
l'organizzazione – organization
il passatempo – pastime, hobby
lo spettacolo – spectacle, show, play, performance
lo spettatore – spectator
lo sport – sport
il teatro – theater
la televisione, la tivù - television
il tempo – time, weather
la tenda – tent
il tempo libero – free time
l'ufficio informazioni turistiche – tourist information office
la vacanza – vacation
la visita – visit, tour
lo zoo – zoo

VERBS - VERBI

Voglio I want…
Devo…   I must…
Non posso…   I can't…

campeggiare – to camp
collezionare – to collect
fotografare – to photograph
guardare la televisione – to watch television (a guard watches)
leggere – to read (think legible)
meditare – to meditate
riflettere – to reflect
rilassarsi – to relax
riposare – to repose, rest
visitare – to visit

ADJECTIVES - AGGETTIVI

affascinante – fascinating
atletico – athletic
divertente – fun (think diversion)
educativo – educational
preferito – preferred, favorite
isolato – isolated
istruttivo – educational (instructive)
soddisfato – satisfied
solo – alone, solo

TRAVEL
VIAGGIO

Io cerco… I'm looking for…
Lei sa dov'è…? Do you where… is?
(use definite or indefinite article as needed)

l'aereo, l'aeroplano – airplane
l'agenzia viaggi – travel agency
l'autobus – bus
l'automobile – automobile
l'arrivo – arrival
l'avventura – adventure
il bagagliaio – baggage compartment
il bagaglio – baggage
il campeggio – camp ground
la camera doppia – double room
la camera matrimoniale – double room
la camera singola – single room
la carta di credito – credit card
il catamarano – catamaran
la città – the city
il/la cliente – client
la comunicazione – communication, message
la conferma – confirmation
il deposito bagagli – baggage deposit, checkroom
la destinazione – destination
la foto/fotografia – photograph
la galleria d'arte – art gallery
il giardino – garden
la guida – guide, guidebook
la guida turistica – tour guide
l'hotel – hotel
le indicazioni – directions (indications)
l'internet point – internet cafè
l'itinerario – itinerary
la macchina – car (machine)
la macchina fotografica – camera
la mappa – map
il monumento – monument
la nave – ship (think naval)
l'ostello – hostel

il panorama – panorama, view
il parco – park
il parco a tema, luna park – theme park
il parco nazionale – national park
il passaporto – passport
il porto – port
la prima classe – first class
il programma – program, plan
il punto internet – internet cafè
i ricordi – souvenirs (un ricordo – think record)
il ristorante – restaurant
il ritardo – delay (think tardy)
il ritorno – return
la seconda classe –second class
la sicurezza – security
la stazione – station
la tariffa – tarrif, fare, price
il taxi, tassì – taxi
il tram – tram
il treno – train
il turismo – turism
il/la turista – tourist
l'ufficio informazioni turistiche – tourist information office
l'ufficio postale – post office
la vacanza – vacation
la valigia – valise, suitcase
la videocamera – videocamera
la visita – visit, tour
la visita accompagnata – guided tour
la visita guidata – guided tour
il visto – visa
lo yacht – yacht

TRAVEL VERBS
VERBI DI VIAGGIO

Devo... I must...
Non posso... I can't...
Vorrei... I would like...

annullare – to annul, cancel
arrivare – to arrive
cancellare – to cancel, delete, erase
confermare – to confirm
fotografare – to photograph
imbarcare – to embark, take off
informarsi – to inform oneself, find out, inquire
pagare – to pay
parcheggiare – to park
partire – to depart
passare – passare, spend
prenotare – to reserve
preparare – to prepare
rilassare – to relax
riposare – to relax, repose
riservare – to reserve
ritornare – to return
visitare – to visit

TRAVEL ADJECTIVES
AGGETTIVI DI VIAGGIO

Questo è...   This is....

completo – complete, full, no vacancy
costoso – costly, expensive
(however, caro is more commonly used)
divertente – fun (think diversion)
educativo – educational
occupato – occupied, busy, taken
privato – private
pubblico – public
puntuale – punctual
rilassante – relaxing
riservato – reserved
tardi – late, tardy
turistico – touristic, touristy
urbano – urban
vicino – close (think vicinity)

SHOPPING
LO SHOPPING

C'è / Non c'è...   There is / There isn't...
Vorrei comprare...   I'd like to buy...
Ho bisogno di...   I need...
(use definite or indefinite article as needed)

gli accessori – accessories
l'acquisto – purchase, acquisition
l'acquisto impulsivo – impulse purchase
l'acquisto vantaggioso – good buy (advantageous buy)
l'articolo – article, item
l'assistenza alla clientela – customer service
il catalogo – catalog
il centro commerciale – shopping area, mall, etc. (commercial center)
il codice a barre – bar code
il/la commerciante – vendor, trader, merchant
il commercio – commerce, business
il consumatore – consumer
il contenuto – contents
la cosmetica – cosmetics
il cotone – cotton
il direttore – manager, director
le istruzioni per l'uso – instructions for use
il lino – linen
la lista della spesa – shopping list
il mercato – market
la misura – measurement, size
la moda – fashion, style (mode)
il modello – model
il/la negoziante – shopkeeper
il negozio – shop, store
il numero – number, size
l'offerta speciale – special offer
il pacco – package
il prezzo – price
il profumo – perfume
la qualità – quality
la quantità – quantity
il resto – change (from a bank note)
la riduzione – reduction

il sacchetto – sack
il sacco – sack
il settore – sector, department
lo sconto – discount
la zona dei negozi – shopping area

SHOPPING VERBS
VERBI DI SHOPPING

Voglio...   I want...

acquistare – to buy, acquire
combinare – to combine, put together
commerciare – to trade, sell
costare – to cost
decidere – to decide
pagare – to pay
rimborsare – to reimburse
spendere – to spend
valutare – to estimate, consider, weigh
vendere – to sell (a vendor sells)

SHOPPING ADJECTIVES
AGGETTIVI DI SHOPPING

Questo è...   This is....

acquistato – bought, acquired
costoso – costly, expensive
(however, caro is more commonly used)
difettoso – defective
delicato – delicate
economico – economical, reasonably priced
garantito – guaranteed
incluso – included
lungo – long
stupendo – stupendous

THE GARDEN
IL GIARDINO

NOUNS OF THE GARDEN
NOMI DEL GIARDINO

Questo è...   This is...
Quello non è...   That isn't...
(use definite or indefinite article as appropriate)

l'annuale – annual
il biennale – biennial
il bulbo – bulb
il cactus – cactus
la conifera – conifer
l'erba – grass, lawn (think herb)
l'erba aromatica – herb
l'erbaccia – weed (think bad herb)
l'erbicida – herbicide
il fiore – the flower
il geranio – geranium
il giardino – garden
un giardino a patio – patio garden
un giardino di erbe – herb garden
un giardino acquatico – water garden
il giardiniere – gardener
l'insetticida – insecticide
l'orchidea – orchid
l'ornamentale – ornamental
l'orticoltura – horticulture
la palma – palm
il perenne – perennial
la pesticida – pesticide
il petalo – petal
la pianta – the plant
la pianta acquatica – water plant
il pino – pine
la pianta – plant
la pianta da fiore – flowering plant
la pianta da vaso – potted plant

il polline – pollen
la rosa – rose
il seme – seed (think seminate)
la specie – species
la spina – spine, thorn
il tronco – trunk
il tubero – tuber, bulb
il tulipano – tulip
il vaso – vase, pot
il vaso portafiori – flowerpot
la vegetazione – vegetation
la violetta – violet

VERBS OF THE GARDEN
VERBI DEL GIARDINO

Devo ... questo/quello.   I must ... this/that.

aerare – to aerate
architettare – to landscape, architect
coltivare – to cultivate
curare – to tend (to cure)
fecondare – to fertilize (fecund, fertile)
fertilizzare – to fertilize
germinare – to germinate
impollinare – to pollinate
piantare – to plant
propagare – to propagate
scavare – to dig (think excavate)
seminare – to seed, to sow

THE ARTS
L'ARTE

ART GENRES – GENERI D'ARTE

l'architettura – architeture
l'arte grafica – graphic art
la danza – dance
il disegno – design, drawing
il film – film
la fotografia – photography
la letteratura – literature
la litografia – lithography
la pittura – painting

ARTISTIC STYLES
GLI STILI ARTISTICI

il barocco – Baroque
l'età del bronzo – Bronze age
il periodo classico – Classical period
l'illuminismo – Enlightenment (luminous = light)
l'espressionismo – Expressionism
il futurismo – Futurism
il periodo gotico – Gothic period
l'arte greca – Greek
il medioevo – Middle Ages
il naturalismo – Naturalismo
l'età neolitica – Neolithic Age
post-modernista – Post modernist
il realismo – Realism
il Rinascimento – Renaissance
il Rococò – Rococo
l'Impero Romano – Roman Empire
il romanticismo – Romanticism
il simbolismo – Symbolism
il surrealismo – Surrealism

ART NOUNS – NOMI D'ARTE

l'affresco – fresco
l'agente – agent
l'antichità – antiquity
l'architetto – architect
l'architettura – architecture
l'armonia – harmony
l'arte – art
l'artefatto – artifact
l'artista – artist
l'atmosfera – atmosphere, mood
l'attrice – actress
l'attore – actor
l'attore comico – comedian
l'auditorio – auditorium
l'autrice – author (f.)
l'autore – author (m.)
l'avanguardia – avant-garde
l'azione – action

il balletto – ballet
il ballo – dance, dancing, ball (think ballet)

la caratteristica – characteristic
la caricatura – caricature
la ceramica – pottery, ceramics
il/la ceramista – potter, ceramist
la collezione – collection
la commedia – comedy, play
il commento – comment
il compositore – composer
il conflitto – conflict
il contrasto – contrast
il contratto – contract
la cornice – cornice, frame
il coro – choir, chorus
la creatività – creativity
il critico d'arte – art critic
la cultura – culture

la decorazione – decoration
il dialogo – dialogue
il disegno – design, drawing, picture, plan, etc.

gli effetti speciali – special effects
l'equilibrio – balance (equilibrium)

la favola – fable
la figura – figure
la forma – form

la galleria – gallery
il genere – genre
il gruppo – group

l'illustruzione – illustration
l'immaginazione – imagination
l'immagine – image
l'interno – interior

la lezione – lesson
la lirica – lyric poetry
la luminosità – luminosity

la melodia – melody
il metallo – metal
il microfono – microphone
la miniatura – miniature
il mito – myth
il modello – model
il monumento – monument
il mosaico – mosaic
il museo – museum
il musicista – musician
la musica – music

il narratore – narrator
la natura – nature
la nota – note

l'opera – work
l'opera d'arte – work of art, masterpiece
l'opera su gran scala – large scale work
l'opinione – opinion
l'orchestra – orchestra
l'originale – original
l'ornamento – ornament, decoration, scenery
l'ovazione – ovation

la pagina – page
la passione – passion
il pastello – pastel
il personaggio – character
il pezzo – piece
il poema – poem
la poesia – poetry
la pittura – picture, painting, paint
la pittura a olio – oil painting
il produttore – producer (film, etc)
la produzione – production
il/la protagonista – protagonist
il pubblico – the public, audience
il punto di vista – point of view

il rapporto – relationship, rapport
il restauro – restoration
la riflessione – reflection
la riproduzione – reproduction
la rima – rhyme
il ritmo – rhythm
il ruolo – role

la satira – satire
la scena – scene
lo scrittore – writer
lo scultore – sculptor
la scultura – scupture
il simbolo – symbol
il soggetto – subject
lo spettacolo – show, play, performance, entertainment
la statua – statue
lo stile – style

il talento – talent
il teatro – theater
la tecnica – technique
il testo – text, lyrics
il titolo – title
il tono – tone, shade
la tragedia greca – Greek tragedy

l'umore – mood, humor

il verso – verse
il volume – volume

ART VERBS – VERBI D'ARTE

acquistare – to acquire
applaudire – to clap, applaud
creare – to create
dirigire – to direct
disegnare – to design, sketch, draw, plan
ispirare – to inspire
rappresentare – to represent
restaurare – to restore
scrivere – to write (scribes write)

ART ADJECTIVES
AGGETTIVI D'ARTE

antico – antique, ancient
appassionato – passionate
armonioso – harmonious
artistico – artistic
astratto – abstract
autentico – authentic, true-to-life
bronzo – bronze
caratteristico – characteristic
classico – classic, classical
colorato – colored, tinted
colto – cultivated
comico – comic
contemporaneo – contemporary
creativo – creative
decorato – decorated
divertente – fun, entertaining (think diversion)
eccitante - exciting
elegante – elegant, stylish
emozionante – exciting, moving
estetico – aesthetic
falso – fake, false
fantastico – fantastic
immaginario – imaginary
intenso – intense
intricato – intricate
ironico – ironic
lirico – lyrical
misterioso – mysterious
moderno – modern
musicale – musical
originale – original
osceno – obscene
ovale – oval
poetico – poetic
realistico – realistic
restaurato – restored
satirico – satirical
splendido – splendid
stravagante – extravagant
stupendo – stupendous
tradizionale – traditional
trasparente – transparent

MUSIC
LA MUSICA

Italian is *the* standard language of musical terminology. Renaissance Italy woke up Europe from its dark-ages hibernation as a result of the explosion of high-calibre composers, artists, architects, sculptors, and writers, etc. Many English speakers have their first contact with the Italian language through music study. Below are tempo, volume and mood markings as well as musical vocabulary of Italian derivation. Although some of the terms below are not cognates, the vocabulary is fundamental to the Italian language.

MUSICAL NOTATION

accelerando – accelerating
accento – accented, emphasised
adagio – slow, stately ("at ease")
affettuoso – with feeling, tenderly, affectionately
agitato – agitated, quick
allegro – happy
altissimo – very high (think altitude)
con amore – with love, lovingly
andante – at a walking pace
animato – animated
appassionato – passionately
assai – very much

ballabile – danceable
con bravura – with skill
brillante – brilliant, brightly
con brio – with spirit, vigor
bruscamente – brusquely

cantabile – in a singing style
coda – tail, end of the piece
crescendo – growing

dolce – sweetly
con dolore – with pain, sadness
doppio movimento – double movement/speed

energetico – energetically
eroico – heroically
con molto espressione – with much expression
espressivo – expressively

con fuoco – with fire
furioso – furiously

giocoso – playfully
gioioso – joyfully
grandioso – grandly, magnificently
grazioso – graciously, gracefully
grave – grave, serious

lacrimoso – tearfully
lamentoso – lamenting, mournfully
largo – wide, broadly
lento – slow
lentamente – slowly
lentando – slowing down

maestoso – majestically, stately
malinconico – sadly, with melancholy
alla marcia – in a march-like manner
meno mosso – less quickly
misterioso – mysteriously
moderato – moderate
in modo di… – in the manner …
molto – very
con moto – with motion

nobilmente – nobly

opera – work

pesante – heavily
più – more
piuttosto – rather
poco – little, slightly
poco a poco – little by little
presto – fast, quickly
prestissimo – very quickly

quasi – almost

saltando – jumping
scherzando – playfully
semplicemente – simply
senza interruzione – without interruption
soave – smoothly, gently
sognando – dreamily
solenne – solemn
sostenuto – sustained, prolonged
subito – suddently

non tanto – not so much
tempo – time, pace
tempo comodo – at a comfortable pace
tempo giusto – at the right speed
tempo semplice – simply, regular speed
con tenerezza – with tenderness
tranquillamente – tranquilly, calmy
trionfante – triumphantly
troppo – too, too much
non troppo – not too much

vivace – vivaciously, lively
vivacissimo – very fast and lively

MUSICAL TERMS
TERMINI DI MUSICA

alto – second highest vocal line
l'armonia – harmony
basso – lowest vocal line
basso profondo – very deep bass voice
a cappella – in chapel style, voice only
cantata – a work for voice and orchestra
basso continuo – continuous bass
contralto – alto, esp. for female singers
coloratura – coloratura, musical flourish
concertino – a little concert
concerto grosso – big concert
mezzo soprano – between soprano and alto
libretto – little book, lyrics of the work
prima donna – first/leading lady
pianoforte – piano (soft-loud)
soprano – highest vocal line

EDUCATION
L'ISTRUZIONE

DEPARTMENTS
I DIPARTIMENTI/LE FACOLTÀ

Io studio... I study...
La mia materia preferita è... My favorite subject is...

l'architettura – architecture
l'arte – art
l'aritmetica – arithmetic
l'educazione – education
l'educazione fisica – physical education
la biologia – biology
la chimica – chemistry
il commercio – commerce
il disegno tecnico, tecnologico – techical design, drawing
l'economia – economics
l'educazione sessuale – sex education
la farmacia – pharmacy
la fisica – physics
la filosofia – philosophy
la geografia – geography
la ginnastica – gymnastic
l'informatica – information, computer studies
l'ingegneria – engineering
l'ingegneria civile – civil engineering
l'ingegneria elettronica – eletronical engineering
l'ingegneria meccanica – mechnanical engineering
la letteratura – literature
le lingue – languages
la linguistica – linguistics
la matematica – mathematics
la medicina – medicine
la musica – music
la pedagogia – pedagogy
la psicologia – psychology
la religione – religion
la scienza – science

la scienza dell'ambiente – environmental science
la scienza nucleare – nuclear science
le scienze politiche – political science
la sociologia – sociology
la storia – history
la storia d'arte – art history
gli studi commerciali – business studies
la teologia – theology

FOREIGN LANGUAGES
LE LINGUE STRANIERE

Lei/lui parla...   S/he speaks...
(definite article is optional)

l'arabo – Arab
il cinese – Chinese
il francese – French
l'inglese – English
l'italiano – Italian
il giapponese – Japanese
il greco – Greek
il mandarino – Mandarin
il russo – Russian
lo spagnolo – Spanish

EDUCATION NOUNS
NOMI EDUCATIVI

l'abilità – skill, ability
l'alfabeto – alphabet
l'ammissione – admission
il capitolo – chapter
la carriera – career
il certificato – certificate
la classe – class
la competenza – skill
la comprensione – comprehension
il concetto – concept
la copia – copy
il corso – course, class
il corso post-laurea – post graduate course
il diploma – diploma
la disciplina – discipline
la dissertazione – dissertation
il dizionario – dictionary
il dottorato – doctorate
l'esame – test, exam
l'esame orale – oral exam
la formula – formula
l'istituto tecnico – technical school
la lezione – lesson
la lista dei libri – reading list
il livello – grade, level
il master – master's
la materia – matter, subject, field (material)
la materia obbligatoria – compulsory subject
la materia preferita – favorite subject
la memoria – memory
la penna – pen
la preparazione – preparation
il preside – principal (of school)
il principale – boss, manager, principal (at work)
il professore – professor, high school teacher
il progetto – project

il punto, punteggio – point
la regola – rule (think regulation)
la ricerca – research
la risposta – response, answer
la scuola – school
la scuola elementare – elementary school
la scuola d'obbligo – compulsory (obligated) schooling
la scuola privata – private school
la scuola secondaria – secondary school, high school
il sistema di votazione – grading system
la studentessa – student (f.)
lo studente – student (m.)
il successo – success, achievement
la sufficienza – passing grade, (sufficiency)
il tema – essay (theme)
la tesi – thesis
il titolo – title
l'università – university
l'unione studentesca – student union
la valutazione – assessment (evaluation)
il voto – grade, mark (vote)

EDUCATION VERBS
VERBI D'ISTRUZIONE

Noi abbiamo bisogno di... We need to....

calcolare – calculate
concentrarsi – to concentrate
contare – to count
copiare – to copy
correggere – to correct
discutere – to discuss
disegnare – to design
dividere – to divide
frequentare – to attend, frequent
leggere – to read (think legible)
memorizzare – to memorize
montare – to mount, set up, assemble
prendere appunti – to take notes/points
programmare – to program, plan
rispondere – to respond
smontare – to dismount, take down
sommare – to sum up, add
scrivere – to write
studiare – to study
ubbidire/obbedire – to obey

ADJECTIVES OF EDUCATION
AGGETIVI D'ISTRUZIONE

Lei/lui è... S/he is...
Lei/lui è uno studente/una studentessa ...
S/he is a ... student.
(make gender agreement as necessary)

abile – capable, able
assente – absent
brillante – brillant

capace – capable
confuso – confused
creativo – creative
curioso – curious
deficiente – mentally slow (deficient)
difficile – difficult
diligente – diligent
disciplinato – disciplined
distratto – distracted
eccellente – excellent
efficiente – efficient
eloquente – eloquent
entusiastico – enthusiastic
ignorante – ignorant
indipendente – independent
industrioso – industrious
innovativo – innovative
intelligente – intelligent
inventivo – inventive
meticoloso – meticulous
metodico – methodical
negativo – negative
negligente – negligent
obbediente – obedient
osservante – observant
ossessionato – obsessed
ottimista – optimistic
paziente – patient
popolare – popular
positivo – positive
preciso – precise
rispettoso – respectful
serio – serious
severo – severe, strict
sicuro – secure, confident
speciale – special
specializzato – specialized, skilled
studioso – studious
stupido – stupid

MATH, ETC.
LA MATEMATICA, ECC.

MATH, SHAPES, MEASUREMENT
LA MATEMATICA, LE FORME, LA MISURA

Some areas of language are more blessed with cognates than others.
Math, shapes and measurement are replete with a multitude of cognates.
Even if you're not a math person, familiarization with this chapter will
benefit your Italian in unforeseen ways, (quite unrelated to math per se)
particularly regarding form, measurement and vocabulary
relating to the physical world.

NOUNS - NOMI

l'addizione – addition
l'aritmetica – arithmetic
il calcolo – calculus
la differenza – difference
la divisione – division
l'equazione – equation
la frazione – fraction
la geometria – geometry
l'incremento – increment
la moltiplicazione – multiplication
il numero – number
la parte – part
la percentuale – percentage
il pezzo – piece
la porzione – portion
la quantità – quantity
la sottrazione – subtraction
la trigonometria – trigonometry

FORMS - LE FORME

l'angolo – angle
l'arco – arc
il centro – center
il cerchio – circle
la circonferenza – circumference
il circolo – circle
il cono – cone
il cubo – cube
il cilindro – cylinder
il diametro – diameter
l'esagono – hexagon
l'ipotenusa – hypotenuse
la linea – line
l'ottagono – octagon
l'ovale – oval
il parallelogramma – parallelogram
il pentagono – pentagon
la piramide – pyramid
il punto – point
il raggio – ray, radius, range
il rettangolo – rectangular
il rombo – rhombus
la sfera – sphere
il trapezio – trapezoid
il triangolo – triangle
il tubo – tube

MEASUREMENTS
LE MISURE

l'altezza – height, altitude
l'altitudine – altitude
la capacità – capacity
il centimetro – centimeter
il chilometro – kilometer
il denominatore – denominator
la dimensione – dimension
la frazione – fraction
il gallone – gallon
la iarda – yard
la larghezza – width
il litro – liter
la lunghezza – length
la massa – mass
il metro – meter
il miglio (pl. le miglia) – mile
il millimetro – millimeter
la misura – size, measurement
il numeratore – numerator
il paio – pair
il pezzo – piece
la pinta – pint
la porzione – portion
la profondità – depth (think profound)
il volume – volume

MATH VERBS
VERBI DI MATEMATICA

Devo... I must...

contare – to count
dividere – to divide
moltiplicare – to multiply
misurare – to measure
numerare – to number
sommare – to add, sum
sottrare – to subtract

MATH ADJECTIVES
AGGETTIVI DI MATEMATICA

primo – first (think primary)
secondo – second (think secondary)
terzo – third (think tertiary)
ultimo – last (think ultimate)

alto – high (think altitude)
basso – low (think base)
circa – circa, about, approximately
completo – complete
concavo – concave
convesso – convex
cubico – cubic
curvo – curved
diagonale – diagonal
largo – wide
lungo – long
orizzontale – horizontal
parallelo – parallel
perpendicolare – perpendicular
profondo – deep (profound)
rotondo – round, rotund
quasi – almost, quasi
sufficiente – sufficient
totale – total

GEOGRAPHY
LA GEOGRAFIA

CONTINENTS - I CONTINENTI

Vive nel continente dell'...
He lives on the continent of...

l'Africa – Africa
l'America del Nord, Nordamerica – North America
l'America del Sud, Sudamerica – South America
l'Antartica - Antartica
l'Asia – Asia
l'Australia – Australia
l'Europa – Europa
l'Oceania – Oceania

DIRECTIONS - LE DIREZIONI

Lui vive... He lives...

al nord – to the north
al sud – to the south
all'est – to the east
all'ovest – to the west

OCEANS AND SEAS
GLI OCEANI ED I MARI

l'oceano antartico – Antartic Ocean
l'oceano artico – Arctic Ocean
l'oceano atlantico – Atlantic Ocean
l'oceano indiano – Indian Ocean
l'oceano pacifico – Pacific Ocean

il mar arabico – Arabian sea
il mar baltico – Baltic sea
il mar caspio – Caspian sea
il mar dei caraibi – Caribbean sea
il mare mediterraneo – Mediterrean sea
il mare del nord – North sea
il mar nero – Black sea
il mar rosso – Red sea

NOUNS – I NOMI

la capitale – capital
la cascata – cascade, waterfall
la caverna – cave, cavern
la colonia – colony, principality
il continente – continent
la costa – coast
il cratere – crater
la crosta – crust
il deserto – desert
il distretto – district
l'emisfero – hemisphere
l'estuario – estuary
la foresta – forest
il lago – lake
la latitudine – latitude
la longitudine – longitude
la montagna – mountain
la nazione – nation
l'oceano – ocean
la penisola – peninsula
il pianeta – planet
il polo – pole
la provincia – province
le rapide – rapids
la regione – region
la stato – state
la superficie – surface (think superficial)
il terreno – soil, ground, terrain
il territorio – territory
i tropici – tropics
la valle – valley
il vulcano – volcano
la zona – zone, area

RELIGION
LA RELIGIONE

PRINCIPAL RELIGIONS
PRINCIPALI RELIGIONI

Io studio… I study…
La mia religione è... My religion is...

il Buddhismo – Buddhism
il Cristianesimo – Christianity
l'Ebraismo – Judaism
l'Induismo – Hinduism
l'Islam, L'Islamismo – Islam

CLASSIFICATIONS
LE CLASSIFICAZIONI

Agnosticismo – Agnosticism
Animismo – Animism
Ateismo – Atheism
Deismo – Deism
Monoteismo – Monotheism
Politeismo – Politheism

RELIGION NOUNS
NOMI DELLA RELIGIONE

l'angelo – angel
il battesimo – baptism
la Bibbia – Bible
la cappella – chapel
il cardinale – Cardinal
la cattedrale – cathedral
il cielo – Heaven

il clero – clergy
il comandamento – commandment
la comunione – communion
la santa communione – Holy Communion
la confessione – confession
il convento – convent
la conversione – conversion
il convertito – convert
il coro – chorus
la coscienza – conscience
il credente – believer (one who has a creed)
la credenza – belief, creed
il credo – creed
la croce – cross
il culto – cult
la dannazione – damnation
il destino – destiny
il diavolo – devil
il discepolo – disciple
la disciplina – discipline
la divina provvidenza – divine providence
la divinità – divinity
il dubbio – doubt (think dubious)
il dogma – dogma
l'eretico – heretic
l'esistenza – existence
il fondamentalismo – fundamentalism
la grazia – grace
l'ideologia – ideology
l'infallibilità – infallibility
l'inferno – Hell, inferno
il laico – lay person
la meditazione – meditation
la messa – mass
il ministro – minister
il ministero – ministry
il miracolo – miracle
la missione – mission
il missionario – missionary
il misticismo – mysticism
il mito – myth
il monaco – monk
la moralità – morality

la moschea – mosque
il paradiso – Heaven, paradise
il pastore – pastor
il perdono – forgiveness (pardon)
la promessa – promise
il rabbino – rabbi
il rito – rite
il rituale – ritual
il sacramento – sacrament
il sacrificio – sacrifice
la salvezza – salvation
il santo – saint
il segno – sign
il segreto – secret
la setta – sect, cult
il simbolo – symbol
la sinagoga – synagogue
la sofferenza – suffering
la spiritualità – spirituality
lo spirito – spirit
la superstizione – superstition
il tempio – temple
la teologia – theology
la tradizione – tradition
la trascendenza – transcendence
la trinità – trinity
l'Ultima Cena – the Last Supper
la virtù – virtue
la visione – vision

RELIGION VERBS
VERBI DI RELIGIONE

assolvere – to absolve
canonizzare – to canonize
confessarsi – to confess
confidare – to confide
convertire – to convert
meditare – to meditate
pregare – to pray
purificare – to purify

sacrificare – to sacrifice
soffrire – to suffer
sopportare – to support, bear
tollerare – to tolerate

RELIGION ADJECTIVES
AGGETTIVI DI RELIGIONE

È ...   He's/It is...
Lei non è...   She is not...
(make gender/number agreement)

ateo – atheist
agnostico – agnostic
carismatico – charismatic
cattolico – Catholic
celeste – Heavenly (celestial)
cosmico – cosmic
cristiano – Christian
devoto – devoted
divino – divine
eretico – heretical
etico – ethical
evangelico – evangelical
morale – moral
pio – pious
protesante – Protesant
ortodosso – orthodox
reverente – reverent
religioso – religious
sacro – sacred
soprannaturale – supernatural
spirituale – spiritual

HEALTH
LA SALUTE

MEDICAL DIVISIONS
DIVISIONI MEDICHE

Lei/lui è un medico della/dell'... S/he is a doctor of...

l'anestesia – anesthesia
la cardiologia – cardiology
l'unità di cura intensiva – intensive care unit
la dermatologia – dermatology
l'endocrinologia – endocrinology
la fisioterapia – physical therapy
la gastroenterologia – gastroenterology
la ginecologia – gynecology
la medicina interna – internal medicine
la maternità – maternity
la neurologia – neurology
l'oftalmologia – ophthalmology
l'oncologia – oncology
l'ortopedia – orthopedics
l'ostetrica – obstetrics
la patologia – pathology
la pediatria – pediatrics
la psichiatria – psychiatry
la radiologia – radiology
l'urologia – urology

SURGICAL DIVISIONS
DIVISIONI CHIRUGICHE

la cardiochirurgia – cardio surgery
la chirurgia vascolare – vascular surgery
la chirurgia generale – general surgery
la chirurgia pediatrica – pediatric surgery
la chirurgia plastica o estetica – plastic surgery

DISEASES, MALADIES, DISTURBANCES
LE MALATTIE, I DISTURBI

Il povero ha…   The poor guy has…
Lei è malata di…   She is sick with...
Lui soffre di...   He suffers from...

l'alcolismo – alcoholism
l'allergia – allergy
la malattia di Alzhiemer – Alzheimer's disease
l'anoressia – anorexia
l'appendicite – appendicitis
l'asma – asthma
un attacco di panico – a panic attack
l'autismo – autism
il blocco mentale – mental block
il botulismo – botulismo
la bronchite – bronchitis
la bulimia – bulimia
il cancro – cancer
le cataratte – cataracts
la cirrosi epatica – cirrhosis
i crampi – cramps
la demenza – dementia
la depressione – depression
la dermatite – dermatitis
la diarrea – diarrhea
l'ebola – ebola
l'eczema – eczema
l'emicrania – migrane
l'emorragia – hemorrhage
l'encefalite – encephalitis
l'epilessia – epilespy
la febbre – fever
la febbre gialla – yellow fever
la frattura – fractura
la gastrite – gastritis
il glaucoma – glaucoma
l'infezione – infection
l'infiammazione – inflammation
l'influenza – influenza, flu
l'ischemia cardiaca – ischemic heart disease

130

l'ipertensione arteriosa – arterial hypertension
la malaria – malaria
una malattia – a malady, disease
la malattia di huntington – Huntington disease
la meningite – meningitis
la mononucleosi – mononucleosis
la miopia – myopia
la nausea – nausea
la polmonite – pulmonary disease, pneumonia
la SARS – SARS
la schizofrenia – schizophrenia
la sclerosi multipla – multiple sclerosis
la trombosi – thrombosis
l'ulcera – ulcer
la vaginite – vaginitis
la varicella – varicella, chickenpox

AT THE PHARMACY - IN FARMACIA

Devo comprare...   I must buy...
Ho bisogno di un/una...   I need...

l'analgesico – analgesic, pain killer
gli antibiotici – antibiotics
l'antinfiammatorio – anti-inflamamatory
l'assorbente – sanitary napkin
la crema – cream
il deodorante – deodorant
il dosaggio – dosage
la farmacia – pharmacy
il/la farmacista – pharmacist
l'indigestione – indigestion
l'igiene femminile – feminine hygiene
l'inalatore – inhaler
il lassativo – laxative
l'insulina – insulin
il medicamento – medication
la medicina – medicine
monouso – disposable [one use]
la pillola – pill
il prodotto – product
i prodotti per i denti – dental care

i prodotti per la pelle – skin care
il sedativo – sedative
lo sciroppo – syrup
lo spray – spray
la supposta – suppository
il tampone – tampon
le vitamine – vitamins

MEDICAL NOUNS
NOMI MEDICI

le analisi – lab tests
un'ambulanza – an ambulance
un appuntamento con il dottore – doctor's appointment
un attaco – attack
la clinica – a clinic
la coagulazione – coagulation
il crampo – cramp
La Croce Rossa – Red Cross
una cura – a cure
la diagnosi – diagnosis
la dieta – diet
la digestione – digestion
un disturbo – disturbance, trouble, disorder
la droga – drug
un emergenza – an emergency
l'energia – energy
la frattura – fracture
un incidente – an accident, incident
l'infezione – infection
l'infiammazione – inflammation
l'iniezione – injection
l'inocculazione – inocculation
la letargia – lethargy
il medico – doctor
la mestruazione – menstruation
la nevrosi – neurosis
l'operazione – operation
l'ospedale – hospital
l'ovulazione – ovulation
la paziente – patient
il polso – the pulse
la puntura – sting, puncture

la respirazione – breathing
il risultato – result
la sindrome – syndrome
la siringa – syringe
la sofferenza – suffering
lo/la specialista – specialist
il sintomo – symptom
la supposta – suppository
la terapia – therapy
l'urina – urine
la vaccinazione – vaccination
il virus – virus
la visita medica – medical exam

MEDICAL VERBS
VERBI MEDICI

ambulare – to ambulate, walk
curare – to cure, treat, take care of
diagnosticare – to diagnose
disinfettare – to disinfect
dislocare – to dislocate
dispensare – to dispense
dosare – to dose
drogarsi – to take drugs
esaminare – to examine
fratturare – to fracture
intubare – to intubate
lacerare – to lacerate
medicare – to medicate
operare – to operate
palpitare – to palpitate
prescrivere – to prescribe
respirare – to breathe (think respiration)
salvare – to save
soffocare – to suffocate, choke
soffrire di – to suffer from
sterilizzare – to sterilize
urinare – to urinate
vaccinare – to vaccinate
vomitare – to vomit

MEDICAL ADJECTIVES
AGGETTIVI MEDICI

Lui è...   *He is...*
Questo è...   *This is...*
Quello è...   *That is...*

contagioso – contagious
debilitato – debilitated
deformato – deformed
depresso – depressed
disinfettato – disinfected
drogato – drugged
efficace – effective
fratturato – fractured, broken
grave – grave, serious
handicappato – handicapped, disabled
imfiammato – inflamed
infettato – infected
igenico – hygenic
paralizzato – paralyzed
resistente – resistent
sterile – sterile

BUSINESS
IL COMMERCIO

BUSINESS NOUNS
NOMI DEL COMERCIO

l'accordo di affari – business deal
gli affari – business (the affairs)
l'agenda – day planner, personal organizer
l'agenda degli appuntamenti – appointment book
l'agenda telefonica – personal phone book
l'amministrazione – administration
l'amministratore delegato – CEO (delegated administrator)
l'appuntamento – appointment
gli appunti – notes (points)

la banca, il banco – bank
il commercio – business, commerce

il canale di distribuzione – channel of distribution
la capacità di produzione/produttiva – manufacturing capacity
il capitale industriale – instrumental capital
il capitale investito – invested capital
il capitale liquido – liquid/working capital/funds
i capitali fissi – fixed capital
il capitalismo – capitalism
la capitalizzazione – capitalization
il capo – head, chief, boss
il capo servizio – foreman
il capo sindicale – labor/union leader
la carriera – career
il catalogo – catalog
il centro – center
il certificato di deposito – certificate of deposit
il ciclo commerciale – business cycle
la clausola – clause
il/la cliente – customer, client
il codice – code
il codice postale – zip code
il collaterale – collateral
il/la collega – the colleague

il commerciante – dealer, trader
il commercio all'ingrosso – wholesale trade
il commercio interstatale – interstate commerce
il commercio libero – free trade
il commercio multilaterale – mulitlaterale trade
il/la cliente – client
il compenso – compensation
la competizione – competition
il componente – component
il computer – computer
le comunicazioni di massa – mass communications
le condizioni di commercio – terms of trade
le condizioni di vendita – terms of sale
la conferenza – conference
il conflitto d'interesse – conflict of interest
il conglomerato – conglomerate
il consorzio – consortium
il consulente – consultant
i conti annuali – annual accounts
i conti creditori – accounts receivable
i conti debitori – accounts payable
i conti garantiti – secured accounts
i conti di gruppo – group accounts
il conto bancario – bank account
il conto capitale a breve/lungo termine – short/long-term capital account
il conto congiunto – joint accout
il conto corrente – checking account, current account
il conto dettagliato – detailed/itemized account
il contratto di lavoro – work contract
il contratto di manutenzione – maintenance/service contract
il controllo – control, check
il controllo del credito – credit control
il controllo dell'inventario – inventory control
il controllo della produzione – production control/check
il controllo di qualità – quality control
il controllo finanziario – financial control
il controllore – comptroller
la copia scritta – hard copy
la correzione – correction
la corrispondenza – correspondence
i costi amministrati – administrative costs
i costi bancari – bank charges
i costi di distribuzione – distribution costs
i costi fissi – fixed costs
i costi iniziali – start-up costs
i costi normali – normal/standard costs
i costi di produzione – production costs

136

i costi di trasporto – shipping costs
i costi variabili – variable costs
il costo della vita – cost of living
il costo diretto – direct cost
il costo e trasporto – cost and freight
il costo medio – average cost
il credito al consumatore – consumer credit
il creditore – creditor, payee

la data – date
i dati – data
la data di maturazione – maturity date
la data di registrazione – record date
il debito – debt
il debito a breve/lungo termine – short/long term debt
il debito attivo – active debt
il debito nazionale – national debt
il deficit – deficit
la demozione – demotion
il deposito – deposit, down payment
il deposito bancario – bank deposit
il diagramma – graph, diagram
il diagramma delle correnti – flow chart
il dibattito costruttivo d'opinioni – brainstorming session
la dichiarazione – declaration, statement, permit
la dichiarazione d'esportazione – exporation permit
la dichiarazione di conto – statement of account
la dichiarazione scritta e giurata – affidavit
il difetto – defect
la differenza – differential
la differenziale dei prezzi – price differential
la dinamica del gruppo – group dynamics
la dinamica del mercato – market dynamics
il direttore – director, manager (masc.)
la direttrice – director, manager (fem.)
il direttore della pubblicità/pubblicitario – advertising manager
il direttore finanziario – financial director
il direttore generale – chief executive
la disputa di lavoro – labor dispute
la diputa salariale – salary/wage dispute
la disputa sindacale – labor, union dispute
il dividendo – dividend
il documento – document

l'economia – economics, economy
l'economia di scala – economy of scale

l'efficienza – efficiency
l' entrata – entry
l'errore – error
l'esame della personalità – personality test
l'esecutore/esecutrice – executor
l'esenzione – exemption
l'esportazione dei capitali – capital exports

il fax – fax
la fabbrica – factory
il fabbricante – manufacturer
la fase negativa – slump, negative phase
il fattore – factor
il fattore dei costi – cost factor
il fattore dei profitti – profit factor
la festività legale – legal holiday
il fiduciario – fiduciary
la filiale – affiliate
il finanziamento a breve termine – short-term financing
i fondi pubblici – public funds
il fondo d'investimento fiduciario – trust fund
il fondo pensionistico – pension fund

la garanzia – guarantee, security, warranty
la giurisdizione – jurisdiction
la giustizia – equity
il governo – government
il grafico – graph, chart
il grafico a barra – bar chart
su grande scala – large scale
il gruppo ammininstrativo – management group

l'imitazione – imitation
l'impatto – impact
l'impatto dei profitti – profit impact
l'importatore – importer
l'importazione – import
l'indennità- indemnity
l'indicatore principale – leading indicator
l'indice – index
l'indice dei prezzi – price index
l'indice dei prezzi al consumo – consumer price index
l'indice di mercato – market index
l'industria di mercato libero – free market industry

l'inflazione – inflation
l'informazione riservata – insider information
l'infrastruttura – infrastructure
insubordinazione – insubordination
l'interesse – interest
l'interesse composto – compound interest
l'intermediario – broker, middleman, intermediary
l'inventario – inventory
l'inventario fisico – physical inventory
l'investimento – investment
l'investimento capitale – capital expenditure
l'investimento diretto – direct investment
l'ispezione – inspection

una lettera di accompagnamento – cover letter
una lettera di garanzia – letter of guaranty
una lettera di presentazione – letter of introduction
il libro paga – payroll
la licenza di importazione – import license
una linea di credito – line of credit
la linea di prodotti – product line
la linea di produzione – production line
la lista di controllo – check list
il listino prezzi – price list
il livello – level, grade
il livello commerciale – commercial grade
il livello di qualità accettabile – acceptable quality level
il livello salariale – salary/wage level
la logistica – logistics

una marca – mark, brand
un marchio registrato – registered trademark
il margine di profitto – profit margine
il margine variabile – variable margine
la materia prima – raw materials
il mercante – merchant
il mercato dei capitali – capital market
un mercato volatile/instabile – volatile market
il mercato nero – black market
il moratorio – moratorium
il movimento di cassa – cash flow
il movimento positivo dei fondi – positive cash flow

il negoziato – negotiation
la norma – norm
la nota – note, comment, list, point, entry

139

la nota di credito – credit note
la nota di debito – debit entry
il numero del conto – account number
il numero di riferimento – reference number

l'obbligazione – obligation, bond
l'obbligazione municipale – municipal bond
le obbligazioni convertibili – convertible bonds
le obbligazioni redimibili – redeemable bonds
l'offerta – offer, tender, bid
l'offerta al pubblico – public offering
l'offerta e la domanda – supply and demand
l'offerta scritta – written bid
l'operatore – operator
l'opzione – option
l'ordine – order

la paga – pay/wage
la paga minima – minimum pay/wage
il pagamento completo – payment in full
il pagamento parziale – partial payment
il pagante – payer
il paradiso fiscale – tax haven
il patto – pact, agreement
il patto collettivo – collective agreement
il patto commerciale – trade agreement
il patto implicito – implied agreement
il periodo – period
il permesso – permit
il personale – personnel, staff
il piano commerciale – business plan
il piano d'azione – action plan
il piano di mercato – market plan
la polizza – policy
la politica di distribuzione – distribution plan
la politica monetaria – monetary policy
la posizione – position
la presentazione – presentation
il prezzo corrente – the current price/going rate
il prezzo di base – base price
il prezzo di listino – list price
il prezzo di mercato – market price
il prezzo iniziale – initial/opening price
il prezzo minimo/massimo – minimum/maximum price
il prezzo medio – medium/average price

il prezzo unitario – unit price
il prodotto – product
il produttore – producer
la produzione – production
il profitto – profit
il progetto – project
il programma – program
la promessa – promise, pledge
la proprietà – property
la pubblicità – publicity, advertising

la quanità – quantity
la qualità – quality

i rapporti sindacali - labor (syndacate) relations
il rapporto annuale – annual report
le relazioni pubbliche/pubbliche relazioni – public relations
la riunione – meeting (reunion)
il rappresentante – representative
la relazione – report, account, relationship
le relazioni con gli investitori – investor relations
le relazioni con il personale – employee relations
il responsabile – person in charge, manager, director, organizer
la responsabilità – responsability, liability
la responsabilità congiunta – joint liability
la responsabilità fissa/limitata – fixed/limited responsibilty
la responsabilità personale – personal responsability
la restrizione – restriction
la richezza – richness, wealth
il ricovero – recovery
la riduzione dei costi – reduction of costs
la riduzione dei prezzi – price reduction
la riforma – reform
la riserva – reserve
la risoluzione – resolution
la risoluzione dei problemi – problem solving
il ritorno sull'investimento – return on investment
la riunione – meeting (reunion)
la riunione generale – general meeting

il salario – salary, wage
i servizi finanziari – financial services
i servizi pubblici – public services
la sicurezza – security

il sindacato – syndicate
il sistema – system, structure, approach, method
la società – company, firm, group, guild, society
la soddisfazione del consumatore – consumer satisfaction
lo specialista – specialist
lo statuto – statute
lo stipendio – salary, wage, stipend
la strategia – strategy
lo strumento – instrument
la struttura – structure
il supervisore – supervisor
lo svantaggio – disadvantage

la tariffa – tariff
la tassa – tax, duty, fee, charge
il tasso – rate
il territorio – territory
il titolo – title, stock
il torto – tort
la transazione – transaction
il trasferimento – transfer

l'ufficio – office, department, bureau
l'ufficio di assistenza al cliente – customer service
l'ufficio contabilità – accounting department
l'ufficio legale – legal department
l'ufficio marketing – marketing department
l'ufficio del personale – personnel office, Human Resources
l'ufficio vendite – sales department
l'unione – union
l'utensile – utensil, tool
l'utilità – utility

il valore – value, worth
il valore di mercato – market value
il valore registrato – register/book value
la valutazione – evaluation, appraisal
il vantaggio competitivo – competitive advantage
la variabilità – variability
la variazione – variation
il volume – volume
la zona – zone

BUSINESS VERBS
VERBI DI COMMERCIO

Dobbiamo... We must...

contare – to count
controllare – to check, control, audit
commerciare – to trade
costare – to cost

derivare – to derive from, accrue
dettagliare – to itemize, detail
disputare – to dispute

economizzare – to save
eliminare – to eliminate
emettere – to emit, issue
esportare – to export

fabbricare – to manufacture
finalizzare – finalize
finanziare – to finance
finire – finish
fissare il prezzo – to fix the price

garantire – to guarantee, warrant

importare – to import
incorporare – to incorporate
incrementare – to increase
industrializzare – to industrialize
investire – to invest
istruire – to instruct

lanciare – to launch
lavorare – to work (think labor)
liquidare – to liquidate, settle

massimizzare - to maximize
maturare – to mature
meccanizzare – to mechanize
misurare – to measure

negoziare – to negotiate

pagare – to pay
partecipare – to participate
presiedere – to preside, chair
produrre – to produce
privatizzare – to privatize
pubblicizzare – to advertise, make public

razionare – to ration
recuperare – to recoup, recover, salvage
revisionare – to revise, amend, edit, overhaul
ridurre – to reduce
rinnovare – to renovate
ristrutturare – to restructure

salariare – to pay salary/wages to
scontare – to discount
sistemare – to organize, settle, fix, take care of
sospendere il pagamento – to suspend payment
specificare – to specify, earmark
speculare – to speculate
standardizzare – to standardize
stipulare – to stipulate

tassare – to tax
trasportare – to transport
terminare – to terminate

validare – to validate
valutare – to value
vendere – to sell (vendors sell)

BUSINESS ADJECTIVES
AGGETTIVI DI COMERCIO

Questo è... This is...
Quello non è... That isn't...

confidenziale – confidential
costoso – costly
(caro is more common)
cumulativo – cumulative
sotto standard – substandard, deficient
difettoso – defective
digitale – digital
economico – economical
efficiente – efficient
garantito – guaranteed
massimo – maximum
minimo – minimum
negativo – negative
negligente – negligent
negoziabile – negotiable
non registrato – not registered, off the books
nullo – null, void
pagato – paid
completamente pagato – paid in full
pagabile – payable
positivo – positive
profittabile – profitable
registrato – registered
utile – useful
valido – valid

TECHNOLOGY
LA TECNOLOGIA

English speakers of foreign languages benefit from the fact that, linguistically, the English language rules the technological world. So much so, that this list of words needs no translation. Foreign language words imported into Italian are generally masculine, thus all the English import words on the following list are all masculine.

IMPORTED ENGLISH
TECHOLOGICAL VOCABULARY

il browser
il byte
il computer
il CPU
il database
l'email
il file
il firewall
l'hard drive
l'hardware
l'home page
l'internet
il link
il modem
il mouse
il monitor
il password
la RAM
lo scanner
il server
il sistema
il software
l'upgrade
il virus

TECHNOLOGICAL NOUNS
NOMI TECHNOLOGICI

l'applicazione – application
la barra di scorrimento - scrollbar
la barra degli strumenti – tool (the instrument bar)
il carattere – font, character
il codice barra – bar code
il codice di identificazione – password
il computer portatile – portable computer, laptop
il dischetto – disk
l'icona – icon
l'intelligenza artificiale – artificial intelligence
la memoria – memory
il motore di ricerca – search engine
la posta elettronica – email
la porta – port
il processore – processor
il programma – program
il sito internet – internet site
il sito web – website
il videogioco – videogame

TECH VERBS
VERBI TECHNOLOGICI

Dobbiamo... We must...

archiviare – to file, archive
communicare – to communicate
copiare – to copy
cancellare – to erase, delete, cancel
categorizzare – to sort, categorize
cliccare – to click
downloadare – to download
immettere – to input
importare – to import
installare – to install
programmare – to program
registrare – to register
ricevere – to receive
salvare – to save (think salvage)

TRANSPORTATION
IL TRASPORTO

MODES OF TRANSPORTATION
MODI DI TRASPORTO

l'aereo – plane
l'aeroplano – airplane
l'autobus – bus
l'automobile – car
l'auto sportiva – sports car
la bicicletta – bicycle
la canoa – canoe
il catamarano – catamaran
l'elicottero – helicopter
la limousine – limousine
la macchina – car, machine
la metropolitana – subway, metro
la motocicletta – motorcycle
la nave – ship (think naval)
il tram – tram
il treno – train
il veicolo – vehicle
lo yacht – yacht

TRANSPORTATION NOUNS
NOMI DI TRASPORTO

l'ancora – anchor
gli arrivi – arrivals
la cabina – cabin
il capitano – captain
il chilometro – kilometer
il controllo passaporto – passport control
la destinazione – destination
la distanza – distance
la deviazione – detour, deviation
il garage – garage
la guardacoste – coastguard
l'incidente – accident (incident)
indicazione – direction, information
la mappa – map
il meccanico – mechanic
il motore – engine, motor
il parchimetro – parking meter
le partenze – departures
il passaporto - passport
il pilota – pilot
il porto – port
il prezzo – price
il radar – radar
il ritardo – delay (think tardy)
il segnale – signal
la sicurezza – security
la stazione – station
la stazione di servizio – gas/service station
la tariffa – fare
il terminal - terminal
la terminale – terminal
la torre di controllo – control tower
il traffico – traffic

TRANSPORTATION VERBS
VERBI DI TRASPORTO

Lui deve… He must…

arrivare – to arrive
avanzare – to advance, get ahead
entrare – to enter
fare il check-in – to check-in
imbarcare – to board (embark)
indicare – to indicate
girare – to turn (gyrate)
guidare – to drive (to guide)
parcheggiare – to park
passare – to pass by
partire – to depart, leave
pendolare – to commute (think pendolum)
sbarcare – to disembark
sorpassare – to pass
ritornare – to return
tornare – to return
trasportare – to transport, ship
visitare – to visit

THE CAR - LA MACCHINA

l'acceleratore – accelerator
l'autoradio – car radio
la batteria – battery
il filtro d'aria – air filter
il motore – engine, motor
l'odometro – odometer
il porta bagali – trunk
il radiatore – radiator
il segnale – signal
il silenziatore – muffler (silencer)
la sospensione – suspension
la trasmissione – transmission
il ventilatore – fan, ventilator

MISCELLANEOUS NOUNS
NOMI VARI

C'è...   There is...
Non c'è...   There's no...
Questo è ...   This is...
Quello non è ...   That's not...
(use definite or indefinite article, as needed)

un'abbondanza – an abundance
un accordo – an agreement, accord
un'alternativa – an alternative
un altro – another (think alternative)
un ambiente – an ambiance, atmosphere
un analisi – an analysis
un angolo – an angle, corner
un animale – an animal
un'area – an area
un aspetto – aspect, appearance, look
un'attività – an activity
un'automobile – an automobile
un autore – an author
un autorità – an authority
un'azione – an action

un balcone – a balcony
una battaglia – a battle
un beneficio – a benefit

un carattere – a character
un caso – a case
una catastrofe – a catastrophe
una categoria – a category
una causa – a cause, reason
un centro – a center
un commento – a comment
una communicazione – a communication
un compagno – a companion
una compagnia – a company, firm, companionship

una condizione – a condition
un consiglio – an advice, council
un contatto – a contact
una conseguenza – a consequence
una considerazione – a consideration
un contrasto – a contrast
una corrente – a current, flow
una costruzione – a construction, building
una crisi – a crisis
una critica – a criticism, comment
una cultura – a culture
una cura – a cure, care, attention

una decisione – a decision
un desiderio – desire
un destino – a destiny
un dettaglio – a detail
una difesa – a defense
una difficoltà – difficulty
una differenza – a difference
un direttore – a director
una direzione – a direction
una disciplina – a discipline
una distanza – a distance
una distinzione – a distinction
un disturbo – a disturbance, a bother
un dottore – a doctor
un dubbio – a doubt (think dubious)

un'eccezione – an exception
un effetto – an effect
un elemento – an element
un'energia – an energy
un'epoca – an era, epoch
un errore – an error
un esame – an exam
un esempio – an example
un'esperienza – an experience
un'espressione – an expression
un eufemismo – euphemism
un evento – an event, occurance

una famiglia – a family
un fatto – a fact
un fattore – a factor
un favore – a favor
un fenomeno – a phenomena
una figura – a figure, shape
una fine – an end, finish (think final)
una forma – a form, shape
una fortuna – a fortune, luck
una frase – a phrase, sentence
una fronte – a front, face, forehead
una frontiera – a frontier, border
una frutta, un frutto – a fruit
una funzione – a function

un gesto – a gesture
un giardino – a garden
un giornale – a newspaper, periodical, journal
un governo – a government
un grado – a grade, rank, level
un gruppo – a group

un'idea – an idea
un'imitazione – an imitation
un'impressione – an impression
un'immagine – an image
un'importanza – an importance
un indicatore – an indicator
un'indicazione – an indicator
un'industria – an industry
un inizio – a beginning (think initally)
un'intenzione – an intention
un istinto – an instict
un istituto – an institute

una legge – a law (think legal)
una leggenda – a legend
una lettera – a letter
un limite – a limit
una linea – a line
un livello – a level

153

una maggioranza – magiority
una maniera – a manner, way
una massa – a mass, lump, bunch, heap
un massimo – a maximum
una materia – a material, matter, subject
un materiale – a material
un medio – a medium, average
un membro – a member
una memoria – a memory
un metodo – a method
un minimo – a minimum
un miracolo – a miracle
un mistero – a mystery
una misura – a measure
un modello – a model
un modo – a way, manner, mode
un momento – a moment
una montagna – a mountain
un motivo – a motive, reason, cause
un movimento – a movement

una natura – a nature
una nazione – a nation
una necessità – a necessity
un nemico – a nemesis, enemy
un nome – a name, noun
una nota – a note
una notizia – news, notice
un numero – a number

un'occasione – an occasion
un odore – an odor
un oggetto – an object
un'operazione – an operation
un'opinione – an opinion
un opzione – an option
un ordine – an order
un'origine - an origin

una pagina – a page

una parte – a part

una passione – a passion

una pena – a pain, sorrow, punishment

un periodo – period

una persona – a person

un pezzo – a piece

un polizotto – a police officer

una posizione – a position

una possibilità – a possibility

un posto – a post, place, spot, seat, job, etc.

una preponderanza – preponderance

una presenza – a presence

una prevalenza – prevalence

un prezzo – a price

un problema – a problem

una procedura – a procedure

un processo – a process, lawsuit

un prodotto – a product

una produzione – production

un progetto – a project, plan

un programma – a program

una promessa – a promise

una proposta – a proposal, suggestion

un protocollo – a protocol

una provincia – a province

una punta – a point (e.g. of a pencil, knife) tip

un punto – a point, period, score, stitch, dot, detail

una qualità – a quality

una quantità – a quantity

un rapporto – a rapport, relationship, connection, proportion

una razza – a race, breed, sort (not a runner's race)

una realtà – a reality

una reazione – a reaction

una regione – a region

una regola – a rule (think regulation)

una relazione – a relationship, connection, report, romance, affair

un resto – a rest (e.g., from currency, not a break) remainder

un rischio – a risk

una risposta – a response

un risultato – a result, outcome, effect, consequence
una rivoluzione – a revolution
un ritmo – a rhythm, tempo, pace
un ritorno – a return
un ruolo – roll, part

un sacrificio – a sacrifice
uno scandalo – a scandal
una scena – a scene
uno scenario –a setting, scenery
un segnale – a signal
un segno – a sign, symbol
un segreto – a secret
una sequenza – a sequence, progression
una sensazione – a sensation
un senso – a sense, feeling, meaning
un sentimento – a sentiment, feeling, emotion
una serie – a series
un servizio – a service
un significato – a meaning, significance
un simbolo – a symbol
un sistema – a system
una situazione – a situation
una società – society, company, club, guild
un soggetto – a subject, topic, theme, matter
un soldato – a soldier
una soluzione – a solution
un sospetto – a suspect, suspiscion
uno spazio – a space
una specie – a type, species
una speculazione – a speculation
uno spettacolo – a spectacle, show
uno stato – state, status
una stazione – a station
una stella – a star (think stellar)
uno stile – a style
una storia – a story, history
una strategia – a strategy
uno strumento – an instrumento
una struttura – a structure
un successo – a success
un suggerimento – a suggestion

156

una tecnica – a technique
una tendenza – a tendency
un territorio – a territory
un tipo – a type
un titolo – a title
un tono – a tone, quality
una traccia – a trace
una tragedia – a tragedy
un treno – a train
un trionfo – a triumph

un ufficiale – an official
un ufficio – an office
un uso – a use
un utensile – a utensil

una vacanza – a vacation
un vantaggio – an advantage, benefit
un vizio – a vice

una zona – a zone

MISCELLANEOUS
ADJECTIVES
AGGETTIVI VARI

Questo è ...   This is...
Quello non è ...   That isn't...
Lui/lei è...   He/she is...

accettabile – acceptable
adeguato – adequate
alto – tall (think altitude)
antico – ancient, antique
artificiale – artificial
assoluto – absolute
automatico – automatic

banale – banal
benevolo – benevolent
bizzarro – bizarre
breve – brief
brillante – brillant

capace – capable
centrale – central
compatto – compact, united
complesso – complex
complicato – complicated
comune – common
concentrato – concentrated
contento – content, happy
continuo – continuous
contrario – contrary, opposite
coraggioso – courageous
corretto – correct
costante – constant
conveniente – convenient
cristiano – Christian
curioso – curious

delicato – delicate
differente – different
difficile – difficult
difficoltoso – difficult
diretto – direct
distante – distant
divertente – fun (think fun diversion)
diverso – different (diverse)

eccessivo – excessive
eccezionale – exceptional
elettrico – electric
economico – economical, cheap
enorme – enormous
esatto – exact
esterno – external, outside
estremo – extreme
evidente – evident

familiare – familiar
famoso – famous
fantastico – fantastic
favorevole – favorable
fermo – firm
finale – final
fondamentale – fundamental
futuro – future

generale – general
giusto – just, right, correct
gigante – gigantic
grave – grave, serious

illegale – illegal
immediato – immediate
implicito – implicit
importante – important
impossibile – impossible
inerente – inherent
innato – innate

159

intelligente – intelligent
intensivo – intensive
intenso – intense
interessante – interesting
internazionale – international
interno – internal, inner
intero – entire, whole

legale – legal
libero – free (think liberated)
limitato – limited
lungo – long

macabro – macabre
magnifico – magnificent
massimo – maximum
maturo – mature
medio – mid, middle
meraviglioso – marvelous
minimo – minimal
minore – minor
misterioso – mysterious
moderno – modern
modesto – modest
morale – moral

naturale – natural
necessario – necessary
negativo – negative
nobile – noble
normale – normal
notevole – notable
nudo – nude
numeroso – numerous

offensivo – offensive
onorevole – honorable
opzionale – optional
originale – original
ottimista – optimist
ottimo – optimal, great
ovvio – obvious

particolare – particular, unique
patetico – pathetic
perfetto – perfect
personale – personal
popolare – popular
positivo – positive
possibile – possible
povero – poor (think poverty)
preciso – precise, exact
presente – present
primo – primary, first
principale – principal, main
privato – private
probabile – probable
problematico – problematic
prodigioso – prodigious, enormous
profondo – deep, profound, intense
puntuale – punctual
puro – pure

rapido – rapid, quick
recente – recent
religioso – religious
repetitivo – repetitive
responsabile – responsible
ricco – rich
ridicolo – ridiculous
rilevante – relevant, also sizable
romantico – romantic
rotondo – round, rotund

sacro – sacred, holy
scettico – sceptical
segreto – secret
semplice – simple
secondo – second, secondary
sensazionale – sensational
sereno – serene
serio – serious
sicuro – sure, secure
silenzioso – silent, quiet
simile – similar, alike
singolare – singular, unique
sociale – social

solo – sole, alone, only
solitario – solitary, lonely
sospettoso – suspicious (think suspect)
speciale – special
splendido – splendid
spirituale – spiritual
storico – historic
strano – strange
straordinario – extraordinary
strano – strange
stupendo – stupendous
stupido – stupid
sufficiente – sufficient
superiore – superior

tardi – late, tardy
tecnico – technical
tenace – tenacious
terribile – terrible
timido – timid
tollerante – tollerant
tranquillo – tranquil, calm

ufficiale – official
uguale, eguale – equal
ultimo – last, ultimate
unico – unique
uniforme – uniform, even, regular, constant
urgente – urgent
utile – useful (think utiliterian)

valido – valid
vantaggioso – advantageous
vario – various, diverse
vasto – vast
veloce – quick (think velocity)
vicino – close (think vicinity)
visibile – visible

FUN PHRASES
FRASI DIVERTENTI

Following is a collection of compound cognate phrases. These constructions are just the tip of the iceberg, a mere introduction of useful expressions, which could facilitate and propel language ability. As you improve your language skills, collect your own phrases. Writing them down as you discover them will help you retain the phrases.

Some very basic vocabulary words are listed here that are not cognates (e.g. *con, senza, qualche, volta*, etc.) but are used, with the assumption that you already know these words. And if you don't, you'll need to learn them anyway, as they are fundamental to the language.

alto – tall, high (think altitude)
alto livello – high grade
alto valore – high value
alta moda – high fashion
alto prezzo – high price
gli alti e bassi della vita – the ups and downs of life
lei è molto alta per la sua età – she's very tall for her age

basso – short, low, shallow, menial
a basso livello – at a low level
a basso prezzo – at a low price
basso e grasso – short and fat
di basso costo – at low cost, affordable
di basso profilo – low profile
di basso stato sociale – of low social status
il punto più basso – the lowest point
un quoziente d'intelligenza basso – a low IQ
un tono basso – a low pitch

base – base, basis, core, foundation
la base lunare – lunar base
la base militare – military base, post
la base operativa – base of operations
il campo base – base camp
in base a – depending on

163

la linea base – base line
il livello base – base level
la paga base – base pay
il salario base – base salary
lo stipendio base – basic wage
la tariffa base – base fee
il prezzo base – base price
una base di comparizione – basis for comparision, standard
la base protettiva/rinforzante – backing, reinforcement

il caso – the case, event, instance, chance
un caso clinico – clinical case
un caso disperato – hopeless/desperate case
un caso esemplare – exemplarary case
un caso estremo – extreme case
un caso isolato – isolated case
il caso in questione – case in question/point
un caso limite – borderline case
un caso medico – medical case
un caso mentale – mental case
il caso precedente – preceding case
un caso sfortunato – unfortunate situation
un caso speciale – special case
un caso tipico – typical case
un caso unico – unique case/situation
in caso di – in case of
in caso di necessità – in case of necessity
in questo caso particolare – in this particular case

con – with
con buone intenzioni – with good intentions
con calma – with calm, calmly
con cordialità – cordially
con decoro – with decorum, dignified
con difficoltà – with difficulty
con entusiasmo – with enthusiasm, enthusiastically
con forza – with force, forcibly, hard
con franchezza – with candor, frankly
con gioia – with joy, joyously
con gratitudine - gratefully
con interesse – with interest

con moderazione – with moderation
con onore – with honor, honorably
con passione – with passion, passionately
con pazienza – with patience, patiently
con semplicità – neatly, simply
con successo – successfully
con il tempo – with time
con una mano sola – singlehandedly
con le mani nel sacco – red handed
(literally, with the hands in the sack)

la decisione – the decision
arrivare ad una decisione – to arrive at a decision
una decisione della corte/del tribunale – court/tribunal decision
una decisione grave – a grave/serious decision
una decisione legale – a legal decision
una decisione storica – historic/landmark decision

la dimensione – the dimension, size, proportion
a dimensione singola – one dimensional
di dimensione eccessiva – of an excessive amount, overgrown
di dimensione regola – regular sized
la quarta dimensione – the fourth dimension
un disastro di bibliche dimensioni – a disaster of biblical proportions

la distanza – the distance, length, extent
una breve distanza – short distance
distanza attraverso – distance through
distanza media – mean distance
distanza perpendicolare – perpendicular distance
distanza verticale – vertical distance
lunga distanza – long distance

l'energia – the energy, force, power
consumo di energia – energy consumption
energia alternativa – alternative energy
energia atomica – atomic power
energia elettrica – electric power
fonte di energia – power source
un'unità di energia – unit of energy
energia solare – solar energy

l'errore – the error, mistake
commettere un errore – to commit an error
un errore evidente – an evident/glaring error
un errore grammaticale – grammatical error
un errore in giudizio – an error in judgement
un errore stupido – a stupid mistake
errore umano – human error

falso – false
denaro falso – counterfeit money
un falso allarme – a false alarm
un falso amico – fair-weather friend, false cognate
un falso nome – a false name
vero o falso – true or false?

la famiglia - family
una famiglia di separati – a broken home
una famiglia felice – a happy family
la famiglia umana – human family
una festa di famiglia – a family party
una grande famiglia – a large family
il medico della famiglia – family doctor
un membro della famiglia – a family member
la prima famiglia – first family
una grande famiglia felice – one big happy family
la famiglia reale – the royal family

la fine – the end (think final, finish)
alla fine – in the end, at last, eventually
alla fine del mondo – at the end of the earth
dall'inizio alla fine – from beginning to end, throughout, head to tail
la fine della vita – end of life
una fine prematura – an untimely end
fino alla fine – to the bitter end, till the end of time
in fin dei conti – in the end, when all is said and done, basically
senza fine – without end, never ending
il fine settimana – the weekend

giusto – just, fair, right, correct, proper

nel modo giusto – in the right way
non proprio giusto – not quite right
essere nel giusto – to be in the right
al momento giusto – at the right time
giusto ed appropriato – right and proper
il conto non è giusto – the check's not right
arrivare al momento giusto – to arrive at the right time
non posso trovare le parole giuste – I can't find the right words

grande – big, large, great

con grande attenzione – with great attention, care
con grande preoccupazione – frantically
di grande importanza – of great importance, momentous
di grande valore – of great value
una grande avversario – archenemy
una grande città – a big city
una grande eccitazione – great excitement, fever pitch
un grande fratello – a big brother
una grande idea – a great idea
un grande magazzino – department store
un grande onore – a great honor
una grande quantità – a large quantity, a lot, a bunch of
con grande rispetto – with great respect
con grande soddisfazione – with great satisfaction
un grande successo – great success
il pubblico generale – the general public
in grande misura – to a great degree

il gruppo – the group, bunch, cluster

criteri di gruppo – group policy, criteria
un gruppo corale, un coro – choral group
un gruppo di amici – group of friends
un gruppo di criminali – gang, group of criminals
un gruppo di esperti – think tank, brain trust
un gruppo di giovani – youth group
un gruppo di interesse – (special) interest group
un gruppo di minoranza – minority group
un gruppo di persone – group of people
un gruppo di pressione – pressure group, lobbyists
un gruppo di studio – study group

un gruppo etnico – ethnic group
un gruppo familiare – family group, household
un gruppo finanziario – financial group
un gruppo musicale – band, music group
metodo di gruppo – group method
parte del gruppo – part of the group

la idea – the idea
buon idea – good idea
ottima idea – great (optimal) idea

l'inizio – the start, beginning, onset (think initial)
all'inizio – at the beginning
un inizio entusiastico – a flying start
un nuovo inizio – a new beginning, a fresh start

intero – entire, whole, complete
un anno intero – a whole year
il latte intero – whole milk
al mondo intero – to the entire world
un numero intero – whole number, integer
l'intero pezzo – the whole piece
a valore intero – full value

il livello – the level, degree, point, layer
a livello mondiale – world wide (at the world wide level)
a livello nazionale – nationwide (at the national level)
al livello più alto, elevato – to the most elevated/highest degree
al massimo livello – to the maximum/hightest degree
di alto livello – at a high level
di basso livello – below standand
famoso a livello mondiale – world famous
linguaggio di basso livello – low level language
linguaggio formale di alto livello – high level language
livello del mare – sea level
livello di tensione – stress level
livello energetico – energy level
livello inferiore –base level
livello più basso – lowest level
livello salariale – pay level

maggiore – major, greater, main, bigger, oldest
per la maggiore parte – for the most part, the majority
il fratello maggiore – big brother
la sorella maggiore – big sister

la maniera – the manner, way, style, fashion
in maniera corrispondente – proportionately
in maniera onesta – in an honest/fair manner/way
in maniera più eccellente – in a most excellent way
in maniera prevedibile – in a foreseeable manner, predictably
in maniera radicale – in a radical manner, radically
nella maniera giusta – in the right way, properly

il modo – the way, manner, fashion, mode
in modo appropiato – in an appropriate way
in un certo modo – in a certain way
in modo comico – comically
in modo competente – professionally, in a competent way
in modo condiscendente – patronizingly, in a condescending way
in modo contemplativo – pensively, in a contemplative way
in modo continuo – continuously, in a continuous way
in modo costante – constantly, in a constant way
in modo convincente – convincingly, in a convincing way
in modo credibile – credibly, in a believable way
in modo diretto – directly, in a direct way
in modo diverso – in a different/diverse way
in modo eloquente – eloquently, in an eloquent way
in modo entusiastico – enthusiastically
in modo evidente/ovvio – in an evident/obvious way
grosso modo – for the most part, roughly speaking
nel modo giusto – in the right way, fairly
in modo imparziale – fairly, in an impartial way
in modo impreciso – imprecisely, inaccurately
in modo inaccettabile – unacceptable
in modo intelligente – in an intelligent way
in un modo interessante – in an interesting way
in modo naturale – in a natural way
in modo onesto – honestly, fairly
in modo relativo – relatively, in a relative way
in modo simile – in a similar way
in modo soddisfacente – in a satisfying way

il movimento – the movement, motion

in movimento – on the go, shifting
in movimento circolare – in swirling circular movement
in movimento costante – in constant motion
un movimento carismatico – a charismatic movement
un movimento di lavoratori – worker's movement
il movimento di liberazione delle donne – women's liberation movement
un movimento massa – a mass movement
un movimento ecumenico – an ecumenical movement
movimento fluido – fluid motion
un movimento intestinale – a bowel movement
un movimento politico – a political movement
un movimento rapido – a rapid movement
un movimento sociale – a social movement
un movimento spasmodico improvviso – a jerky/spastic movement

la natura – the nature

forze della natura – forces of nature
la natura della bestia – the nature of the beast
le leggi della natura – the laws of nature
la natura animale – animal nature
la natura interiore – inner nature
la natura umana – human nature
la madre natura – mother nature

ogni – each, every

da ogni parte – from every part, from everywhere
in ogni caso – in any case, anyway, at any rate
in ogni modo – in any case, besides, anyhow
in ogni senso pratico – for all practical purposes
ogni cosa – everything
ogni altra cosa – everything else
ogni genere – all sorts
ogni giorno – every day, daily
ogni notte – every night, nightly
ogni ora – every hour, hourly
ogni sera – every evening, nightly
ogni settimana – every week, weekly
ogni pezzo – every piece, bit
in ogni direzione – in all directions

l'opinione – the opinion, thought
una bassa opinione – a low opinion
un opinione commune – a common opinion
un'opinione negative – a negative opinion
un'opinione positiva – a good opinion
l'opinione pubblica – public opinion
una seconda opinione – second opinion

ottimo – great, best, optimal
un'ottima idea – a great idea
un ottimo lavoro – a first-rate job
ottimo livello – optimal level
un'ottima memoria –a great memory
in ottima salute –in excellent health
in ottimo stato – in excellent condition
è di ottimo umore – he's in a very good mood
la macchina è in ottimo stato – the car is in excellent condition

la parte – the part, side
la parte centrale – the central part
la parte essenziale – the essential part
la parte esterna – the external/outer part
in gran parte – to a great extent
la parte più importante – the most important part
la parte inferiore – the underside
la parte interiore – the inner part
la parte interna – the inner part
per la maggior parte – for the most part
la parte opposta – the opposite side
la parte posteriore – the back side
la parte superiore – the top part
l'ultima parte – the last part

la persona – the person
una persona d'affari – a business person
una persona di contatto – a contact person
una persona con disturbi mentali – a psychotic
una persona molto importante – a bigwig, VIP
una persona con integrita' morale – a moral person
una persona dalle idee conservatrici – a narrow minded person
una persona onesta – an honest person
una persona strana – an oddball, strange person

posto – post, place, spot, job, workspace, seat, site, station, etc.

un posto al sole – a place in the sun
al posto di – in place of, instead of
al proprio posto – in its (own) place
al primo/secondo/terzo/ultimo posto – in 1st/2nd/3rd/last place
avere un posto in prima fila – to have a ringside seat
cambiare posto – to changes places
una coscienza a posto – a clear conscience
fare posto – to make space
fuori posto – out of place
in ogni posto – in every place, everywhere
in quel posto – in that place
in questo posto – in this place
mettere al posto giusto – to put in the right spot
un posto alla moda – a hot spot
un posto di lavoro – a workplace
un posto dimenticato da Dio – a godforsaken place
il posto di polizia – police station
un posto vacante – a vacancy
mettere a posto qualcosa – to set something right
tutto a posto – good, OK, alright (everything's in place)

qualche – some, any, a few
(nouns that follow are always in the singular)
in qualche altra occasione – at some other time
in qualche maniera – in some manner, somehow
in qualche misura – to some degree, somewhat
in qualche modo – in some way, somehow
in qualche altro posto – in some other place, somewhere else
per qualche motivo – for some motive/reason
qualche cosa – something
qualche tempo dopo – some time after
qualche tempo fa – some time ago

quasi – almost, just about, nearly
quasi lo stesso – nearly the same
quasi mai – almost never
quasi niente – almost nothing
quasi perfetto – almost perfect
quasi pronto – almost ready
quasi troppo tardi – almost too late
quasi impossibile – almost impossible

172

la ragione – reason, cause

il potere della ragione – the power of reason
per qualche ragione – for some reason
la ragione di fondo – underlying reason
ragione di preoccupazione – matter of concern
la ragione pratica – practical reason
la ragione principale – main reason
una ragione valida – a good reason
una buona ragione – good reason

la regola – rule (think regulation)

un eccezione alla regola – exception to the rule
la regola di maggioranza – majority rule
la regola generica/generale – general rule
una regola speciale – a special rule

il senso – the sense, feeling, meaning

buon senso – good sense, common sense
senso commune – common sense
un senso di dolore – a feeling of pain
un senso del dovere/d'onore – a sense of duty, of honor
il senso di un frase – the meaning of a phrase
un senso di gioia – a feeling of joy
un senso di giustizia – a sense of justice/right and wrong
in senso giusto – in the right way/direction
un senso di gratitudine – a sense of gratitude
un senso di gusto – a sense of taste
in senso opposto/contrario – in the opposite way
un senso morale/pratico – a moral/practical sense
un senso di piacere – a feeling of pleasure
un senso di responsabilità – a sense of responsibility
un senso d'umorismo – a sense of humor
senso unico – one way only
il senso della vita – the meaning of life
avere senso – to make sense
avere il senso di – to have the sense that
in ogni senso pratico – for all practical purposes
in un certo senso – in a certain sense/way
questo non ha senso – this doesn't make sense
i cinque sensi – the five senses
il sesto senso – the sixth sense

senza – without

senza alternative – without alternative
senza assistenza – without help/assistance
senza attenzione – carelessly, without attention
senza base – baseless
senza capo né coda – without rhyme or reason
senza casa – homeless
senza cerimonie – without ceremony
senza considerazione – without regard, consideration
senza difficoltà – without difficulty
senza dubbio – without a doubt (dubbio – think dubious)

il sistema – the system

battere il sistema – to beat the system
l'analista di sistema – systems analyst
il sistema di allarme – alarm system
il sistema di bassa pressione – low-pressure system
sistema di communicazione – communications system
il sistema di controllo – control system
sistema di governo – government system
il sistema legale – legal system
il sistema postale – postal system
sistema del liberalismo economico – free enterprise system
il sistema numerico – number system
il sistema di selezione – selection system

lo stile – the style

lo stile di famiglia – family style
lo stile di prosa – prose style
lo stile di scrittura – writing style
lo stile di vita – lifestyle
lo stile letterario – literary style
lo stile linguistico – language style
lo stile libero – freestyle
lo stile musicale – musical style
lo stile ornamentale – decorative style
lo stile personale – personal style

sotto – down, below, beneath, under, sub, downstairs

di sotto – below, underneath, downstairs
avere la situazione sotto controllo – to have the situation under control
lavorare sotto pressione – to work under pressure
nato sotto una buona stella – born under a lucky star
sotto la custodia di – in custody of
sotto falso nome – under a false name
sotto l'influenza di - under the influence of
sotto i piedi – underfoot
sotto una nuvola di sospetto – under a cloud of suspicion
sotto ogni punto di vista – in all respects
sotto la protezione di – under the protection of
sotto la responsabilità – under the responsibility of
sotto il sole – under the sun
sotto la superficie – under the surface
sotto terra – underground

su – up on, over, above, atop, about, regarding

su e giù – up and down
su richiesta – upon request
basato su probabilità – based on probability
basato/fondato su – based/founded on
commento su – comment on
fatto su misura – made to order
giuro su Dio – I swear to God
mettere su peso – to put on weight

tutto – all, everything

è tutto per il meglio – it's all for the best
è tutto sotto controllo – everthing's under control
fai tutto quello che puoi – do all you can
fare di tutto – to make every effort
in tutto il creato – in all creation
in tutto il mondo – all over the world
in tutto il suo splendore – in all its splendor
per tutto il mondo – for all the world, for everyone
tutto il resto – all the rest, everything else
per tutto il tempo – for all time
per tutto l'anno – year-round
prima di tutto – first of all
quasi tutti – almost all
tutto bene – OK

tutto il giorno – all day long
tutto incluso – all included
tutto intorno – all round
tutto insieme – all together
tutto nella mente – all in the mind
tutto considerato – all things considered
tutto sommato – in summary, in short, in brief

umano – human
il corpo umano – the human body
l'errore umano – human error
l'essere umano – human being
il fattore umano – human factor
la natura umana – human nature
il progresso umano – human progress/development
un sacrificio umano – a human sacrifice

l'uso – the use
in uso – in use
per uso pubblico – for public consumption
l'uso attivo – active use
l'uso eccessivo – eccessive use
l'uso errato – wrong use
l'uso finale – final use
uso illecito – abuse, illicit use
per l'uso personale – for personal use

vero – true, real (think verily, veracity)
un vero amico – a true friend
vero amore – true love
vero e proprio – out and out
vero o falso – true or false
un vero problema – a real problem
il vero significato – true meaning

176

la volta – the time, one time, once

alla volta – at a time
ancora una volta – once more, another time, again
c'era una volta – once upon a time
di volta in volta – from time to time
fino alla prossima volta – until next time
la volta precedente – the previous time
ogni volta – every time
per la prima volta – for the first time
qualche volta – sometimes
questa volta – this time
quella volta – that time
solo una volta – just once
un po' per volta – a little at a time
un'altra volta – another time
una volta nella vita – once in a lifetime
una volta o due – once or twice
una volta per tutte – once and for all
uno alla volta – one by one

la zona – the zone, area, region

la zona dei negozi – shopping area
una zona d'interesse – an area of interest
una zona grigia – a grey area
la zona euro – the euro zone
la zona protetta – safe haven, protected zone

RANDOM PHRASES
(alphabetized by noun)

un falso allarme – false alarm
un angolo interno – an inner angle/corner
un approccio positivo/negativo – a positive/negative approach
l'area di servizio – service area
un argomento molto convincente – a very convincing argument
l'aspetto generale – general appearance/aspect/look
l'aspetto personale – personal appearance
attenzione costante – constant attention
l'attività del gruppo – group activity
l'autorità suprema – supreme authority
azione legale – legal action

una base militare – a military base
un salario base – base pay/salary

causa ed effetto – cause and effect
la causa probabile – probable cause
il centro di cultura – the cultural center
un circolo vizioso – a viscious circle
una civiltà antica – an ancient civilization
prima/seconda classe – first/second class
un colore delicato/dominante – subtle/dominant color
un colore fondamentale – a primary color
una compagnia teatrale – a theatrical company, troupe
il compagno di cella in prigione – prison cell mate
la comunicazione elettronica – electronic communication
il concetto principale – the principal concept/idea
condizioni favorevoli – favorable conditions
una conseguenza naturale/inevitabile – a natural/inevitable consequence
la conservazione di energia – energy conservation
il consumo di energia – consumption of energy
una persona di contatto – a contact person
il contatto fisico – physical contact
assumere il controllo – to assume control, take charge
la ferma convizione – firma conviction
il coraggio morale – moral courage
una corrente d'aria – a current of air
la corte di giustizia – court of justice
la corte di opinione pubblica – the court of public opinion

una critica costruttiva – a constructive criticism
una crisi isterica – a nervous breakdown/hysterical fit/crisis
una cultura letteraria/della droga – literary/drug culture

una decisione coragiosa – a courageous decision
una decisione personale – a personal decision
un desiderio insaziabile – an insatiable desire
un desiderio intenso – an intense desire
accettare il proprio destino – to accept one's fate/destiny
una differenza d'opinioni – a difference of opinion
in direzione opposta/contraria – in the opposite direction
la dinamica del gruppo – the group dynamic
una breve/lunga distanza – a brief/long distance

un effetto domino – a domino effect
un effetto positivo/negativo – a positive/negative effect
un elemento chimico – a chemical element
l'elemento di sorpresa – the element of surprise
un'energia alternativa – alternative energy
durante l'epoca di pubertà – during (the time of) puberty
commettere un errore – to commit an error
un errore grammaticale – a grammatical error
un segnale di errore – an error signal
un errore umano – human error
l'esame di coscienza – examination of conscience
un esame medico – a medical exam
un esempio specifico – a specific example
l'esperienza precedente – the previous/preceding experience
un'esperienza traumatica – a tramatic experience
un'espressione idiomatica – an idiomatic expression

un fenomeno naturale – natural phenomena
una figura leggendaria – a legendary figure
la forma di governo – form of government
con forza brutale – with brute force
una forza della natura – a force of nature
una frase famosa – a famous phrase
la struttura della frase – structure of the phrase/sentence
la fronte di battaglia – the battlefront
una funzione vitale – a vital function

179

in genere – in general, usually
la giustizia infinita – infinite justice
un governo democratico – a democratic government
un grado superiore – a superior grade
un gruppo di discussione – discussion group
un gruppo etnico – ethnic group

un'idea astratta/generale/originale – abstract/general/original idea
un'immagine distorta – a distorted image
un'immagine pubblica – a public image
della massima importanza – of utmost/maximum importance
di minore/minima importanza – of minor/minimal importance
un'ottima impressione – an excellent (optimal) impression
con l'intenzione giusta/ostile – right, good/hostile intention
una persona di interesse – a person of interest
un istinto naturale – a natural instinct

un limite estremo – an extreme limit
il limite di velocità – speed/velocity limit
stabilire un limite superiore – to establish an upper limit
livello di tensione – stress level

il magnetismo animale – animal magnetism
in maniera meccanica – in a mechanical way, mechanically
una massa critica – a critical mass
una materia liquida/solida – a liquid/solid matter
una medaglia per il merito – merit badge/medal
una memoria di breve/lungo termine – a short/long term memory
una menzione speciale – a special mention
ricevere un messaggio – to receive a message
un audio messaggio – audio message
all'ultimo minuto – at the last minute
in una certa misura – to a certain degree
un breve momento in tempo – a brief moment in time
il morale della storia/favola – moral of the story/fable
un buon motivo – a good reason/motive

la natura della bestia – the nature of the beast
la natura essenziale – essential nature
la natura umana – human nature
una nazione indipendente – an independent nation
una necessità urgente – urgent need/necessity
la notizia allarmante – alarming news

un'occasione speciale – a special occasion
un odore ripugnante – a repugnant/foul odor
un oggetto d'arte – an art object
un oggetto sessuale – a sex object
un omicidio premeditato – premeditated murder
un grande onore – a great honor
un operazione di emergenza – an emergency operation
l'opinione popolare – popular opinion
in ordine descendente – in descending order
in ordine numerologico – in numerological order
l'origine della specie – origin of the species

la parte centrale – the center part, middle
un passaggio segreto – a secret passage
la pazienza al limite – patience at its limit
per un breve/lungo periodo – for a brief/long time
una persona ambiziosa – an ambitious person
una persona molto importante – a VIP
l'intero pezzo – whole/entire piece
un piano d'azione – a plan of action
una posizione favorevole – a favorable position
una remota possibilità – a remote possibility
una presenza soprannaturale – a supernatural presence
il prezzo della fama – the price of fame
un processo mentale – a mental process
il prodotto finale – final product, end product, output
produzione in serie/di massa – mass production
un programma musicale – a musical prgram
un progetto a larga scala – a large scale project
una proposta indecente – an indecent proposal
una proposta di matrimonio – a marriage proposal
un punto di vista – a point of view
un punto di interesse – a point of interest
il punto di non ritorno – the point of no return

una lunga tradizione di qualità – *a long tradition of quality*
una quantità sufficiente – *a sufficient quantity/adequate amount*
una questione di necessità – *a question/matter of necessity*

una reazione chimica – *a chemical reaction*
una reazione esagerata/ecessiva – *an overraction*
una regione agricola – *an agricultural region*
una relazione inversa – *inverse relationship*
il resto è storia – *the rest is history*
il riscaldamento globale – *global warming*
(*riscaldare* – to heat, warm up; think to scald)
una risposta immediata – *an immediate response*
una risposta ambigua/vaga – *ambiguous/vague response*
il risultato finale – *end result, outcome, bottom line*
il risultato logico – *logical outcome*

offrire in sacrificio – *to offer in sacrifice*
un sacrificio umano – *human sacrifice*
sano e salvo – *safe and sound* ("*healthy and safe*")
un segnale d'allarme – *an alarm signal*
un segno positivo – *a positive sign*
un segno rivelatore – *a telltale (revealing) sign*
in un certo senso – *in a certain sense, in a way*
in ogni senso pratico – *for all practical purposes*
il sentimento religioso – *religious sentiment/feeling*
una sequenza logica – *a logical sequence*
una serie di eventi – *a series of events*
il servizio diplomatico – *diplomatic service*
un servizio pubblico – *a public service*
il sistema di sicurezza – *security system*
una situazione difficile – *a difficult situation*
la soluzione di un problema – *the solution to a problem*
nello spazio cosmico – *in outer/cosmic space*
uno spettacolo di talento – *a talent show*
un spirito libero – *a free spirit*
lo spirito di competizione – *the spirit of competition*
una storia di interesse umano – *a human interest story*
uno strumento medico/ottico – *a medical/optical instrument*
una struttura di supporto – *a support structure, framework*
un grande successo – *a great success*

una tendenza naturale – a natural tendency
il territorio neutrale – neutral territory
il territorio vergine – virgin territory
il tipo di carattere – character type
il tipo ideale – ideal type
il titolo dell'articolo – the title of the article
il trasporto pubblico – public transportation

l'ufficio del direttore – office of the director

di valore sentimentale – of sentimental value
alla velocità della luce – at the speed of light
viceversa – vice versa

una zona di bassa pressione – a low pressure system
una zona commerciale – commercial/shopping zone

FALSE COGNATES

FALSE FRIENDS

FALSE COGNATES

Although false cognates, otherwise known as false friends or *falsi amici*, certainly do exist in Romance language, statistically, these account for a very small percentage of vocabulary. However, as you advance in linguistic ability and sophistication, you'll find that certain words are just not what they seem. Here are common false cognates.

attualmente – currently; not actually
If you want to say *actually,* your best bets are
in realtà, in effetti, effettivamente.
la moda attuale – the current fashion
all'ora attuale, al momento attuale – at the present moment

l'argomento – topic, subject matter,
issue, statement, content; not an argument
The word doesn't have the bite that *argument* has in English. *Argomento* can mean *argument* in the sense of debate or reasoning, but not in the angry, heated sense. If you want to indicate argument, that's
un litigio, un lite, una lotta or una disputa, and
at times… *una discussione…* (see next page.)
un buon argomento – a good point
un argomento delicato – a delicate issue
l'argomento del giorno – topic of the day
argomento di meditazione – food for thought
un argomento molto persuasivo – a very persuasive argument
l'argomento principale – main point
cambiare argomento – to change the subject

bravo – good, skilled, capable; not brave
The word bravo is packed with nuance and meaning.
It can mean good, smart, fine, capable, skilled, clever and morally upright.
brave is coraggioso or valoroso

la camera – room, bedroom, chamber;
not a photographic camera
Camera indicates bedroom, and not the memory documentation device that we think of. The Italian term for that is un macchina fotografica. If you've studied Spanish, remember that the word for bed is cama.
la camera matrimoniale – master bedroom
una camera singola – a single room

casuale – coincidental, by chance, random; not casual
casual - informale

il collegio – boarding school; not college
the college - l'università

la confidenza – intimacy; not confidence
the confidence - la fiducia

crudo – raw, uncooked, unrefined; not crude
crude - volgare, non raffinato (not refined, crude)

la delusione – disappointment; not a delusion
a delusion - un'illusione

la discussione – discussion, but more commonly, an argument, quarrel
It generally connotes a more heated discussion than in English.
una discussione unilateral – one-sided discussion
in discussione – in debate, in dispute

educato – polite, well mannered, well bred; not educated
educated - colto, istruito
well bred - ben educato

eventuale – possible, potential, any; not eventual
eventualmente – possibly, maybe, perhaps; not eventually
eventually - alla fine

la fabbrica – factory; not fabric
the fabric - il tessuto, la stoffa

fame – hunger; not fame
the fame - la fama, la celebrità

la fattoria – farm; not factory
the factory - la fabbrica (where things are fabricated)
to manufacture, fabricate – fabbricare

187

fastidioso – irritating, bothersome; not fastidious

If you want to indicate *fastidious*, use *meticoloso or pignolo*.
So if you say, (thinking you're giving your accountant a big compliment,)
"Lei è molto fastidioso!" what you are really saying is, "You're a big pain
in the butt/You're getting on my nerves!" Beware the false cognate!

fastidiare, verb – to irritate, bother
un fastidio, noun – a bother, annoyance
fastidioso, adj. – annoying, tedious

la firma – signature; not firm

the firm/company – la ditta, l'azienda, l'impresa, la compania, società
firmare – to sign
firm, adj. – rigido

gentile – kind, nice; not gentle

gentle – dolce, leggero

incidente – accident

Incidente can mean incident, but generally translates as accident.
un incidente bizzarro – a freak accident
un incidente industriale – an industrial accident
un incidente mortale – a fatal accident
un incidente aereo – an airplane crash

largo – wide; not large

large – grande

la lettura – the reading; not lecture

lecture – la conferenza

libreria – bookstore; not library

library – la biblioteca

il magazzino – storage unit; not a magazine

Un magazzino is a storage unit, whether it's a bin, closet or warehouse.
Remember that the container holding bullets is a magazine.
The magazine that you read is *una rivista*.
un grande magazzino – department store
depositare in magazzino – to warehouse

il mare – the sea; not a mare

the mare – la cavalla

morbido – soft; not morbid
Yeah, where did this one come from?!!
If you want to say *morbid*, use *morboso or patologico.*

noioso – boring, annoying, tedious; not noisy
noisy – rumoroso

palazzo – building, palace
Yes, do think of palace. But just as commonly, it simply refers to an
apartment or office building. So if a guy asks you back to
his palazzo after a date, don't get your hopes up...
un palazzo senza ascensore – a walk-up, building without an elevator
il palazzo di municipio – municipal building, town hall, city hall
il palazzo di giustizia – court house
la guardia di palazzo – palace guard
il palazzo d'uffici – office building

parenti – relatives; not parents
The term for parents is *i genitori.* FYI, in colloquial Italian, Italians
generally refer to their parents as *"i miei,"* dropping the noun.

la patente – driver's license; not patent
a patent – un brevetto

pavimento – floor, surface; not pavement
Yes, think of pavement, because it helps you remember, but this word
actually means floor, on the inside of a building, not outside.
the pavement - marciapiede (sidewalk,) strada (street,)
or terra (ground, dirt, land and earth.)

i pepperoni – bell or hot peppers;
not pepperoni, as in the pizza sausage
The *pepperoni* we put on our pizza is *salame piccante.*

preservativo – condom
From the Latin verb, *preservare*, which means *to preserve*, well, not just
food, but also, um...certain bodily fluids. Its vernacular meaning is
condom. To obtain food without preservatives or snickering from the
locals, use *cibo senza conservanti, cibo biologico or cibo organico.*

proprio – own, one's own; not proper
proper – appropriato

ricoverato – to be admitted, hospitalized
 not *recovered*

recovered, healed – recuperato, guarito (healed)
ritrovato (found; after being lost)

rumore – a sound, noise; **not** *rumor*

rumor – una voce, un pettegolezzo

il sale – salt; **not** *sale*

sale – la vendita, l'occasione

sensibile – sensitive; **not** *sensible*

sensible – ragionevole

simpatico – nice; **not** *sympathetic*

sympathetic, understanding – comprensivo

tremendo – terrible, frightening, excessive, severe

This word in Italian carries negative connotations regarding its subject matter, whereas in English it often has just as often has positive overtones.   It's therefore, highly ill-advised to tell your hostess, after a delightful dinner, "Era un pasto tremendo!"
(It was a terrible meal!)

la vacanza – vacation; **not** *vacancy*

vacancy – stanza libera, posto vacante

PART THREE

ESSENTIAL VOCABULARY

THE THOUSAND ESSENTIAL ITALIAN VOCABULARY WORDS

ESSENTIAL VOCABULARY
VOCABULARIO ESSENZIALE

The 1000 or so most commonly used Italian words enable 80% of everyday speech.

So you wanna speak this gorgeous language? Absorbing Italian through the use of those warm, fuzzy twin words will expedite the language process for you, but there are other nuts and bolts that still need tightening. Can you say, *"Grammar, Pronunciation and Vocabulary?"* Besides having a good grasp of grammar and pronunciation, there's simply a certain critical mass of additional basic vocabulary which makes fluency possible. This section presents essential vocabulary with example sentences.

Broad strokes, the 1000 or so most commonly used Italian words enable about 80% of everyday speech. Wow. So it stands to reason then, that the better command you have of these gold-bullion, high-frequency words, the more your speech will glide along, assuming commensurate grammar and pronunciation skills.

So what are the thousand most common Italian vocabulary words? The answer to that question is somewhat subjective, but the following four chapters are a reasonable response to that deeply stirring, existential question. This extensive vocabulary list of over 1000 words is divided into nouns, verbs, adjectives and miscellaneous grammatical words (pronouns, articles, prepositions, etc.) Accompaning those 1000 plus vocabulary words are sample sentences. Many vocabulary words have multiple connotations; however, emphasis has been placed on the more frequently used aspects of the vocabulary.

The following sentences are simple and straightforward; the intention is to provide clear constructions in order to reinforce basic grammar and vocabulary.   In keeping with the premise with this book, cognates have been used as much as possible for easy vocabulary expansion and to demonstrate how pervasively twin words exist between Italian and English.

The sentences are at times quite literal in translation; these sometimes word-for-word translations are used intentionally to aid the beginning student and may be a significant aid in terms of vocabulary expansion and grammar consolidation. Note that Italian capitalization differs from its English counterpart, as the Italian language doesn't capitalize as much as English does. Days of the week, months of the year, etc., are not capitalized as in English.

COGNATES VS. ESSENTIAL VOCABULARY

As you know by now, *a cognate*, or *twin word*, is a word that's basically the same in two languages: "interessante" or "interesting;" you know the drill... Tweak the spelling or pronunciation a bit, and boom, it's a show... The cool thing about cognates is, once you realize how pervasive and easy they are to learn, you've got an extra, oh, 2000 or so words to throw around at cocktail parties.

The thing about cognates... linguistically, they're *so easy*. They're in your comfort zone... Cognates are by far the easiest vocabulary to remember because they're intimately related to your own language are many of the words you've used all your life. Linguistically, they feel like family, because they've been rolling around in your head since childhood, but without that funny foreign accent... Reading words like, *il sistema nervosa centrale (central nervous system)* are comprehensible. Relatively speaking, they lack the hard-core "foreignness," of a foreign language. And they are hands down the best shortcut to learning a language.

However, in order to speak Italian (ahem, "the world's most beautiful language,") with some fluency, you need a *basic vocabulary* of 1000 essential words or so to get through the day. This essential vocabulary is comprised of a gnarly assortment of nouns, verbs, adjectives and miscellaneous words. Between the "cognates" and "essential vocabulary," the essential vocabulary is definitely the more difficult of the two groups to absorb, since the words are, well... foreign. But this "essential group," is critical to your goal of speaking this lusty, zesty, drop-dead gorgeous language. The bottom line is, with practice and exposure, it all comes together.

Yep, the sad truth is, "twin words" and "essential vocabulary" don't always overlap. But the really cool thing is, once you start using Italian cognates, you can beef up your vocabulary while treading water and fine tuning the "essential vocabulary" group. Cognates will facilitate the language process while you hone your skills with grammar, pronunciation and the more difficult, "essential vocabulary."

THE
SEVEN
VERBS
YOU CAN'T
LIVE
WITHOUT

THE SEVEN VERBS YOU CAN'T LIVE WITHOUT

These are the all-singing, all-dancing verbs of the world.
Without these verbs, you've got Project Mayhem...

We start this section with verbs because they are linguistically *The Essence of Life*. There are just certain things you need in life... Food, Water, Love and Chocolate... Well, if you want to speak Italian, verbs are that warm gooey center.

That said, there are seven Italian verbs that are just so essential that their importance can't be overstated. The seven verbs are broken into two groups. The first group... (drum roll:)

THE ESSENTIAL FOUR

essere – to be
avere – to have
andare – to go
fare – to do, to make

Since you're reading this book, it's presumed that you'd like to speak Italian fluently. Huh... imagine a foreigner who's trying to learn English, but has a shaky grasp of verbs, particularly the most common verbs, *to be, to have, to go, to do and to make*. Every time he wants to say phrases like, *I am... you have... he's going... we're making... they're doing*, etc., he has to hesitate, cogitate, fumble, hem and haw to remember these basic phrases. Now imagine how much more fluent his speech would be if he just had these verbs down cold. Ease with these verbs would improve his English by *a quantum leap*.

Not surprisingly, thus is the situation with *essere, avere, andare and fare*. If you want a command of Italian, these verbs are *the starting point of the language*. These verbs really tie the language together... They're also high-octane auxiliary verbs and used in endless, important idiomatic expressions. Yes, they're wildly irregular and untamed, hence more difficult to memorize, but hey... that's part of their *zesty Italian charm*... Their high frequency demands your attention. Bottom line, command of these verbs will set you apart from those who will always fumble with the language.

THE MODAL VERBS

dovere – to need to, must, ought, should
potere – to be able to, can
volere – to want

This second group of verbs is equally valuable. Why are they verbs *so* important? While communicating with earthlings, a substantial amount of what you need to convey in life has to do with what you need, can or want to do. As well as the negative therein; what you don't need, can't, or don't want to do. What makes these verbs easy is that only the modal verb is conjugated; the verb that follows is always in the infinitive, taking the pressure off of conjugating dozens, and ultimately hundreds of verbs essential for fluency.

In your quest for Italian fluency, you'll eventually want to master verb conjugations, but fluency with *dovere, potere and volere* will give you time to sideswipe literally hundreds of verbs and coast until you've gotten a handle on verb conjugations. A good grasp of these verbs will *transform* your Italian. As for traveling, these verbs are a enormous help. As a tourist, the power of being able to say, "I want to... I can't... I need to..." (followed by the infinitive verb) is "Survival Italian." Memorize these verbs, and then you can link them with a multitude of infinitives, thusly:

Devo usare il bagno. I need to use the bathroom.
Non devo mangiare più. I shouldn't eat anymore.
Non devi mai andare lì. You should never go there.

Posso pagare con la carta di credito? Can I pay with a credit card?
Posso parcheggiare qui? Can I park here?
Non posso trovare l'autobus. I can't find the bus.
Può chiamarmi un tassì? Can you call me a taxi?
Ci può fare una foto? Can you take a photo of us?
Mi può aiutare? Can you help me?

Voglio prendere la metropolitana. I want to the subway.
Voglio confermare la prenotazione. I want to confirm the reservation.
Vogliamo trovare un bel ristorante. We want to find a nice restaurant.
Non vogliamo spendere troppo. We don't want to spend too much.

Initially, memorizing all those pesky verb conjugations can be daunting for language learners. If you're struggling with verb conjugations, focus particularly on the first person singular, or the "io/I" conjugation, as in *devo/posso/voglio*. The first person singular is the most frequently used among emerging speakers and thus the most practical verb tense to concentrate on during the initial stages of language acquisition.

THE ESSENTIAL FOUR

ESSERE	_AVERE_
io sono	io ho
tu sei	tu hai
lui è	lui ha
noi siamo	noi abbiamo
voi siete	voi avete
loro sono	loro hanno

ANDARE	_FARE_
io vado	io faccio
tu vai	tu fai
lui va	lui fa
noi andiamo	noi andiamo
voi andate	voi andate
loro vanno	loro vanno

THE MODAL VERBS

DOVERE	_POTERE_	_VOLERE_
io devo	io posso	io voglio
tu devi	tu puoi	tu vuoi
lui deve	lui può	lui vuole
noi dobbiamo	noi possiamo	noi vogliamo
voi dovete	voi potete	voi volete
loro devono	loro possono	loro vogliono

ESSENTIAL VERBS

VERBI ESSENZIALI

ESSENTIAL VERBS
VERBI ESSENZIALI

Do you want another lecture about how important verbs are? Philologically speaking, verbs are the center of the universe, the linguistic limelight, the wine and the cheese. You wanna try to speak Italian without using verbs? *Fuggedaboutit!*

We start this section with verbs because verbs are where it's at. This chapter, *Essential Verbs*, is abuzz with inspirational quotes, words to live by, proverbs and movie lines to enhance your high frequency verb learning pleasure. The second chapter in this section, *Essential Adjectives*, is pure fun -- pithy quips and witty quotes. The third chapter, *Essential Nouns*, is a mix of inspirational quotes and vocabulary-rich sentences. The fourth chapter, *Miscellaneous Vocabulary*, focuses on both general and thematic vocabulary. If your Italian tends toward the beginner level, start with the last chapter of this section, *Miscellaneous Vocabulary*.

abitare – to live, dwell
Un nevrotico costruisce castelli in aria, uno psicotico
li abita e lo psichiatra riscuote l'affitto.
*A neurotic builds castles in the air, a psychotic
lives in them, and the psychologist collects the rent. – Anon*

accadere – to happen
I miracoli accadranno a quelli che credono in loro.
Miracles will happen to those who believe in them. – Paul Coelho

accendere – to turn on, light
Se hai conoscenza, lascia che gli altri accendano le candele con quella.
*If you have knowledge, let others light their candles with it.
– Margaret Fuller*

accettare – to accept
La maturità comincia quando iniziamo ad accettare le nostre debolezze.
Growth begins when we begin to accept our own weaknesses. – Jean Vanier

accompagnare – accompany
Meglio solo che mal accompagnato.
Better alone than to be in bad company. – Proverbio

accogliere – to accept, receive, welcome
Quello che non puoi evitare, accoglilo.
What you cannot avoid, welcome. – Anon

accorgersi – to realize
Il tessuto cicatriziale è più forte rispetto al tessuto
normale. Accorgiti della sua forza e procedi.
Scar tissue is stronger than regular tissue.
Realize the strength, move on. – Henry Rollins

affrontare – to face, confront
L'Eterno Nulla va perfettamente bene se sei
disponibile ad affrontarlo con un abito adatto.
Eternal Nothingness is fine if you happen
to be dressed for it. – Woody Allen

aggiungere – to add
La vita è come un panino, più si aggiunge, meglio diviene.
Life is like a sandwich; the more you add to it,
the better it becomes. – Anon

aiutare – to help
Nessuno può sinceramente cercare di aiutare
un'altra persona senza aiutare se stesso.
No man can sincerely try to help another
without helping himself. – Emerson

alzare – to raise, lift
La discrezione è essere capace di alzare il sopracciglio invece della voce.
Discretion is being able to raise your eyebrow instead of your voice. – Anon

amare – to love
Se non ci amiamo, ci distruggiamo.
If we don't love ourselves, we destroy ourselves. – Raoul Follereau

ammettere – to admit, accept, grant, allow
Nessuna regola è così generale che non ammette qualche eccezione.
No rule is so general, which admits not some exception. – Robert Burton

andare – to go
La cosa che preferisco in assoluto è andare dove non sono mai stata.
My favorite thing is to go where I've never been. – Diane Arbus

appartenere – to belong
Il futuro appartiene a coloro che credono
alla bellezza dei propri sogni.
The future belongs to those who believe in the
beauty of their dreams. – Eleanor Roosevelt

aprire – to open

I maestri aprono l'uscio, ma devi entrare da solo.
Teachers open up the doorways, but you must enter alone. – Anon

arrestare – to arrest, halt

Il segreto della giovinezza eterna è lo sviluppo arrestato.
The secret to eternal youth is arrested development.
– Alice Roosevelt Longworth

arrivare – to arrive

L'ambizione è la strada per il successo.
La persistenza è il veicolo con cui arrivi.
Ambition is the path to success.
Persistence is the vehicle you arrive in. – Bill Bradley

ascoltare – to listen

Dio ci ha dato due orecchie ed una sola bocca
per ascoltare almeno il doppio di quanto diciamo.
God gave us two ears and just one mouth to listen
to at least twice as much as what we say. – Proverbio

aspettare – to wait

Non aspettare. Il tempo non sarà mai assolutamente giusto.
Don't wait. The time will never be just right. – Napolean Hill

assicurare – to assure, secure

Il potere ha solo un dovere:
assicurare la sicurezza sociale della gente.
Power has only one duty: to secure the social
welfare of the people. – Benjamin Disraeli

assistere – to assist, help, attend, witness

Il baseball è come la chiesa.
Molti assistono, ma pochi capiscono.
Baseball is like church. Many attend
but few understand. – Wes Westrum

assumere – to assume, undertake, hire, engage

Chi assume molte cose alla volta raramente fa tutto bene.
He who undertakes many things at once seldom does anything well. – Anon

attendere – to wait, expect

Si attende con ansia il futuro se non si sa vivere il presente.
Man awaits anxiously the future if he doesn't
know how to live in the present. – Anon

aumentare – to raise, enhance, augment
Mentre la conoscenza aumenta, la meraviglia si intensifica.
As knowledge increases, wonder deepens. – Charles Morgan

avanzare – to advance
L'errore è la disciplina attraverso la quale noi avanziamo.
Error is the discipline through which we advance. – William Channing

avere – to have
"Houston, abbiamo un problema."
"Houston, we have a problem." – Apollo 13, 1995

avvenire – to happen, occur, come about, take place
Sii il cambiamento che vuoi vedere avvenire nel mondo.
Be the change you wish to see in the world. – Gandhi

avvicinare – to approach
La vera eleganza diventa sempre di più mentre si avvicina alla semplicità.
True elegance becomes even more so as it approaches simplicity.
Henry Ward Beecher

baciare – to kiss
"Baciami. Baciami come se fosse l'ultima volta."
"Kiss me. Kiss me as if it were the last time." – Casablanca, 1942

badare – to take care of, nurse, pay attention
Chi non bada a ciò che mangia diffilcilmente baderà a qualsiasi altra cosa.
He who does not mind his belly, will hardly mind anything else.
– Samuel Johnson

bastare – to suffice, to be enough
I denari non bastano, bisogna saperli spendere.
Money isn't enough, you have to know how to spend it. – Anon

battere – to beat, strike, hit, bang, bat, pound, hammer, knock, win
Batti il ferro quando è caldo.
Strike while the iron is hot. – Proverbio

bere – to drink
È stato accertato che bere alcolici significa
una morte lenta. E chi ha fretta?
It's been ascerted that drinking alcohol means
a slow death. So who's in a hurry? – Anon

bisognare – to need

Bisogna essere seri almeno riguardo a qualcosa,
se si vuole avere qualche divertimento nella vita.
One needs to be serious at least about something
if one is to have any amusement in life. – Oscar Wilde

bruciare – to burn

Chi brucia i libri, presto o tardi arriverà
a bruciare anche gli esseri umani.
He who burns books, sooner or later will also
burn human beings. – Heinrich Heine

buttare – reject, to discard, throw, toss, cast

Io da sola non posso cambiare il mondo,
ma posso buttare un sassolino
nel mare, per creare molte ondulazioni.
I alone cannot change the world, but I can cast a stone
across the waters to create many ripples. – Mother Teresa

cadere – to fall

Il frutto non cade lontano dall'albero.
The fruit doesn't fall far from the tree. – Proverbio

cambiare – to change

Concedimi la serenità di accettare le cose che non posso cambiare,
il coraggio per cambiare quelle che posso e la saggezza
per riconoscerne la differenza.
Grant me the serenity to accept the things that I can't change,
the courage to change what I can, and the wisdom to know the difference.
attributed to Reinhold Neibuhr and many others

camminare – to walk

"Ehi! Sto camminando qui!"
"Hey! I'm walkin' here!" – Midnight Cowboy, 1969

cantare – to sing

L'acqua fa male e il vino fa cantare.
Water makes you sick and wine makes you sing. – Proverbio

capire – to understand

La vita si può capire solo all'indietro ma si vive in avanti.
Life can only be understood backwards but
it must be lived forwards. – Kierkegaard

capitare – to happen

È meglio impiegare la nostra mente a sopportare le sventure
che ci capitano, che a prevedere quelle che ci possono capitare.
_It's better to use our minds to deal with the misfortunes
that happen upon us, rather than to predict what
may happen. – Francois de La Rochefoucauld_

celebrare – to celebrate

L'arte celebra l'uomo.
Art celebrates man. – Keith Haring

cercare – to look for, search, seek

Chi cerca, trova. _He who seeks, finds. – Proverbio_
Il vero viaggio di scoperta non consiste nel cercare
nuove terre, ma nell'avere nuovi occhi.
_The true voyage of discovery does not consist in seeking
new lands, but in having new eyes. – Voltaire_

chiamare – to call

Gli amici che chiamano troppo spesso e troppo poco si perdono.
Friends are lost by calling too often and too seldom. – Anon

chiedere – to ask

Vuoi sapere chi sei? Non chiedere. Agisci! L'azione ti definirà.
_Do you want to know who you are? Don't ask. Act!
Action will define you. – Thomas Jefferson_

chiudere – to close

Se vuoi che la roba si faccia, chiudi la bocca e muovi le braccia.
If you want stuff to get done, close your mouth and move your arms. – Anon

colpire – to strike, hit, blow

La potenza non consiste nel colpire forte o spesso, ma nel colpire giusto.
_Power does not consist in striking with force or frequency,
but in striking true. – Honoré de Balzac_

cominciare – to begin, start

Ogni viaggio comincia con il primo passo.
Every journey begins with a single step. – Proverbio

compensare – to compensate, make up for

Gli amici sono il modo che Dio compensa per i parenti.
Friends are God's way of making up for the relatives. – Anon

compiere – to complete, accomplish, fulfill, achieve, carry out

Parole gentili non costano molto.
Ma compiono molto.
Kind words do not cost much.
Yet they accomplish much. – Blaise Pascal

comporre – to compose, create, make up

Le sensazioni sono i dettagli che compongono la storia della nostra vita.
Feelings are the details that make up the story of our life. – Oscar Wilde

comprare – to buy

Chi compra un magistrato vende la giustizia.
He who buys a judge sells justice. – Anon

comprendere – to comprehend, understand

L'uomo superiore comprende ciò che è giusto,
l'uomo inferiore ciò che vende.
The superior man understands what is right,
the inferior man understands what sells. – Anon

concludere – to conclude

Chi ascolta troppa gente conclude poco o niente.
He who listens to too many people concludes little or nothing. – Proverbio

confessare – to confess

Confesso che nel 1901 ho detto a mio fratello Orville
che l'uomo non avrebbe volato per altri 50 anni.
I confess that in 1901 I said to my brother Orville that
man would not fly for another 50 years. – Wilbur Wright

conoscere – to know (be familiar with, to know a person or sphere of knowledge)

Un amico è colui che conosce tutto di te,
e nonostante tutto, ti vuole bene.
A friend is someone who knows all about you,
and loves you anyway. – Anon

conservare – to conserve, keep

Se vuoi conservare un amico osserva tre cose:
onoralo in sua presenza, lodalo in assenza, aiutalo nel bisogno.
If you want to keep a friend, observe three things: honor him in his
presence, praise him in his absence and help him in need. – Anon

208

considerare – to consider, see, regard
Le cose che una generazione considera un lusso,
la generazione successiva le considera necessità.
*What one generation sees as a luxury, the next
generation sees as a necessity. – Anthony Crossland*

consistere – to consist of
La buona educazione consiste nel nascondere quanto
bene pensiamo di noi stessi e quanto male degli altri.
*Good breeding consists in concealing how much we think of ourselves
and how little we think of the other person. – Mark Twain*

contare – to count
Non sono gli anni della tua vita che
contano, ma la vita nei tuoi anni.
*It's not the years in your life that count,
but the life in your years. – Molière*

contenere – to contain
Una casa non è una vera casa se non contiene
nutrimento e fuoco per la mente oltre che per il corpo.
*A house is not a home unless it contains food and fire for
the mind as well as for the body. – Ben Franklin*

continuare – to continue
A volte l'uomo inciampa nella verità, ma nella maggiore parte dei casi,
si rialza e continua per la sua strada.
*Man will occasionally stumble over the truth, but most of the time
he will pick himself up and continue on. – Winston Churchill*

coprire – to cover
Il successo copre una miriade di errori.
Success covers a multitude of blunders. – George Bernard Shaw

costituire – to constitute, compose, form, consist of
La parte migliore della vita di una persona è costituita dalle sue amicizie.
The better part of one's life consists of friendships. – Abe Lincoln

costruire – to construct, build
"Se lo costruisci, verranno." – Campo dei Sogni, 1989
"If you build it, they will come." – Field of Dreams, 1989

209

convincere – to convince
Quello che convince è la convinzione.
What convinces is conviction. – LBJ

correre – to run
Il mondo è nelle mani di coloro che hanno il coraggio di sognare e
di correre il rischio di vivere i propri sogni.
*The world is in the hands of those who have the courage to dream and
run the risk of living their dreams. – Paulo Coelho*

creare – to create
La vita è piacevole. La morte è pacifica.
È la transizione che crea dei problemi.
*Life is pleasant. Death is peaceful. It's the transition
that creates problems. – Isaac Asimov*

credere – to believe
"Toto, credo che non siamo più in Kansas." – Il Mago di Oz, 1939
*"Toto, I have a feeling we're not in Kansas any more."
– The Wizard of Oz, 1939*

crescere – to grow
L'uomo cresce secondo la grandezza del compito.
Man grows according to the magnitude of his duty. – Carl Jung

cucinare – to cook
Cucinare male è una forma di peccato.
Cooking badly is a kind of sin. – Martino Ragusa

dare – to give
Creare è dare una forma al proprio destino.
Creating is giving form to one's destiny. – Albert Camus

decidere – to decide
Non si può scegliere il modo di morire. O il giorno.
Si può soltanto decidere come vivere. Ora.
*You can't choose the way you die. Or the day.
You can only decide how to live. Now. – Joan Baez*

dedicare – to dedicate
Sii più dedicato a fare conquiste invece di seguire
una contentezza rapida ma sintetica.
*Be more dedicated to making solid achievements than in
running after swift and synthetic happiness. – Abdul Kalam*

descrivere – to describe
Un uomo non svela mai così chiaramente il proprio carattere
come quando descrive quello di un altro.
A man never discloses his own character so clearly
as when he describes another's. – Jean Paul Richter

desiderare – to desire
Le persone che hanno successo in questo mondo sono quelle che vanno
alla ricerca delle condizioni che desiderano, e se non le trovano, le creano.
The people who get on in this world are the people who get up and
look for the circumstances they want, and if they can't find them,
make them. – George Bernard Shaw

determinare – to determine
L'abilità è ciò che sei capace di fare.
La motivazione determina ciò che fai.
L'atteggimento determina quanto lo fai bene.
Abililty is what you're capable of doing.
Motivation determines what you do.
Attitude determines how well you do it. – Lou Holtz

dichiarare – to declare
Gli uomini più vecchi dichiarano la guerra;
ma sono i giovani che devono combattere e morire.
Older men declare war. But it is the youth that
must fight and die. – Herbert Hoover

difendere – to defend
Un patriota deve essere sempre pronto a difendere
il suo paese dal suo governo.
A patriot must always be ready to defend
his country against his government. – JFK

dimenticare – to forget
Perdonare è umano, dimenticare è divino.
To forgive is human, to forget divine. – James Grand

dipendere – to depend
Non dipendere dagli altri, ma conta invece su te stesso.
La vera felicità nasce dalla fiducia in se stessi.
Don't depend on others, but instead on yourself.
True happiness is born of faith in yourself. – Codice di Manu

dire – to say, tell
Chi ha detto che i soldi non possono comprare
la felicità non sa dove fare le spese...
Whoever said that money doesn't buy
happiness doesn't know where to shop... – Anon

dirigere – to direct
Dirigi la tua rabbia verso i problemi, non le persone;
concentra le tue energie sulle soluzioni, non sulle scuse.
Direct your anger towards problems, not people; focus your energies
on answers, not excuses. – William Arthur Ward

discutere – to discuss
Le grandi menti discutono le idee; le menti ordinarie discutono
gli avvenimenti; le piccole menti discutono la gente.
Great minds discuss ideas; average minds discuss events;
small minds discuss people. – Eleanor Roosevelt

distinguere – to distinguish
L'uomo si distingue da tutte le altre creature per la facoltà di ridere.
Man is distinguished from all other creatures
by the faculty of laughter. – Joseph Addison

distruggere – to destroy
La morte distrugge un uomo, l'idea della morte lo salva.
Death destroys a man, the idea of death saves him. – E.M. Forster

divenire/diventare – to become
Non cercare di divenire un uomo di succcesso,
ma piuttosto un uomo di valore.
Try not to become a man of success,but
rather try to become a man of value. – Einstein

divertirsi – to enjoy oneself
L'uomo consiste di due parti, la mente e il corpo.
Solo che il corpo si diverte di più.
Man consists of two parts, his mind and his body.
Only the body has more fun. – Woody Allen

dividere – to divide
L'amicizia raddoppia la nostra gioia e divide la nostra pena.
Friendship doubles our joy and divides our grief. – Proverbio

domandare – to ask
Domanda consiglio a chi ben si corregge.
Ask advice of him who rules himself well. – Leonardo da Vinci

dormire – to sleep
Pensa al mattino. Agisci nel pomeriggio.
Mangia di sera. Dormi di notte.
Think in the morning. Act in the afternoon.
Eat in the evening. Sleep at night. – William Blake

dovere – must, ought, should
Chi vuole ben parlare, deve ben pensare.
He who wants to speak well, must think well. – Proverbio

dubitare – to doubt
Dubitare di se stesso è il primo segno dell'intelligenza.
Doubting oneself is the first sign of intelligence. – Ugo Ojetti

elevare – to elevate
Qualsiasi cosa che eleva la mente è sublime.
Anything that elevates the mind is sublime. – John Ruskin

entrare – to enter
Lasciate ogni speranza, voi ch'entrate.
Abandon hope, all ye who enter here. – Dante Alighieri, L'Inferno

errare – to err, make a mistake
Errare è umano, ma per veramente incasinare tutto,
ci vuole un computer.
To err is human, but to really screw up,
you need a computer. – Murphy's Law

escludere – to exclude
Due eccessi: escludere la ragione, non ammettere che la ragione.
Two excesses: to exclude reason, to admit nothing
but reason. – Blaise Pascal

esistere – to exist
La bellezza delle cose esiste nella mente di chi le osserva.
The beauty of things exists in the mind
of he who observes. – David Hume

esprimere – to express

Come non vorrei essere uno schiavo, non vorrei neanche essere
un padrone. Questo esprime la mia idea di una democrazia.
As I would not be a slave, so I would not be a master. This
expresses my idea of democracy. – Abraham Lincoln

essere – to be

"Essere o non essere, ecco la questione."
"To be or not to be, that is the question." – Hamlet
"Luca, io sono tuo padre!" *"Luke, I am your father!" – Darth Vader*

evitare – to avoid

Evita la popolarità se vorresti la pace.
Avoid popularity if you would have peace. – Abraham Lincoln

fare – to do, to make

Tutto ciò che merita di essere fatto merita di essere fatto bene.
Everything worth doing deserves to be done well. – Lord Chesterfield

fermare – to stop, arrest

"Fermate i soliti sospetti."
"Round up the usual suspects." – Casablanca, 1942

fidare – to trust

So che Dio non mi darà niente che non sarò in grado di affrontare.
Vorrei solo che non si fidasse tanto di me…
I know God will not give me anything I can't handle.
I just wish He didn't trust me so much… – Mother Teresa

finire – to finish

Tutto è bene quel che finisce bene.
All's well that ends well. – Shakespeare

fornire – to furnish, supply, provide

È il nutrimento che fornisci alla mente che
determina l'intero carattere della tua vita.
It is the food which you furnish to your mind that
determines the whole character of your life. – Emmet Fox

fumare – to smoke

Smettere di fumare è facile.
L'ho fatto un centinaio di volte.
It's easy to quit smoking. I've done it
hundreds of times. – Mark Twain

funzionare – to function, work
La mente è come un paracadute. Funziona solo quando è aperta.
The mind is like a parachute. It works only when it is open. – Einstein

giocare – to play
Lei aveva un corpo da clessidra e volevo giocare nella sabbia.
She had an hourglass figure, and I wanted to
play in the sand. – Woody Allen

giudicare – to judge
Non giudicare un libro dalla copertina.
Don't judge a book by its cover. – Proverbio

godere – to enjoy
Saper godersi la vita è importante per la salute.
Knowing how to enjoy life is important for one's health. – Proverbio

guidare – to drive
Se la passione ti guida, lascia che la ragione tenga le redini.
If passion drives you, let reason hold the reins. – Ben Franklin

guardare – to watch, look at
Ogni volta che mi guardo allo specchio, mi convinco sempre
di più che Dio abbia un ottimo senso dell'umorismo.
Every time that I look at myself in the mirror, I'm convinced
even more that God has a great sense of humor. – Matteo Molinari

immaginare – to imagine
Ho sempre immaginato il Paradiso come una sorta di biblioteca.
I have always imagined Paradise as a kind of library. – JL Borges

imparare – to learn
Chiunque smetta di imparare è vecchio, che abbia 20 o 80 anni.
Chiunque continua ad imparare resterà giovane.
Anyone who stops learning is old, whether 20 or 80,
anyone who keeps learning stays young. – Henry Ford

impedire – to impede, prevent, block
Le difficoltà fanno più forti i coraggiosi piuttosto che impedire.
Difficulties embolden, rather than impede, the brave. – Anon

importare – to matter, be important

La vita è come una commedia: non importa
quanto è lunga, ma come è recitata.
Life is like a play: it doesn't matter how long it is,
but how it is performed. – Seneca

incontrare – to meet

Sono pronto ad incontrare il mio Creatore.
Se Lui è pronto a vedermi, questa è un'altra storia.
I am ready to meet my Maker. As for whether my Maker
is prepared for the great ordeal of meeting me
is another matter. – Winston Churchill

indicare – to indicate, show, point to

Quando il saggio indica la luna, lo sciocco vede il dito.
When the wise man points to the moon,
the fool looks at the finger. – Anthony de Mello

iniziare – to begin, start

Ci sono due errori che si possono fare lungo la strada verso la verità…
non andare fino in fondo, e non iniziare.
There are two mistakes one can make along the road to truth…
not going all the way and not starting. – Buddha

insegnare – to teach

Dai un pesce a un uomo e lo nutrirai per un giorno.
Insegnagli a pescare e lo nutrirai per tutta la vita.
Give a man a fish and you'll feed him for a day.
Teach him to fish and you'll feed him for a lifetime. – Lao Tzu

interessare – to interest, be of interest

Sono curioso di tutto.
Anche di argomenti che non mi interessano.
I'm curious about everything.
Even subjects that don't interest me. – Alex Trebek

invitare – to invite

Siamo tutti invitati alla festa della vita, dimentica i giorni
dell'oscurità, qualsiasi cosa possa essere successa non è la fine.
We're all invited to the party of life, forget the dark days,
whatever may have happened is not the end. – Augusto Daolio

lasciare – to permit, allow

Non lasciare che una piccola disputa offenda una grande relazione.
Don't let a little dispute injure a great friendship. – Dalai Lama

lavorare – to work

Ogni giorno leggo la "Forbes list" della gente più ricca
d'America. Se non sono nell'elenco, vado a lavorare.
Every day I get up and look through the Forbes list of the richest people
in America. If I'm not on the list, I go to work. – Robert Orben

leggere – to read

Un classico è qualcosa che tutti vorrebbero aver
letto e che nessuno vuole leggere.
A classic is something that everyone would like to have
read and no one wants to read. – Mark Twain

liberare – to free

L'unico modo per liberarsi da una tentazione è cedervi.
The only way to get rid of a temptation is to yield to it. – Oscar Wilde

limitare – to limit, curb, restrain

La rabbia, se non limitata, è spesso più dannosa
che la ferita che l'ha provocata.
Anger, if not restrained, is frequently more hurtful
than the injury that provoked it. – Seneca

lottare – to fight

Chi lotta può perdere, chi no lotta ha già perso.
He who fights may lose, he who doesn't
fight has already lost. – Che Guevara

mancare – to be lacking

Dove manca la natura, l'arte provvede.
Where nature is lacking, art provides. – Anon

mandare – to send

Un bambino di cinque anni capirebbe questo.
Manda qualcuno a prendere un bambino di cinque anni.
A child of five would understand this.
Send someone to fetch a child of five. – Groucho Marx

mangiare – to eat

Leggere senza riflettere è come mangiare senza digerire.
Reading without reflecting is like eating
without digesting. – Edmund Burke

mantenere – to maintain, keep

Il successo è raggiunto e mantenuto da quelli che provano e riprovano.
Success is achieved and maintained by those who try
and keep trying. – W. Clement Stone

meritare – to merit, deserve

Ognuno ha ciò che merita.

Everyone has what they deserve./You get what you deserve. – Anon

mescolare – to mix, stir, blend, shuffle

Il destino mescola le carte e noi giochiamo.

Destiny shuffles the cards and we play. – Schopenhauer

mettere – to put, place

Tra moglie e marito non mettere il dito.

Don't put/stick your finger/don't get involved
in a wife and husband's business. – Proverbio

migliorare – to improve

Migliorare è cambiare, essere perfetto è cambiare spesso.

To improve is to change, to be perfect is to change often. – Churchill

morire – to die

Non voglio realizzare l'immortalità attraverso l'arte...
La voglio realizzare non morendo.

I don't want to achieve immortality through my work...
I want to achieve it through not dying. – Woody Allen

mostrare – to show, display

L'amore è mostrato dalle tue azioni, non dalle parole.

Love is shown in your deeds, not words. – Fr. Jerome Cummings

muovere – to move

La vita è come andare in bicicletta:
se vuoi stare in equilibrio devi muoverti.

Life is like riding a bicycle. To keep your balance
you must keep moving. – Einstein

nascere – to be born

Dove sono troppi a comandare, nasce la confusione.

Where there are too many in command, confusion is born. – Luigi Einaudi

nuotare – to swim

Se i miei critici mi vedessero mentre cammino sul Thames,
direbbero che era perchè non sapevo nuotare.

If my critics saw me walking over the Thames they would
say it was beause I couldn't swim. – Margaret Thatcher

nascondere – to hide

Chi non beve vino ha qualcosa da nascondere.

He who doesn't drink wine has something to hide. – Baudelaire

odiare – to hate
Non odio le persone. Solamente mi sento meglio
quando non mi sono intorno.
I don't hate people. It's just that I feel better
when they aren't around. – Charles Bukowski

offendere – to offend
Si può scherzare ma non offendere.   *Joke, but don't offend. – Anon*

offrire – to offer
La vita è una scuola in cui c'è molto da apprendere e tanto da offrire.
Se avremo fede in noi stessi saremo ottimi alunni ed efficaci docenti.
Life is a school where there's much to learn and so much to offer.
If we have faith in ourselves, we'll be great students and
effective teachers. – Giuseppe D'Oria

opporre – to oppose
Tutto in eccesso è opposto alla natura.
Everything in excess is opposed to nature. – Hippocrates

ordinare – to order
L'ottimista è un uomo che, senza una lira in tasca, ordina delle ostriche
nella speranza di poterle pagare con la perla trovata.
An optimist is a man who, without a lire in his pocket, orders oysters
in the hope of being able to pay with the pearl he finds. – Ugo Tognazzi

organizzare – to organize
La scienza è conoscenza organizzata.
La saggezza è vita organizzata.
Science is organized knowledge.
Wisdom is organized life. – Immanuel Kant

osservare – to observe
Chi legge sa molto; chi osserva sa molto di più.
He who reads knows much; he who observes
knows much more. – Alexandre Dumas Jr.

ottenere – to obtain, to get
Chi ha pazienza può ottenere ciò che vuole.
He that can have patience can have what he will. – Ben Franklin

pagare – to pay
Un investimento nella conoscenza sempre paga l'interesse migliore.
An investment in knowledge always pays the best interest. – Ben Franklin

paragonare – to compare

Non paragonarti mai agli altri. Paragonati
solo alla versione migliore di te stesso.
*Don't ever compare yourself to others. Only compare
yourself to the best version of yourself. – Anon*

parere – to seem

Pare che più vecchio divengo, più irreale diviene il mondo.
*It seems like the older I get, the more unreal
the world becomes. – Rufus Wainwright*

parlare – to speak

Meglio tacere e passare per idiota che parlare e dissipare ogni dubbio.
*It's better to remain silent and be thought a fool than to
open one's mouth and remove all doubt. – Mark Twain*

partecipare – to participate

L'importante non è vincere ma partecipare.
*The important thing isn't winning but
participating. – Pierre de Couberin*

partire – to leave, depart

Per essere creativo, non bisogna partire dalle buone
vecchie cose, bensì dalle cattive cose nuove.
*To be creative, you don't have to leave the good old things,
rather the bad new things. – Bertolt Brecht*

passare – to pass, spend

Il successo è l'abilità di passare da un fallimento
all'altro senza perdere l'entusiasmo.
*Success is the ability to go from one failure
to another with no loss of enthusiasm. – Winston Churchill*

pensare – to think

Se pensi che puoi fare una cosa, o pensi
che non la puoi fare, hai ragione.
*If you think you can do a thing or think that
you can't, you're right. – Henry Ford*

perdere – to lose

Chi perde del denaro, perde molto; chi perde un amico,
perde molto di più; chi perde la fede, perde tutto.
*He who loses money, loses much; he who loses a friend,
loses much more; he who loses faith, loses all. – Eleanor Roosevelt*

perdonare – to pardon, forgive, excuse

Perdona i tuoi nemici, ma non dimenticare mai i loro nomi.
Forgive your enemies, but never forget their names. – John F. Kennedy

permettere – to permit, allow

La diplomazia è l'arte di permettere a qualcun altro di fare a modo tuo.
Diplomacy is the art of letting somebody else
have your way. – David Frost

piacere – to be pleasing

Se vuoi farlo, è proibito; se non ti piace, è obbligatorio.
If you want to do it, it's prohibited; if you don't like it,
it's obligatory. – Anon

piangere – to cry

L'uomo che non piange mai fa piangere un sacco di persone.
The man who never cries makes many others cry. – Bruno Franchi

piantare – to plant

Fai sempre del tuo meglio. Quello che
pianti adesso, lo raccoglierai più tardi.
Always do your best. What you plant now,
you will harvest later. – Og Mandino

porre – to put, position, set

Le uniche limitazioni della vita sono quelle che tu poni a te stesso,
perchè finchè ti impegni, qualsiasi cosa è raggiungibile.
Life's only limitations are those you set upon yourself, for as long as
you strive hard enough, anything is achievable. – Chad Williams

portare – to carry, bring, take

C'è una fonte della giovinezza: è nella tua mente, nei tuoi talenti, nella
creatività che porti nella vita. Quando impari ad attingere a questa
sorgente, avrai davvero sconfitto l'età.
There is a fountain of youth: it's in your mind, in your talents,
in the creativity that you carry with you through life. When you learn
to draw from this source, you will truly have defeated age. – Sophia Loren

possedere – to possess

Il comunismo non funziona perchè a la gente piace possedere la roba.
Communism doesn't work because people like to own stuff. – Frank Zappa

potere – to be able to, can

"Tu non puoi reggere la verità!"
"You can't handle the truth!" – A Few Good Men, 1992

preferire – to prefer
Preferisco la follia dell'entusiasmo all'indifferenza della saggezza.
*I prefer the folly of enthusiasm to the indifference
of wisdom. – Anatole France*

pregare – to pray
Prega come se tutto dipendesse da Dio e lavora
come se tutto dipendesse da te.
*Pray as if all depended upon God and work as
if all depended upon you. – Ignazio di Loyola*

prendere – to take, get
Un leader è uno che conosce il cammino,
prende il cammino e mostra il cammino.
*A leader is one who knows the way, goes the way,
and shows the way. – John Maxwell*

preoccupare – to worry
Non si può cambiare il passato, ma si può rovinare
il presente preoccupandosi del futuro.
*You can't change the past, but you can ruin
the present by worrying about the future. – Isak Dinesen*

preparare – to prepare
L'istruzione è il nostro passaporto al futuro, perchè il domani
appartiene a quelli che si preparano oggi.
*Education is our passport to the future, for tomorrow
belongs to those who prepare for it today. – Malcolm X*

presentare – to introduce, offer, present
L'avversità presenta un uomo a se stesso.
Adversity introduces a man to himself. – H.L. Mencken

procedere – to proceed
L'ambizione è il germe dal quale tutta la crescita di nobiltà procede.
*Ambition is the germ from which all growth of
nobleness proceeds. – Oscar Wilde*

produrre – to produce
Ogni causa produce più di un effetto.
Every cause produces more than one effect. – Herbert Spencer

promettere – to promise
Dio promette un atterraggio sicuro ma non un passaggio tranquillo.
God promises a safe landing but not a calm passage. – Anon

proporre – to propose

L'uomo propone ma Dio dispone.
Man proposes but God disposes. – Proverbio

provare – to try, test, prove, attempt, experience

A provare non si perde nulla.
You don't lose anything/There's no harm in trying. – Proverbio

provocare – to provoke, cause, force, bother, challenge, taunt

La differenza tra l'amore e il sesso è che il sesso allevia
le tensioni e l'amore le provoca.
*The difference between love and sex is that sex alleviates
tension and love provokes it. – Woody Allen*

provvedere – provide, supply

La famiglia è l'associazione istituita dalla natura
per provvedere alle necessità dell'uomo.
*The family is the association established by nature
for the supply of man's everyday needs. – Aristotle*

raccontare – to tell, recount

Devo fermarmi per raccontarvi brevemente della contraccezione orale.
Ho chiesto a una ragazza di dormire con me e lei ha risposto: "No."
*I must pause and say a fast word about oral contraception.
I asked a girl to go to bed with me and
she said, "No." – Woody Allen*

raggiungere – to reach, contact, join, catch up with

Punta verso le stelle e forse raggiungerai il cielo.
Aim for the stars and maybe you'll reach the sky. – Anon

rappresentare – to represent

La ricchezza dei poveri è rappresentata dai loro figli;
quella dei ricchi dai loro genitori.
*The wealth of the poor is represented by their children;
that of the rich, their parents. – Jean-Jacques Rousseau*

reagire – to react

La vita è dieci percento quello che ti succede e
novanta percento di come tu le reagisci.
*Life is ten percent what happens to you and ninety
percent how you respond to it. – Lou Holtz*

rendere – render, make

"Carpe diem, cogliete l'attimo ragazzi.
Rendete straordinarie le vostre vite."
"Carpe diem, Seize the day, boys. Make your lives
extraordinary." – Dead Poets Society, 1989

resistere – to resist

Posso resistere a tutto tranne alla tentazione.
I can resist anything but temptation. – Oscar Wilde

restare – to stay, remain

Non restare neutrale di fronte al dolore e al male.
Don't stay neutral in the face of pain and evil. – Proverbio

ricevere – to receive

L'istruzione non è ricevuta. È realizzata.
Education is not received. It is achieved. – Anon

richiedere – to require

Come qualsiasi altra cosa vivente e crescente,
l'amore richiede lavoro per mantenerlo sano.
Like any other living, growing thing, love requires
effort to keep it healthy. – Leo Buscaglia

riconoscere – to recognize

L'intelligenza riconosce quello che è accaduto.
Il genio riconosce quello che accadrà.
Intelligence recognizes what has happened.
Genius recognizes what will happen. – John Ciardi

ricordare – to remember

Chi non può ricordare il passato è condannato a ripeterlo.
Those who cannot remember the past are
condemned to repeat it. – George Santayana

ridere – to laugh

Ridi ogni volta che puoi. È una medicina a buon mercato.
Laugh every chance you get. It's cheap medicine. – Lord Byron

ridurre – to reduce

Il matrimonio riduce a metà i tuoi diritti e raddoppia i tuoi doveri.
Marriage reduces your rights by half and doubles
your duties. – Alexander Graham Bell

riferire – to refer
È crudele riferire a quelle cose che causano pena.
It is cruel to refer to those things which cause sorrow. – Anon

riflettere – to reflect
La bellezza è come ti senti dentro, e si riflette nei tuoi occhi.
Non ha niente a che vedere con l'aspetto fisico.
Beauty is how you feel inside, and it reflects in your eyes.
It has nothing to do with the physical appearance. – Sophia Loren

riguardare – to regard, concern, pertain to
Per quanto riguarda la carriera, stai sempre preparato, niente
scorciatoie; il lavoro duro è l'unica alternativa che veramente funziona.
Regarding one's career: always be prepared, no short cuts;
hard work is the only alternative that really works. – Kiana Tom

rimanere – to remain
Chi non ama il vino, le donne e la musica per
tutta la vita rimane un buffone.
He who loves not wine, women and song, remains
a fool his whole life long. – Martin Luther

ripetere – to repeat
La storia si ripete. Lo deve fare. Nessuno ascolta.
History repeats itself. It has to. Nobody listens. – Steve Turner

riportare – bring again, quote, relate, annount, report
Abbiamo tutti le nostre macchine del tempo. Alcune ci riportano indietro,
e si chiamano ricordi. Alcune ci portano avanti, e si chiamano sogni.
We all have our time machines. Some take us back, they're call memories.
Some take us forward, they're called dreams. – Jeremy Irons

rispondere – to respond
Rispondere a stupide domande è più facile
che correggere stupidi errori.
Responding to stupid questions is easier
than correcting stupid errors. – Anon

risolvere – to resolve
L'amore è il problema che risolve tutti gli altri problemi.
Love is the problem that resolves
all the other problems. – Matteo Romitelli

risultare – to result
Tutto il progresso autentico risulta dalla ricerca di nuovi fatti.
All genuine progress results from finding new facts. – Wheeler McMillen

ritornare – to return
Tutto quello che viene dal cuore ritorna al cuore.
All that comes from the heart returns to the heart. – Proverbio

riuscire – to be able to, succeed
Chi non riesce più a provare stupore e meraviglia è già come morto.
He who can no longer pause to wonder and stand rapt
in awe is as good as dead. – Einstein

rivelare – to reveal
Il successo forma il carattere, il fallimento lo rivela.
Success builds character, failure reveals it. – Dave Checkett

rompere – to break
Il cuore forte rompe la cattiva sorte.
A strong heart breaks bad luck. – Proverbio

salire – to rise, go up, climb
Il successo è una scala che non può essere salita con le mani in tasca.
Success is a ladder that cannot be climbed with your hands
in your pocket. – Anon

saltare – to jump, leap, skip
Guarda prima di saltare.
Look before you leap. – Proverbio

salvare – to save
Uomo avvisato, è mezzo salvato.
Forewarned is forearmed./A man warned, is half saved. – Proverbio

sapere – to know (facts)
È bene sapere un po' di tutto.
It's good to know a little about everything. – Proverbio

scappare – to escape
Il modo migliore di scappare da un problema è di risolverlo.
The best way to escape from a problem is to solve it. – Alan Saporta

scegliere – to choose
È l'abilità di scegliere che ci fa umani.
It's the ability to choose that makes us human. – Madeleine L'Engle

scherzare – to joke, play around

Scherzando, si può dire tutto, anche la verità.
In jest, you can say anything, even the truth. – Sigmund Freud

scoprire – to discover

La perfezione dell'uomo consiste proprio nello
scoprire le proprie imperfezioni.
*The perfection of man really consists in
discovering one's own imperfections. – Saint Augustine*

scrivere – to write

La storia sarà gentile con me perchè intendo scriverla.
History will be kind to me for I intend to write it. – Winston Churchill

scusare – to excuse, apologize, forgive, pardon

I cattivi uomini scusano i loro difetti;
gli uomini buoni li abbandonano.
*Bad men excuse their faults;
good men abandon them. – Anon*

sedere – to sit

Una cura sicura per il mal di mare è di sedersi sotto un albero.
A sure cure for seasickness is to sit under a tree. – Spike Milligan

seguire – to follow

L'idealismo è quello che precede l'esperienza,
cinismo è quello che la segue.
*Idealism is what precedes experience,
cynicism is what follows. – David Wolf*

sembrare – to seem

Se tutto sembra andare bene, sicuramente si è trascurato qualcosa.
*If everything seems to be going well, you have obviously
overlooked something. – Murphy's Law*

sentire – to feel, sense, hear, smell

Quando faccio del bene, mi sento bene.
Quando faccio del male, mi sento male.
Questa è la mia religione.
*When I do good, I feel good. When I do bad,
I feel bad. That's my religion. – Abe Lincoln*
Il pettegolezzo è quando senti qualcosa che
ti piace di qualcuno che non ti piace.
*Gossip is when you hear something you like
about someone you don't. – Earl Wilson*

servire – to serve, to be useful

I futuri governanti devono essere eletti per
servire tutti, non per essere serviti.
*Future govenors should be elected to serve all,
not to be served. – Hernan Mamani*

significare – to signify, to mean

Il segreto del genio è di portare lo spirito del bambino alla
vecchiaia, che significa non perdere mai il tuo entusiasmo.
*The secret of genius is to carry the spirit of the child into old age,
which means never losing your enthusiasm. – Adlous Huxley*

smettere – to stop, quit

Renoir è un ragazzo senza alcun talento.
Ditegli, per favore, di smettere di dipingere.
*Renoir is a fellow without any talent. Tell him,
please, to stop painting. – Edourd Manet*

soffrire – to suffer

Chi ha paura di soffrire soffre sempre di paura.
He who fears suffering suffers always of fear. – Paurat

sognare – to dream

Quando smetti di sognare, smetti di vivere.
When you cease to dream, you cease to live. – Malcolm Forbes

sopportare – to tolerate, bear, endure, deal with

Impara a sopportare serenamente
qualsiasi cosa la sorte ti richiederà.
*Learn to serenely tolerate anything that
fate requires of you. – Publio Terenzio*

sorprendere – to surprise

Aspetta il meglio, progetta per il peggio e
preparati ad essere sorpreso.
*Expect the best, plan for the worst, and
prepare to be surprised. – Denis Waitley*

sorridere – to smile

Io amo l'uomo che può sorridere nel guaio, può raccogliere la forza
dalla pena e crescere coraggioso dalla riflessione.
*I love the man that can smile in trouble, that can gather strength
from distress, and grow brave by reflection. – Thomas Paine*

sostenere – to sustain, support
Il cibo è preso per sostenere la vita.
Il vino è bevuto per arricchire la vita.
Preso insieme, aiutono a soddisfare la vita.
Food is taken to support life. Wine is drunk to enrich life.
Taken together, they help fulfill life. – Anon

spegnere – to turn off, extinguish
La gelosia spegne l'amore come le ceneri spengono il fuoco.
Jealosy extinguishes love just as ashes put
out a fire. – Ninon de Lencios

spendere – to spend
La maggior parte degli uomini spende la prima metà
della propria vita a rendere infelice l'altra metà.
The majority of men spend the first half of their
life making the second half unhappy. – La Bruyere

sperare – to hope
Spera nel bene, ma preparati al peggio.
Hope for the best, but prepare for the worst. – Anon

spiegare – to explain
Vorrei che lui spiegasse la sua spiegazione.
I wish he would explain his explanation. – Lord Byron

spingere – to push
È stata sopratutto la passione
a spingermi in questo mondo.
Above all, it was passion that pushed me
forward in this world. – Lina Wertmüller

sposare – to marry
Mi sono sposato davanti a un giudice.
Avrei dovuto chiedere una giuria.
I was married by a judge. I should have
asked for a jury. – Groucho Marx

stare – to be, stay, remain
Nel mondo nulla di grande è stato fatto senza passione.
Nothing great in the world has ever been accomplished
without passion. – Friedrich Hegel

succedere – to happen
La buona fortuna è quello che succede quando
l'opportunità si trova con la programmazione.
*Good fortune is what happens when opportunity
meets with planning. – Thomas Edison*

suonare – to play (a song or musical instrument)
"Suonala, Sam. Suona, 'Mentre il tempo passa.'"
"Play it, Sam. Play, 'As Time Goes By.'" – Casablanca, 1942

svegliare – to wake up
Il migliore modo di far diventare veri i tuoi sogni è di svegliarti.
The best way to make your dreams come true is to wake up. – Paul Valery

tenere – to keep, hold
La vita dev'essere vissuta e la curiosità tenuta viva.
Non si deve mai, per qualsiasi ragione, voltare la schiena.
*Life must be lived and curiosity kept alive. One must never,
for whatever reason, turn his back on life. – Eleanor Roosevelt*

tentare – to try, attempt, strive, seek
La storia è un incubo dal quale sto tentando di svegliarmi.
*History is a nightmare from which I am
trying to awake. – James Joyce*

toccare – to touch
Guardare e non toccare è una cosa da imparare.
To look and not touch is a thing to learn. – Proverbio

togliere – to remove, take off
In ogni attività la passione toglie gran parte della difficoltà.
In every activity, passion removes a substantial part of the difficulty. – Anon

tornare – to return, come back
"Io tornerò!" – *"I'll be back!" Terminator, 1984*

trasformare – to transform
La funzione principale di una città è di trasformare il potere in
strutture, l'energia in cultura, elementi morti in simboli viventi
d'arte, e la riproduzione biologica in creatività sociale.
*The chief function of the city is to convert power into form,
energy into culture, dead matter into the living symbols of art,
biological reproduction into social creativity. – Lewis Mumford*

trattare – to treat, examine, deal with, negotiate, handle

Essere donna è terribilmente difficile perchè consiste
principalmente nel trattare con gli uomini.
*Being a woman is a terribly difficult task, since it consists
principally in dealing with men. – Joseph Conrad*

trovare – to find

Se vuoi trovare l'arcobaleno…
devi sopportare la pioggia.
*If you want to find the rainbow…
you have to put up with the rain. – Dolly Parton*

trascinare – to drag

Il destino conduce quelli che accettano
e trascina quelli che non accettano.
*Fate leads the willing and drags
along the unwilling. – Seneca*

uccidere – to murder, kill

Quello che non mi uccide, mi fortifica.
What doesn't kill me makes me stronger. – Nietzsche

unire – to unite

L'amore, l'amicizia e il rispetto non uniscono
la gente tanto come l'odio comune per qualcosa.
*Love, friendship and respect do not unite people as much
as a common hatred for something. – Anton Chekhov*

usare – to use

Soltanto i re, i presidenti, editorialisti e persone con i
vermi solitari hanno il diritto di usare il "noi" editoriale.
*Only kings, presidents, editors and people with tapeworms
have the right to use the editorial "we." – Mark Twain*

uscire – to exit, leave

Il lavoro non arriva da solo; serve uscire e cercarlo.
*Work doesn't come to me, I have to go out
and look for it. – Whoopi Goldberg*

vedere – to see

"Vedo la gente morta."
"I see dead people." – The Sixth Sense, 1999

vendere – to sell

Il cuore è una ricchezza che non
si vende e non si compra, ma si regala.
The heart is a treasure that is neither sold nor
bought, but given as a gift. – Flaubert

vestire – to dress

Da quattro cose l'uomo si fa capire:
dal parlare, dal mangiare, dal bere e dal vestire.
Man makes himself understood in four ways:
in the way he speaks, eats, drinks and dresses. – Anon

vincere – to win

Un campione ha bisogno di motivazione oltre alla vincita.
A champion needs a motivation above and
beyond winning. – Pat Riley

vivere – to live

Tutti gli uomini muoiono. Ma non tutti vivono veramente.
Every man dies. But not every man truly lives. – William Wallace

volare – to fly

Abbiamo imparato a volare come gli uccelli, a nuotare come
i pesci, ma non abbiamo imparato l'arte di vivere come fratelli.
We have learned to fly the air like birds and swim the sea like fish, but
we have not yet learned the simple art of living together as brothers. – MLK

volere – to want

Non è che ho paura di morire, solo che
non voglio esserci quando accadrà.
I am not afraid of death, I just don't want to
be there when it happens. – Woody Allen

ESSENTIAL ADJECTIVES

AGGETTIVI ESSENZIALI

ESSENTIAL ADJECTIVES
AGGETTIVI ESSENZIALI

This collection of high frequency adjectives is
dedicated to humor, wit and wisdom.

alcuno – some, any, anyone
Alcuni causano la felicità dovunque vanno,
altri tutte le volte che vanno via.
Some cause happiness wherever they go,
others whenever they go. – Oscar Wilde

alto – tall, high
La disciplina deve cominciare dall'alto se
si vuole che sia rispettato in basso.
Discipline must start from high up
if you want to be respected from below. – Anon

altro – other
Una coscienza è la cosa che ti fa male quando
tutte le altre parti si sentono così bene.
A conscience is what hurts when all
your other parts feel so good. – Hemingway

amoroso – amorous, pertaining to love
La mia vita amorosa è terribile. L'ultima volta che ero dentro
una donna è quando ero dentro la Statua della Libertà.
My love life is terrible. The last time I was inside a woman was
when I visited the Statue of Liberty. – Woody Allen

antico – ancient, antique, old
Gli ebrei non danno importanza alle rivalità antiche.
Ci preoccupiamo dell'umidità a Miami.
Jews don't care about ancient rivalries. We worry
about humidity in Miami. – Evan Sayet

aperto – open
Il cervello, una volta aperto ad una nuova idea,
non riprende mai la dimensione originiale.
One's mind, once stretched by a new idea,
never regains its original dimensions. – Anon

artificiale – artificial
La contentezza è la ricchezza naturale, il lusso è la povertà artificale.
Contentment is natural wealth, luxury is artificial poverty. – Socrates

assoluto – absolute
La fede assoluta corrompe assolutamente, come il potere assoluto.
Absolute faith corrupts as absolutely as absolute power. – Eric Hoffer

attento – careful
Di solito, un uomo è più attento con il suo denaro che con i suoi principi.
A man is usually more careful of his money than
he is of his principles. – Ralph Waldo Emerson

attraente – attractive
Io domando alla gente come mai hanno teste di cervi sulle pareti.
Dicono sempre è perché, come animale, è tanto bello.
Io penso che mia mamma sia attraente, ma ho delle foto di lei.
I ask people why they have deer heads on their walls.
They always say because it's such a beautiful animal...
I think my mother is attractive, but I have
photographs of her. – Ellen DeGeneres

attuale – current
La tua situazione attuale non è
un'indicazione del tuo potenziale finale.
Your current situation is not an indication
of your ultimate potential. – Anthony Robbins

avanti – forward, ahead, before
Un passo avanti, due passi indietro.
One step forward, two steps back.

azzurro – blue
Picasso ha avuto il suo periodo rosa e il suo periodo
azzurro. Sono nel mio periodo biondo adesso.
Picasso had his pink period and his blue period.
I'm in my blonde period right now. – Hugh Hefner

basso – low
Oltre gli omicidi, D.C. ha uno dei tassi di criminalità più bassi nel paese.
Aside from the murders, D.C. has one of the lowest crime rates in
the country. – Former D.C. Mayor Marion Barry

bello – pretty, handsome, good looking
Che alcuni amino gli animali più degli umani,
non sarà bello, ma è comprensibile.
*That some love animals more than humans isn't nice,
but it is understandable. – Giovanni Sorian*

bianco – white
Una volta ero Biancaneve, ma ho fatto una deviazione.
I used to be Snow White, but I drifted. – Mae West

biondo – blonde
Non sono offesa da tutte le barzellette sulle bionde sciocche,
perchè so che non sono sciocca… e anche so che non sono bionda.
*I'm not offended by all the dumb blond jokes, because I know
I'm not dumb… and I also know I'm not blond. – Dolly Parton*

bravo – good, skilled, capable, accomplished
La felicità: un buon conto bancario, un
bravo cuoco e una buona digestione.
*Happiness: a good bank account, a good cook and
a good digestion. – Jean Jacques Rousseau*

breve – brief, short
La distanza più breve tra due punti è probabilmente sotto costruzione.
*The shortest distance between two points is probably
under construction. – Noelie Alito*

brutto – ugly
Il femminismo è semplicemente un modo per le donne brutte
per entrare nella corrente principale di America.
*Feminism is just a way for ugly women to get into the
mainstream of America. – Rush Limbaugh*

buio – dark
Per ogni notte buia, c'è un giorno più luminoso.
For every dark night, there's a brighter day. – Tupak Shakur

buono – good
Hai solo una possibilità per fare una buona prima impressione.
You only have one chance to make a good first impression. – Anon

caldo – hot, warm
La felicità è un cucciolo caldo.
Happiness is a warm puppy. – Charles Schultz

capace – capable

Se pianifichi di essere qualcosa meno di quello di cui sei capace,
sarai probabilmente scontento tutti i giorni della tua vita.
If you plan on being anything less than you are capable of being, you
will probably be unhappy all the days of your life. – Abraham Maslow

caratteristico – distinctive

Ogni cultura ha il suo caratterisco sistema normale di governo.
Il tuo è la democrazia, moderato dalla corruzione.
Il nostro è il totalitarismo, moderato dall'assassinio.
Every culture has its distinctive and normal system of government.
Yours is democracy, moderated by corruption. Ours is totalitarism,
moderated by assassination. – Russian Official, Unknown

carino – cute

Non ero la più carina né la più dotata,
ma me la sono cavata nel periodo di domande e risposte.
I wasn't the cutest or the most talented,
but I could get through the question-and-answer period.
Oprah Winfrey, on beauty pagents

caro – expensive

Sii il tuo eroe, è meno caro di un biglietto del cinema.
Be your own hero, it's cheaper than a movie ticket. – Doug Horton

cattivo – bad

È cattiva fortuna essere superstizioso.
It's bad luck to be superstitious. – Anon

cattolico – Catholic

Sono cattolica, lui è ebreo, è stato semplicemente più facile fuggire insieme.
I'm Catholic, he's Jewish, it was just easier to elope. – Marg Helgenberger

certo – certain

Sono completamente a favore della separazione tra Chiesa e Stato.
Queste due instituzioni ci rovinano abbastanza da sole,
allora tutte e due insieme è morte certa.
I'm completely in favor of the separation of Church and State.
These two institutions screw us up enough on their own,
so both of them together is certain death. – George Carlin

centrale – central

Il lavoro della banca centrale è di preoccuparsi.
The job of the central bank to worry. – Alice Rivlin

chiaro – clear
Una coscienza chiara è il segno sicuro di una cattiva memoria.
A clear conscience is the sure sign of a bad memory. – Anon

ciascuno – each, every
La politica è l'arte gentile di ottenere voti dai poveri e fondi elettoriali
dai ricchi, promettendo di proteggere ciascuno dagli altri.
*Politics is the gentle art of getting votes from the poor and campaign funds
from the rich by promising to protect each from the other. – O. Ameringer*

cieco – blind
La scienza senza la religione è zoppa.
La religione senza la scienza è cieca.
*Science without religion is lame. Religion
without science is blind. – Einstein*

civile – civil
Sii civile con tutti; socievole con molti; familiare con pochi.
Be civil to all; sociable to many; familiar to few. – Ben Franklin

civilizato – civilized
Un visitatore da Marte potrebbe facilmente identificare le
nazioni civilizate. Hanno i mezzi di guerra migliori.
*A visitor from Mars could easily pick out the civilized nations.
They have the best implements of war. – Herbert Prochnow*

comodo – comfortable
La bellezza, secondo me, è di essere comoda nella propria
pelle. Quello, oppure un fortissimo rossetto rosso.
*Beauty, to me, is about being comfortable in your own skin.
That, or a kick-ass red lipstick. – Gwyneth Paltrow*

comune – common
Il senso comune è il genio vestito negli abiti da lavoro.
Common sense is genius dressed in its working clothes. – Emerson

contento – happy, contented
Mia moglie ed io siamo stati contenti per 20 anni.
Poi ci siamo conosciuti.
*My wife and I were happy for 20 years.
Then we met. – Rodney Dangerfield*

continuo – continuous
La vita è un esercizio continuo per risolvere problemi creativamente.
Life is a continuous exercise in creative problem solving. – Michael Gelb

contrario – opposite, contrary
Sono religiosamente contrario alla religione.
I'm religiously opposed to religion. – Victor Hugo

corto – short
La risata è la distanza più corta tra due persone.
Laughter is the shortest distance between two people. – Victor Borge

cristiano – Christian
Andare in chiesa non ti rende Cristiano, così come
stare in un garage non fa di te una macchina.
*Going to church doesn't make you Christian any more
than standing in a gararge makes you a car. – Anon*

decente – decent
"Sai quanto difficile è trovare un uomo decente in questa città?
La maggior parte di loro pensano che la monogamia
è qualche tipo di legno."
*"Do you know how hard it is to find a decent man in this town?
Most of them think monogamy some kind
of wood." – The Mask (1994)*

difficile – difficult
È difficile capire come un cimitero può aumentare
i costi di sepoltura e dare la colpa al costo della vita.
*It is difficult to understand how a cemetery can raise
its burial costs and blame it on the cost of living. – Anon*

diretto – direct, straightforward
La motivazione di un impiego è il risultato diretto
di tutti le interazioni con il suo capo.
*An employee's motivation is a direct result of the sum
of interactions with his or her boss. – Bob Nelson*

diritto – straight
Un sorriso è una curva che può mettere un mucchio di cose diritte.
A smile is a curve that can set a whole lot of things straight. – Victor Borge

disponibile – ready, available
I desideri espandono in proporzione diretta alle risorse
disponibili per la loro gratificazione.
*Wishes expand in direct proportion to the resources
available for their gratification. – Robert Dato*

diverso – different

L'insanità: facendo la stessa cosa ripetutamente e
aspettando risultati diversi.
*Insanity: doing the same thing over and over again and
expecting different results. – Albert Einstein*

divertente – fun

Non ho fatto mai un giorno di lavoro in vita mia. Era tutto divertente.
I never did a day's work in my life. It was all fun. – Thomas Alva Edison

diviso – divided

La gente può essere divisa in tre gruppi: quelli che fanno succedere le cose,
quelli che guardano le cose, e quelli che vogliono sapere cos'è successo.
*People can be divided into three groups: those who make things happen,
those who watch things happen, and those wonder
what happened. – John W. Newbern*

dolce – sweet, gentle, kind

Il caffè, per esser buono, dev'essere nero come la notte,
dolce come l'amore e caldo come l'inferno.
*Coffee, in order to be good, must be black as night,
sweet as love and hot as hell. – Mikhail Bakunin*

duro – hard

Circondati con la gente che prende il proprio lavoro seriamente,
ma non se stessi, quelli che lavorano duro e giocano duro.
*Surround yourself with people who take their work seriously, but not
themselves, those who work hard and play hard. – Colin Powell*

eccellente – excellent

La religione è roba eccellente per tenere la gente comune zitta.
*Religion is excellent stuff for keeping common
people quiet. – Napolean Bonaparte*

economico – economical, cheap

Nel mondo del Rock, c'è un assoluto
vantaggio economico di autodistruzione.
*In rock stardom, there's an absolute economic
upside to self-destruction. – Courtney Love*

efficace – effective

"Il punto chiave qui, credo, è di non pensare alla morte come una fine.
Ma, pensarla di più come un modo molto efficace di ridurre le spese.
"The key here, I think, is to not think of death as an end."
But, think of it more as a very effective way of cutting down
on your expenses." – Love and Death, 1975

elettrico – electric

Se non fosse per l'elettricità, staremmo tutti
guardando la tivu a lume di candela.
If it weren't for electricity, we'd all be watching
television by candlelight. – George Gobal

enorme – enormous

La sola cosa che rimpiango è che il mio lavoro richiedeva
una quantità enorme del mio tempo e molti viaggi.
The one thing that I regret was that my work required an
enormous amount of my time and a lot of travel. – Neil Armstrong

estremo – extreme

Il Congresso sembra drogato, e inerte per la maggior parte del
tempo... la sua idea di affrontare un problema è di tenere
udienze o in casi estremi, di nominare una commissione.
Congress seems drugged and inert most of the time... its idea
of meeting a problem is to hold hearings or in extreme cases,
to appoint a commission. – Shirley Chisholm

europeo – European

Comprerò qualsiasi crema, cosmetico o elisir
da una donna con accento europeo.
I will buy any creme, cosmetic, or elixir from a woman
with a European accent. – Erma Bombeck

facile – easy

Figli. Non sono facili. Ma ci dev'essere
qualche punizione per fare sesso.
Kids. They're not easy. But there has to be
some penalty for sex. – Bill Maher

famoso – famous

Non sei famoso finchè tua madre
non abbia sentito parlare di te.
You're not famous until your mother
has heard of you. – Jay Leno

felice – happy

Il vino è la prova costante che Dio ci ama e vuol vederci felici.
Wine is constant proof that God loves us and
wants to see us happy. – Ben Franklin

forte – strong

Sono soltanto tanto forte come il vino che bevo,
il formaggio che mangio, e gli amici che ho.
I am only as strong as the wine that I drink, the cheese that
I eat, and the friends that I have. – Internet Wisdom

francese – French

Il francese è la lingua che trasforma il fango in romanza.
French is the language that turns dirt into romance. – Stephen King

freddo – cold

Teste calde e cuori freddi non hanno mai risolto niente.
Hot heads and cold hearts never solved anything. – Billy Graham

generale – general

Ho fatto la conoscenza del Chirugio Generale.
Mi ha offerto una sigaretta.
I met the Surgeon General. He offered me
a cigarette. – Rodney Dangerfield

gentile – nice, kind

Sii gentile con i tuoi figli.
Sceglieranno la tua casa di riposo.
Be nice to your children. They'll choose
your rest home. – Phyllis Diller

giallo – yellow

Ho detto al mio dentista che i miei denti stanno diventando
gialli. Mi ha detto di portare una cravatta marrone.
I told my dentist that my teeth are going yellow.
He told me to wear a brown tie. – Rodney Dangerfield

giovane – young

Sono determinato a rimanere giovane
per sempre anche se devo morire provando.
I'm determined to remain forever young even if I die trying. – Anon

giusto – just, right, correct

Il tempo è sempre giusto per fare la cosa giusta.
The time is always right to do the right thing. – Martin Luther King

grande – great, big

Senza questione, la più grande invenzione nella storia dell'umanità
è la birra. Oh, ti concedo che la ruota era una grande invenzione, ma
la ruota non si accompagna neanche lontanamente tanto bene con la pizza.
*Without question, the greatest invention in the history of mankind
is beer. Oh, I grant you that the wheel was also a fine invention, but
the wheel does not go nearly as well with pizza. – Dave Barry*

gratis – free

Uno psichiatra è un tizio che ti fa un sacco di
domande costose che vostra moglie ti fa gratis.
*A psychiatrist is a fellow who asks you a lot of expensive questions
that your wife asks you for nothing. – Joey Lauren Adams*

grave – grave, serious

Ogni tipo di ambizione ha questo
grave difetto: non guarda dentro.
*Every type of ambition has a serious defect:
it doesn't look within. – Seneca*

grosso – big, large, fat, major

La mia idea del Paradiso è una grande grossa
patata al forno e qualcuno con cui dividerla.
*My idea of Heaven is a great big baked potato
and someone to share it with. – Oprah Winfrey*

importante – important

Non avevo mai progettato di fare male di proposito a nessuno, a meno che
fosse, sai, importante. Come una partita di lega o qualcosa di simile.
*I never set out to hurt anybody deliberately unless it was, you know, important.
Like a league game or something. – Dick Butkus*

impossibile – impossible

È impossibile vincere i grandi premi della vita senza correre rischi.
*It is impossible to win the great prizes of life without
running risks. – Theodore Roosevelt*

industriale – industrial
La politica è il riflesso del mondo d'affari ed industriale.
Politics is the reflex of the business and
industrial world. – Emma Goldman

infelice – unhappy
La filosofia è uno studio che ci lascia stare infelici più intelligentemente.
Philosophy is a study that lets us be unhappy more intelligently. – Anon

inglese – English
Le parole più terrificanti nella lingua inglese sono,
"Sono dal governo e sto qui per aiutare."
The most terrifying words in the English language are,
"I'm from the Government and I'm here to help." – Ronald Reagan

intelligente – intelligent
L'efficenza è la pigrizia intelligente.
Efficiency is intelligent laziness. – David Dunham

interessante – interesting
Io bevo per rendere gli altri interessanti.
I drink to make other people interesting. – George Best

interno – internal, inner, inside
La parola è il pensiero esterno, e il pensiero è la parola interna.
Speech is external thought, and thought
internal speech. – Antoine Rivarol

intero – entire
Venezia è come mangiare un'intera scatola
di cioccolati di liquore tutta in una volta.
Venice is like eating an entire box of chocolate
liqueurs in one go. – Truman Capote

inutile – useless
È inutile mettere i freni quando sei sotto sopra.
It is useless to put on your brakes when you're upside down.
Paul Newman, Actor, Racecar Driver

irritante – irritating
La consapevolezza – quel periodo irritante tra i sonnellini.
Consciousness – that annoying time between naps. – Anon

italiano – Italian

La vita è troppo breve, e sono italiana. Vorrei molto di più
mangiare la pasta e bere vino che essere di misura 0.
Life is too short, and I'm Italian. I'd much rather
eat pasta and drink wine than be a size 0. – Sophia Bush

latino – Latin

Ah, si, divorzio…dalla parola latina… che significa strappare
via i genitali dell'uomo attraverso il portafoglio.
Ah, yes, divorce… from the Latin word… meaning to rip out
a man's genitals through his wallet. – Robin Williams

leggero – light

Non pregare per carichi più leggeri ma per schiene più forti.
Don't pray for lighter burdens but for stronger backs. – Anon

lento – slow

La buona salute è semplicemente
il tasso più lento alla quale si può morire.
Good health is merely the slowest possible
rate at which one can die. – Samuel Johnson

letterario – literary

Sono l'equivalente letterario di un Big Mac e patate fritte.
I am the literary equivalent of a Big Mac and Fries. – Stephen King

libero – free

L'indicatore di ricchezza di un uomo sarà sempre più
la quantità di tempo libero piuttosto che la quantità di denaro.
The wealth index of a man will always reflect more so how much
free time he has rather than how much money he has. – Marco Duso

loro – their

L'essenza di tutte le religioni è una.
Soltanto i loro approcci sono diversi.
The essence of all religions is one. Only their
approaches are different. – Gandhi

lungo – long

Un buon sermone dev'essere come la gonna di una donna: corta abbastanza
per suscitare l'interesse ma lunga abbastanza per coprire gli essenziali.
A good sermon should be like a woman's skirt: short enough to arouse interest
but long enough to cover the essentials. – Ronald Knox

maggiore – major, bigger, greater, chief

Il maggiore pericolo nella vita consiste
nel prendere troppe precauzioni.
*The chief danger in life is in taking
too many precautions. – Alfred Adler*

magro – thin

C'è una ragazza magra dentro di me,
ma di solito la posso zittire con il cioccolato.
*There's a skinny girl inside me, but I can usually
shut her up with chocolate. – Anon*

massimo – maximum

Il successo è l'utilizzazione massima dell'abilità che hai.
*Success is the maximum utilization
of the ability that you have. – Zig Ziglar*

medio – medium, average, middle

Sono soltanto un uomo medio, ma per Giove, io lavoro
più duramente a questo che l'uomo medio.
*I am only an average man but, by George, I work
harder at it than the average man. – Theodore Roosevelt*

mezzo – half, middle, medium

La mezza età è quando la tua età comincia a far vedere nel mezzo.
*Middle age is when your age starts to show
around the middle. – Bob Hope*

migliore – better

Accanto all'acquisto di buoni amici,
l'acquisto migliore è quello di buoni libri.
*Next to acquiring good friends, the best acquisition
is that of good books. – Charles Caleb Colton*

minore – minor

Un senso di umorismo è una maggiore
difesa contro problemi minori.
*A sense of humor is a major defense against
minor troubles. – Mignon McLaughlin*

mio – my

Il mio interesse è nel futuro perchè passerò il resto della mia vita lì.
*My interest is in the future because I'm going to spend
the rest of my life there. – Charles Kettering, Inventor*

moderno – modern

L'arte moderna è quello che accade quando i pittori smettono di
guardare le ragazze e si convincono che hanno una idea migliore.
*Modern art is what happens when painters stop looking at girls and
persuade themselves that they have a better idea. – John Ciardi*

molto – many, much

Amore è stare svegli tutta la notte con un bambino malato.
O con un adulto molto in salute.
*Love is staying up all night with a sick child.
Or with a very healthy adult. – David Frost*

morale – moral

Le opinioni variano, i comportamenti cambiano, credi salgono
e cadono, ma le leggi morali sono scritte sulla tavola dell'eternità.
*Opinions alter, manners change, creeds rise and fall, but the
moral laws are written on the table of eternity. – Lord Acton*

morto – dead

Impariamo a dimostrare la nostra amicizia per
un uomo quando è vivo e non dopo che è morto.
*Let us learn to show our friendship for a man when he is
alive and not when he is dead. – F. Scott Fitzgerald*

naturale – natural

I bambini sono la nostra risorsa naturale più pregiata.
Children are our most valuable natural resource. – Herbert Hoover

nazionale – national

Ho trovato questo debito nazionale, raddoppiato, confezionato con un
grande fiocco ad aspettarmi quando sono entrato nell'ufficio ovale.
*I found this national debt, doubled, wrapped in a big bow waiting for me
as I stepped into the Oval Office. – Barack Obama*

necessario – necessary

Se hai un giardino e una biblioteca, hai tutto il necessario.
If you have a garden and a library, you have everything that you need. – Cicero

nero – black

È molto più facile essere nero che gay. Almeno
se sei nero, non lo devi dire ai tuoi genitori.
*It's a lot easier being black than gay. At least if you're
black, you don't have to tell your parents. – Judy Carter*

nessuno – no, none
Il problema con le persone che non hanno nessun vizio è che di solito
puoi essere ben sicuro che avranno alcune virtù assai irritanti.
The problem with people who have no vices is that generally
you can be pretty sure they're going to have
some pretty annoying virtues. – Liz Taylor

nobile – noble
La gratitudine è il segno di anime nobili.
Gratitude is the sign of noble souls. – Aesop

noioso – boring
Senza la musica per decorarlo, il tempo è soltanto un mucchio di noiose
scadenze di produzione o date alla quali le bollette devono essere pagate.
Without music to decorate it, time is just a bunch of boring production
deadlines or dates by which bills must be paid. – Frank Zappa

normale – normal
Tutti sono normali, finchè inizi a conoscerli.
Everyone is normal until you get to know them. – Dave Sim

nostro – our
È diventato terribilmente ovvio che la nostra tecnologia
ha superato la nostra umanità.
It has become appallingly obvious that our technology
has exceeded our humanity. – Albert Einstein

notevole – remarkable, notable, considerable
Trovo tutti questi soldi un notevole onere.
I find all this money a considerable burden. – J. Paul Getty

nudo – nude
Dormivo nuda – fino al terremoto.
I used to sleep nude – until the earthquake. – Alyssa Milano

numeroso – numerous
Nella politica, ogni giorno è pieno di numerose
opportunità per un serio fallimento.
In politics, every day is filled with numerous
opportunities for serious failure. – Donald Rumsfeld

nuovo – new

L'esperienza è quello che induce una persona
a fare nuovi sbagli invece dei vecchi.
*Experience is what causes a person to make new
mistakes instead of old ones. – Anon*

occupato – busy

Il successo viene di solito a quelli che
sono troppo occupati per cercarlo.
*Success usually comes to those who are too
busy to be looking for it. – H.D. Thoreau*

ogni – each, every

Ogni uomo è l'architetto del proprio destino.
Each man is the architect of his own fate. – Appius Claudius

parecchio – several, many, a lot

Parecchie scuse sono sempre meno convincenti che una.
Several excuses are always less convincing than one. – Aldous Huxley

pazzo – crazy

Non sono pazzo della realtà, ma è ancora l'unico
posto per avere un pasto decente.
*I'm not crazy about reality, but it's still the only
place to get a decent meal. – Groucho Marx*

perfetto – perfect

La pratica non rende perfetti, soltanto
la pratica perfetta rende perfetti.
*Practice does not make perfect, only perfect
practice makes perfect. – Vince Lombardy*

pericoloso – dangerous

È pericoloso avere ragione in faccende
quando le autorità stabilite hanno torto.
*It is dangerous to be right in matters when the
established authorities are wrong. – Voltaire*

perso – lost

Quante strade deve viaggiare un uomo
prima di ammettere di essere perso?
*How many roads must a man travel before
he admits he's lost? – Anon*

personale – personal

La comunicazione, il contatto umano,
è la chiave del successo personale e della carriera.
Communication, the human connection,
is the key to personal and career success. – Paul J. Meyer

piccolo – little

L'atteggiamento è una piccola cosa che fa una grande differenza.
Attitude is a little thing that makes a big difference. – Winston Churchill

pieno – full

Gli sbagli sono parte della quota che si deve pagare per una vita piena.
Mistakes are part of the dues one pays for a full life. – Sophia Loren

più – more

Tutto nella vita è sperimento. Più esperimenti fai, meglio è.
All of life is an experiement. The more experiments you
make, the better. – Ralph Waldo Emerson

politico – political

Non sono un membro di nessun partito
politico organizzato. Sono un democratico.
I am not a member of any organized political party.
I am a Democrat. – Will Rogers

possibile – possible

Senza l'amore di se stesso, non è possibile nemmeno amare gli altri.
Without love for self, it is not possible to love others. – Anon

povero – poor

Dicono che è meglio essere povero e contento che ricco e infelice,
ma cosa ne dite di un compromesso, per esempio,
moderatamente ricco e appena capriccioso?
They say it is better to be poor and happy than rich and miserable,
but how about a compromise like moderately rich
and just moody? – Princess Diana

preciso – precise

La storia non fornisce nessuna linea precisa di guida.
History provides no precise guidelines. – Douglas Hurd

preferito – preferred, favorite

La bistecca è il mio animale preferito.
Steak is my favorite animal. – Fran Liebowitz

primo – first
Io so che la verità è tra il primo e quarantesimo drink.
I know the truth is in between the first and 40th drink. – Tori Amos

principale – principal, main, first, major
Il punto principale di saggezza è di sapere come
valutare le cose precisamente come meritano.
*The principal point of cleverness is to know how to value
things just as they deserve. – Francois de La Rochefoucauld*

privato – private
Dio entra da una porta privata in ogni individuo.
God enters by a private door into every individual. – R.W. Emerson

profondo – deep
Le spugne crescono nel mare. Mi chiedo quanto più profondo
sarebbe il mare se questo non accadesse.
*Sponges grow in the ocean. I wonder how much deeper
the ocean would be if that didn't happen. – Stephen Wright*

pronto – ready, prompt
Il matrimonio è un grande istituto, ma non sono pronta
per vivere in un istituto.
*Marriage is a great institution, but I'm not ready
to live in an institution. – Mae West*

proprio – own
Ogni uomo ha il proprio destino: l'unico imperativo è quello
di seguirlo, accettarlo, non importa dove lo porta.
*Every man has his own destiny: the only imperative is to follow it,
to accept it, no matter where it leads him. – Henry Miller*

prossimo – next
La morte è semplicemente la prossima grande avventura della vita.
Death is just life's next big adventure. – J.K. Rowling

pubblico – public
Un uomo saggio prende le proprie decisioni, un uomo
ignorante segue l'opinione pubblica.
*A wise man makes his own decisions, an ignorant man
follows public opinion. – Thomas Jefferson*

puro – pure

Il sesso è la cosa più bella, naturale e
pura che i soldi possono comprare.
*Sex is the most beautiful, natural and pure
thing that money can buy. – Steve Martin*

qualche – some

Perchè non vieni su a vedermi qualche volta?
Why don't you come up and see me sometime? – Mae West

quale – which

Miei compatrioti americani, sono lieto di annunciarvi che ho appena
firmato la legislazione nella quale si bandisce la Russia per sempre.
Il bombardamento comincia fra cinque minuti.
*My fellow Americans, I am pleased to tell you I just signed legislation
which outlaws Russia forever. The bombing begins in five minutes.
Ronald Reagan, goofing off, unaware the mike was on…*

qualsiasi – any

Le uniche limitazioni sono quelli che dai a te stessa, purchè tu
ti impegni abbastanza duramente, qualsiasi cosa è possibile.
*Life's only limitations are those you set upon yourself, as long as
you strive hard enough, anything is possible. – Chad Williams*

qualunque – any, whichever, whatever

L'amore, di qualunque specie, non è mai triste.
Love, of any kind, is never sad. – Aldo Palazzeschi

quanto – how many, much

Quanti mariti ho avuto? Vuoi dire oltre ai miei?
*How many husbands have I had?
You mean apart from my own? – Zsa Zsa Gabor*

quarto – fourth, quarter

L'amore è un pianoforte caduto dalla finestra del quarto piano e
tu eri nel posto sbagliato al tempo sbagliato.
*Love is a piano dropped from a fourth story window, and
you were in the wrong place at the the wrong time. – Ana DiFranco*

quello – that

L'entusiasmo è per la vita quello che la fame è per il cibo.
*What hunger is in relation to food, zest is
in relation to life. – Bertrand Russell*

questo – this

O mangiare questa minestra o saltar questa finestra.
*Take it or leave it. (Literally: Eat this soup
or go jump out the window.) – Proverbio*

rapido – rapid, quick

Centomila spermatozoi e tu eri il più rapido?
100,000 sperm and you were the fastest? – Anon

raro – rare

Gli amici sono quelle rare persone che chiedono
come stiamo e poi aspettano la risposta.
*Friends are those rare people who ask how we are
and then wait to hear the answer.*

reale – real, authentic, actual, royal

L'unica sicurezza reale che un uomo possa avere in questo mondo
è una riserva di conoscenza, esperienza e capacità.
*The only real security that a man can have in this world
is a reserve of knowledge, experience and ability. – Henry Ford*

recente – recent

Tutte le grandi innovazioni della civiltà erano
dubitate quando erano ancora recenti.
*All of civilization's great innovations were
doubted when they were still recent. – Anon*

regolare – regular

Realizzare l'impossibile vuol dire soltanto che il tuo capo
lo aggiungerà ai tuoi doveri regolari.
*Accomplishing the impossible means only that your boss will
add it to your regular duties. – Doug Larson*

religioso – religious

Chissà se altri cani pensano che i barboncini
sono membri di qualche strano culto religioso.
*I wonder if other dogs think poodles
are member of a weird religious cult. – Rita Rudner*

ricco – rich

Nessun uomo è abbastanza ricco per comprare il suo passato.
No man is rich enough to buy back his past. – Anon

romano – Roman

Il Sacro Romano Impero era nè sacro, nè romano nè un impero.
The Holy Roman Empire was neither holy,
nor Roman, nor an empire. – Voltaire

rosso – red

Elizabeth è di nuovo alla Croce Rossa, e io porto fuori il cane.
Elizabeth's back at the Red Cross, and I'm walking the dog. – Bob Dole

russo – Russian

La fortuna, come una macchina russa, di solito funziona solo se la spingi.
Luck, like a Russian car, generally only works if you push it. – Tom Holt

sacro – sacred

Capisci che il diritto di scegliere la propria strada è un privilegio sacro.
Understand that the right to choose your own path
is a sacred privilege. – Oprah

schifoso – disgusting, gross

Pescare è noioso, a meno che prendi un vero pesce, e poi è schifoso.
Fishing is boring, unless you catch an actual fish,
and then it is disgusting. – Dave Barry

scuro – dark

Una tibia è una cosa per trovare mobili in una stanza scura.
A shin bone is a device for finding furniture in a dark room. – Anon

secco – dry

Perchè non ti cambi da quel capotto bagnato ad un martini secco?
Why don't you get out of that wet coat and into
a dry martini? – Peter Benchley

secondo – second

"Mio marito e io ci siamo innamorati a prima vista…
forse avrei dovuto dare un secondo sguardo."
"My husband and I fell in love at first sight… maybe I should have
taken a second look." – Crimes and Misdemeanors, 1989

segreto – secret

Tutti i viaggi hanno destinazioni segrete delle quali
il viaggiatore è ignaro.
All journeys have secret destinations of which
the traveler is unaware. – Martin Buber

semplice – simple
Quando la soluzione è semplice, Dio sta rispondendo.
When the solution is simple, God is answering. – Albert Einstein

sereno – serene, calm
Ragione e giudizio sereno: le qualità che
appartengono particolarmente ad un leader.
*Reason and calm judgment: the qualities
especially belonging to a leader. – Tacitus*

serio – serious
L'umorismo ha una maniera di unire la gente...
Infatti, sono ben serio quando suggerisco che qualcuno
deve piantare alcuni whoopee cushion nelle Nazioni Uniti.
*Humor has a way of bringing people together...
In fact, I'm rather serious when I suggest that someone
should plant a few whoopee cushions in the UN. – Ron Dentinger*

sicuro – sure
L'unica cosa sicura della fortuna è che cambierà.
The only sure thing about luck is that it will change. – Anon

simile – similar
Il giornalismo obiettivo e una rubrica d'opinione sono
più o meno simili come la Bibbia e la rivista Playboy.
*Objective journalism and an opinion column are about as
similar as the Bible and Playboy magazine. – Walter Cronkite*

sociale – social
Il femminismo è un movimento sociale, contro-famiglia, un movimento
politico che incoraggia le donne a lasciare i loro mariti, uccidere i loro figli,
praticare stregoneria, distruggere il capitalismo e diventare lesbiche.
*Feminism is a socialist, anti-family, political movement that
encourages women to leave their husbands, kill their children,
practice witchcraft, destroy capitalism and
become lesbians. – Pat Robertson*

solido – solid
La burocrazia: un metodo di transformare l'energia in rifiuti solidi.
Bureaucracy: a method for transforming energy into solid waste. – Anon

solito – usual
Come di solito, c'è una grande donna dietro ogni idiota.
As usual, there is a great woman behind every idiot. – John Lennon

255

sospettoso – suspicious

Ho paura del buio, e sono sospettoso della luce.
I'm afraid of the dark, and suspicious of the light. – Woody Allen

sottile – subtle, thin

Non importa quanto sottile lo affetti, è ancora sciocchezza.
No matter how thin you slice it, it's still baloney. – A.E. Smith

speciale – special

Non ho nessun talento speciale.
Sono solamente appassionatamente curioso.
I have no special talent.
I am only passionately curious. – Albert Einstein

specifico – specific

Non ho nessun bisogno di guardie del corpo, ma ho un uso molto
specifico per due qualificatissimi ragionieri abilitati.
I have no use for bodyguards, but I have very specific use for two
highly trained certified public accountants. – Elvis Presley

splendido – splendid, marvelous, wonderful

Non mi interessa essere Signora Splendida
nella sala parto. Dammi la droga.
I'm not interested in being Wonder Woman in the
delivery room. Give me drugs. – Madonna

stanco – tired

Quando Dio creò l'uomo, era già stanco. Ciò spiega molto.
When God created man, he was already tired.
That explains a lot. – Mark Twain

straniero – foreign

Personalmente, mi piacciono due tipi
di uomini – domestico e straniero.
Personally, I like two types of men –
domestic and foreign. – Mae West

strano – strange

Abbiamo un rapporto strano e meraviglioso –
lui è strano ed io sono sono meraviglioso.
We have a strange and wonderful relationship –
he's strange and I'm wonderful. – Mike Ditka

stesso – same
La ragione per cui le donne non giocano al football è perchè undici
di quelle non si vestirebbero mai con la stessa tenuta in pubblico.
The reason women don't play footall is because
11 of them would never wear the same outfit in public. – Anon

straordinario – extraordinary
Una delle cose straordinarie degli eventi
umani è che l'impensabile diviene pensabile.
One of the extraordinary things about human events is
that the unthinkable becomes thinkable. – Salman Rushdie

stupido – stupid
Ognuno ha il diritto di essere stupido, ma alcuni abusano del privilegio.
Everyone is entitled to be stupid, but some abuse the privilege. – Anon

sufficiente – enough
Una volta che hai accumulato sufficiente conoscenza per cavartela,
sei troppo vecchio per ricordarlo.
Once you've accumulated sufficient knowledge to get by,
you're too old to remember it. – Anon

suo – its, his, her, your/formal
Nessuno è in grado di governare un altro senza il suo consenso.
No one is able to govern another without his consent. –Anon

superiore – superior
Un uomo superiore è modesto
come parla ma eccede nelle sue azioni.
A superior man is modest in his speech
but exceeds in his actions. – Confucius

tale – such
Vivi in tale maniera che non avresti vergogna di
vendere il tuo pappagallo alla pettegola del paese.
Live in such a way that you would not be ashamed to sell
your parrot to the town gossip. – Will Rogers

tanto – much, so much
Chiedo solo l'opportunità di dimostrare che avere
tanto denaro non porta la felicità...
All I ask is a chance to prove that having a lot of
money doesn't buy happiness... – Anon

tecnico – technical

Gli uomini sono solo bravi come il loro
sviluppo tecnico gli permette di essere.
*Men are only as good as their technical
development allows them to be. – George Orwell*

tedesco – German

Ho sposato un uomo tedesco. Ogni
notte mi vesto come la Polonia e mi invade.
*I married a German. Every night I dress up as
Poland and he invades me. – Bette Midler*

terzo – third

La prima volta sposi per amore, la seconda
volta per denaro, e la terza volta per compagnia.
*The first time you marry for love, the second time for money,
and the third for companionship. – Jackie Kennedy*

tranquillo – calm, serene, quiet, tranquil

Chiunque può pilotare una nave quando il mare è tranquillo.
Anyone can pilot a ship when the sea is calm. – Navjot Sidhu

triste – sad

Il triste dovere della politica è di stabilire
la giustizia in un mondo di peccato.
*The sad duty of politics is to establish justice
in a sinful world. – Reinhold Niebur*

troppo – too

La sorte è per quelli troppo deboli
per determinare il loro destino.
*Fate is for those too weak to determine
their own destiny. – Kamran Hamid*

tuo – your

L'età non è una barriera. È una
limitazione che ti metti sulla mente.
*Age is no barrier. It's a limitation you put
on your mind. – Jackie Joyner-Kersee*

tutto – all

Il 47.2 percento di tutti i dati statistici sono creati all'improviso.
42.7 percent of all statistics are made up on the spot. – Anon

uguale – equal

Il vizio inerente del capitalismo è la divisione ineguale dei beni;
la virtù inerente del socialismo è l'uguale condivisione della miseria.
The inherent vice of capitalism is the unequal sharing of blessings.
The inherent virtue of Socialism is the equal sharing
of miseries. – Winston Churchill

ultimo – last, ultimate

Spero di essere l'ultimo uomo sulla Terra...
voglio vedere se tutte le donne mi mentivano.
I hope I'm the last guy on earth... I want to see if
all those women were lying to me. – Anon

umano – human

La razza umana ha un'arma molto efficiente, e quella è la risata.
The human race has one really effective weapon,
and that is laughter. – Mark Twain

unico – unique, sole, only

Può darsi che il tuo unico scopo nella vita sia semplicemente
di servire come avvertimento agli altri.
It may be that your sole purpose in life is simply
to serve as a warning to others. – Anon

utile – useful

Le virtù più grandi sono quelle che sono le più utile agli altri.
The greatest virtues are those which are the most useful to others. – Aristotle

vario – various

Fare più cose alla volta vuol dire incasinare varie cose alla volta.
Multitasking means screwing up several things at once. – Anon

vasto – vast

La storia è un vasto sistema di allerta precoce.
History is a vast early warning system. – Norman Cousins

vecchio – old

Il miglior modo per convincere mio marito a fare qualcosa
è insinuare che forse è troppo vecchio per farlo.
The best way to convince my husband to do something is
to insinuate that maybe he's too old to do it. – Anon

vegetariano – vegetarian

Non ho lottato per arrivare in cima
della catena del cibo per diventare vegetariano.
*I didn't fight my way to the top of the food chain
to become vegetarian. – Anon*

vero – real, true

Non puoi essere un vero paese a meno che non abbia una birra e una
compagnia aerea. Aiuta se hai qualche tipo di squadra di football,
o qualche arma nucleare, ma al minimo assoluto,
hai bisogno di avere una birra.
*You can't be a real country unless you have a beer and an airline.
It helps if you have some kind of a football team, or some nuclear weapons,
but at the very least, you need a beer. – Frank Zappa*

vicino – close

La politica è stata definita la seconda più antica professione del mondo.
Certe volte trovo che ha una somiglianza molto vicina alla prima.
*Politics is supposed to be the second oldest profession. I have come to
realize that it bears a very close resemblance to the first. – Ronald Reagan*

vivo – alive

Ho finalmente capito che l'unico motivo
per essere vivo è quello di godere.
*I finally figured out the only reason
to be alive is to enjoy it. – Rita Mae Brown*

vostro – your

Stati disattenti per quanto riguarda il vostro
abbigliamento se volete, ma mantenete un'anima ben tenuta.
Be careless in your dress if you will, but keep a tidy soul. – Mark Twain

vuoto – empty

Il sesso senza amore è una esperienza vuota, ma per
quanto riguarda le esperienze vuote, è una delle migliori.
*Sex without love is an empty experience, but, as empty
experiences go, it's one of the best. – Woody Allen*

zitto – silent, quiet, hushed

Ci sono due segreti per mantenere vivo il matrimonio:
quando hai torto, ammettilo; quando hai ragione, stai zitto.
*There are two secrets for keeping a marriage alive:
when you're wrong, admit it; when you're right, shut up. – Anon*

ESSENTIAL NOUNS

NOMI ESSENZIALI

ESSENTIAL NOUNS
NOMI ESSENZIALI

The following is a mix of quotes, proverbs
and vocabulary-rich sentences.

l'acqua – water
Mia madre mi ha servito il vino con
l'acqua da quando avevo tre anni.
*My mother served me wine and water from
the time I was 3 years old. – Robert Mondavi*

l'affare – business matter, concern,
problem, affair, deal, interest
Un affare in cui si guadagna
soltanto del denaro non è un affare.
*A business that makes nothing but money
is a poor business. – Henry Ford*

l'aiuto – help, aid, assistance
Se volete avere molte persone in aiuto, cercate di non averne bisogno.
If you want many people to help you, try not being in need. – Proverbio

l'albergo – hotel
Un gentiluomo è colui che tiene aperta la porta dell'albergo
affinchè la moglie possa portare dentro i bagagli.
*A gentleman is someone who holds the hotel door open
so that the wife can carry in the bags. – Peter Ustinov*

l'albero – tree
L'ira è un'erbaccia, l'odio è l'albero.
Anger is a weed, hatred is the tree. – Saint Augustine

l'ambiente – environment, atmosphere
Stiamo imparando che l'organismo che
distrugge il proprio ambiente distrugge se stesso.
*We're learning that the organism that destroys its own
environment destroys itself. – Gregory Batesman*

l'amicizia – friendship
La vita non è niente senza l'amicizia.
Life is nothing without friendship. – Cicero

l'amico – friend
L'unico modo per avere un amico è essere un amico.
The only way to have a friend is to be one. – Emerson

l'amore – love
La risposta al problema dell'esistenza è l'amore.
The response to the problem of existence is love. – Erich Fromm

l'animale – animal
L'uomo è un animale che ragiona.
Man is an animal that reasons. – Seneca

l'angolo – angle, corner
Un'opera d'arte è un angolo della
creazione visto attraverso un temperamento.
*A work of art is a corner of creation seen
through a mood. – Émile Zola*

l'anno – year
Vivo in quella solitudine che è penosa in
gioventù ma deliziosa negli anni della maturità.
*I live in that solitude that is painful in youth
but delicious in the years of maturity. – Einstein*

l'argomento – topic, matter, subject
Fanatico è colui che non può cambiare idea
e non intende cambiare argomento.
*A fanatic is someone who can't change his mind
and won't change the subject. – Winston Churchill*

l'arte – art
Franca è estremamente creativa e fa molti diversi tipi d'arte.
Lei fa l'arte visiva; la ceramica, la pittura, la scultura; e l'arte
dalla performance; la danza, la musica e il teatro.
*Franca is extremely creative and does many different types of art.
She does visual art; ceramics, painting, sculture and
performance art; dance, music and theatre.*

l'articolo – article, item
La non-violenza è il primo articolo della mia fede.
È anche l'ultimo articolo del mio credo.
*Non-violence is the first article of my faith.
It is also the last article of my creed. – Gandhi*

l'aspetto – look, appearance, aspect, countenance
Meglio un povero di aspetto sano e forte
che un ricco malato nel suo corpo.
Better a poor man of healthy and strong countenance
than a rich man sick in body. – Siracide

l'attenzione – attention
Tutto ciò che non contribuisce in niente alla tranquillità
dell'animo è indegno della nostra attenzione.
All that does not contribute to the tranquility of the mind
is unworthy of our attention. – Alex Oxenstierna

l'attimo – moment
Vive ogni attimo come se fosse l'ultimo.
Live every moment as if it were the last. – La Donna Bifronte

l'attività – activity, business, interest, industry
L'interpretazione dei sogni è la strada maestra
verso la conoscenza delle attività inconsce della mente.
The interpretation of dreams is the royal road to a knowledge
of the unconscious activities of the mind. – Sigmund Freud

l'atto – act, effort, feat, fact, event, record
Era una commedia di tre atti. Il primo atto era divertente, il secondo un
po' lento, ma l'ultimo pieno di azione e secondo me, era esilarante.
It was a play in three acts. The first act was fun, the second a little slow,
but the last one full of action and in my opinion, was exhilarating.

l'attore – actor   l'attrice – actress
L'attore era sul tappeto rosso con la sua fiamma più recente.
The actor was on the red carpet with his latest flame.
Lei non è un'attrice molto valida, ma più una stellina e oggetto sessuale.
She's not an actress of any great merit, more so a starlet and sex object.

l'automobile – automobile, car
L'automobile è diventata un articolo di vestiario
senza il quale ci sentiamo incerti, nudi, e incompleti.
The car has become an article of dress without which we feel
uncertain, unclad and incomplete. – Marshall McLuhan

l'autorità – authority
Oggi la chiave di successo del
comando è l'influenza, non l'autorità.
The key to successful leadership today is
influence, not authority. – Ken Blanchard

264

l'avvocato – attorney, lawyer
"Esistono due tipi di giustizia: gli avvocati che conoscono
bene la legge e gli avvocati che conoscono bene il giudice."
*"There are two types of justice: lawyers who know the law well,
and lawyers who know the judge well." – Le Chômeur, 1986*

l'azione – action
Bisogna pensare da uomo d'azione e agire da uomo di pensiero.
Think like a man of action, act like a man of thought. – Henri Bergson

il bagno – bath, bathroom, restroom, bathing
La lunghezza di un minuto dipende dal
lato della porta del bagno da cui ti trovi.
*The length of a minute depends upon the side
of the bathroom door you're on. – Arthur Bloch*

la bambina, il bambino – baby, toddler, child
Per far crescere un bambino ci vuole un intero villaggio.
It takes a village to raise a child. – Proverbio

la base – base, basis, foundation, reason, grounds
La libertà è la base di uno stato democratico.
Liberty is the basis of a democratic state. – Aristotle

la bellezza – beauty
La vera bellezza sta nella purezza del cuore.
True beauty lies in the purity of the heart. – Gandhi

la birra – beer
Nel vino c'è la saggezza, nella birra
c'è la libertà, nell'acqua ci sono batteri.
*In wine there is wisdom, in beer there is freedom,
in water there is bacteria. – Ben Franklin*

il bisogno – need
L'uomo di buon gusto dev'essere semplice nei suoi bisogni.
The man of good taste should be simple in his needs. – Honoré de Balzac

la bocca – mouth
In bocca al lupo! *Good luck!*
Gli occhi ti dicono quello che uno è,
la bocca quello che è diventato.
*One's eyes are what one is, one's mouth is
what one becomes. – John Galsworthy*

il braccio – arm
Se gli dai un dito, si prende tutto il braccio.
If you give him a finger, he'll take the whole arm.
Give him an inch an he'll take a mile. – Proverbio

il caffè – coffee, café, bar
Il caffè è il balsamo del cuore e dello spirito.
Coffee is the balm for the heart and the spirit. – Giuseppe Verdi

il calcio – soccer, kick, calcium
I ragazzi stanno giocando sul campo di calcio.
The kids are playing on the soccer field.
Mio fratello mi ha dato un calcio alla gamba quando
ho rivelato la sua bugia alla mamma.
My brother kicked my leg when I revealed his lie to mom.
Il latte è un'eccellente fonte di calcio.
Milk is an excellent source of calcium.

la camera – room, bedroom, chamber
La nuova casa è spaziosa: ha una grandissima camera
matrimoniale, tre camere da letto per i figli e una
camera degli ospiti dove sta nonna quando visita.
*The new house is spacious: it has a very large master
bedroom, three bedrooms for the children and a
guestroom where Grandma stays when she visits.*

la campagna – countryside, campaign, drive, effort
La nostra casa si trova nella campagna, sul lago.
Our home is in the countryside, on the lake.
Il politico ha fatto una campagna di
diffamazione contro il suo avversario.
The politician ran a smear campaign against his adversary.

il campo – field, camp, department
Il campo dietro la nostra casa è pieno di fiori selvatici.
The field behind our house is full of wildflowers.
Lui lavora nel campo della biologia.
He works in the field of biology.

il cane – dog
Mio fratello è cieco e ha un cane guida e un cane da guardia.
Io ho, d'altra parte, un cane pastore.
My brother is blind and has a guide dog and a guard dog.
I have, on the other hand, a sheep dog.

il capello – hair

C'è solo una cura per i capelli grigi. È stata
inventata da un francese. È chiamata ghigliottina.
*There is only one cure for grey hair. It was invented by a
Frenchman. It is call the guillotine. – PG Wodehouse*

il capo – head, boss, leader, chief

Il vero capo è sempre guidato.
The true leader is always driven. – Carl Jung

il carattere – character, nature, quality

Il vero carattere si mostra sempre nelle grandi circostanze.
True character always shows itself in great circumstances. – Napolean

la carne – meat

La carne rossa non ti fa male.
È quella blu e verde che non fanno bene...
*Red meat is not bad for you. It's that blue and green
that isn't good for you. – Tommy Smothers*

la carta – paper, map, card, document

Questa fabbrica produce una varietà di prodotti di carta:
carta per scrivere, carta copiativa, carta per appunti, carta per progetti,
carta da regalo, carta filtrante, carta igenica, carta assorbente, ecc.
*This factory produces a variety of paper products:
writing paper, copy paper, note paper, construction paper,
gift wrap, filter paper, toilet paper, paper towels, etc.*
Posso pagare con la carta di credito?
Can I pay with a credit card?

la casa – house, home

La carità comincia a casa propria. *Charity starts at home.*
La casa è dove si trova il cuore. *Home is where the heart is.*
Non c'è posto come la casa. *There's no place like home.*
Proverbi

il caso – case, event, instance

Un caso che finisca bene è provvidenza,
un caso che termini male è destino.
*When good befalls a man he calls it providence,
when evil, fate. – Knut Hamsun*

la causa – cause, reason, trial, lawsuit, case, campaign

Morire per una causa non fa che questa causa sia giusta.
It's only worth dying for a cause if it's a just cause. – Anon

267

la cena – dinner
Dieta suggerita per la salute e il benessere:
Colazione da re, pranzo da regina e cena da povero.
Recommended diet for good health and well being: Breakfast like
a king, lunch like a queen and dinner like a pauper. – Anon

il centro – center, core, heart, middle, downtown
Il centro dell'intelligenza non sta nel cervello, ma in fondo al cuore.
The center of intelligence isn't in the brain, but deep
in the heart. – Vannuccio Barbaro

la chiave – key
Non so quale sia la chiave del successo, ma la
chiave del fallimento è il cercare di far piacere a tutti.
I don't know the key to success, but the key to failure
is trying to please everybody. – Bill Cosby

la chiesa – church
Questa è la chiesa dove sono stata battezzata, confermata e sposata.
This is the church where I was baptized, confirmed and married.

il chilometro – kilometer
Non importa se vinci di un centimetro o di
un chilometro, l'importante è vincere.
It doesn't matter if you win by a centimeter or by
a kilometer, the important thing is to win.- Anon

il cibo – food
L'arte è cibo dell'anima.
Art is food for the soul. – Proverbio
Il cibo è la forma più primitiva di conforto.
Food is the most primitive form of comfort. – Sheila Graham

il cielo – sky, heavens
Insieme possiamo affrontare qualsiasi sfida
profonda come l'oceano e alta come il cielo.
Together we can face any challenge, as deep as the
ocean and as high as the sky. – Sonia Gandhi

la città – city
La felicità è avere una grande famiglia, amorevole,
premurosa e unita in un'altra città.
Happiness is having a large, loving, close-knit
family in another city. – George Burns

civiltà – civilization, culture

Il compito principale della civiltà, la sua propria
ragione d'essere, è di difenderci contro la natura.
*The principal task of civilization, it's actual raison
d'être, is to defend us against nature. – Sigmund Freud*

la classe – class, classroom, family,
grade, status, order, style, department

L'uomo che pratica una sola classe sociale, è come
lo studioso che non legge altro che un libro.
*The man who associates with only one social class is like
a student who reads only one book. – Edmondo De Amicis*

il colore – color

Il quadro era pieno di colore: c'erano varie gradazioni di
grigio, blue, verde, rosso, giallo ed arancione.
*The painting was full of color: there were various shades of
gray, blue, green, red, yellow and orange.*

la colpa – fault, guilt, blame

Il senso di colpa è semplicemente il modo che
Dio ha di farti sapere che ti stai divertendo troppo.
*Guilt is simply God's way of letting you know
that you're having too good a time. – Dennis Miller*

il colpo – hit, strike, blow, stroke, shock, bang, coup

L'essenza dello snobismo è che vuoi far colpo sugli altri.
*The essence of snobbery is that you wish to impress
[strike a blow to] others. – Virginia Woolf*

il commercio – commerce, marketing, trade, deal, business

Come uomo d'affari, si occupa di commercio all'ingrosso e d'esportazione.
As a business man, he's involved in wholesale and export trade.

la commissione – errand, committee, board

Torno fra un'oretta. Devo fare una commissione.
I'll be back in a bit. I have to run an errand.
Mio zio è capo della commissione elettorale.
My uncle is the head of the board of elections.

il compagno – companion, partner, associate, comrade

Era il mio compagno di scuola elementare, di liceo, e adesso di università.
He was my classmate in elementary school, high school and now in college.

269

la compagnia – company, group, corporation, firm
Devo chiamare la compagnia telefonica perchè il telefono non funziona.
I have to call the phone company because the phone's not working.
In questi giorni tengo compagnia con un gruppo di lavoro.
These days I keep company with a group from work.

la comunicazione – communication, language, contact
La cosa più importante nella comunicazione
è di ascoltare quello che non è detto.
The most important thing in communication
is hearing what isn't said. – Peter Drucker

il concetto – concept, idea, notion
Io ho un mio personale concetto di dieta: evito
rigorosamente tutti i cibi che non mi piacciono.
I have my own personal concept of diet: I rigorously
avoid all foods that I don't like. – Milan Kundera

la condizione – condition, state
La civiltà è un movimento e non una
condizione, un viaggio e non un porto.
Civilization is a movement and not a condition,
a voyage and not a harbor. – Arnold Toynbee

il confronto – comparision, match
Dobbiamo fare un confronto con questi due prodotti
per decidere cosa comprare in grande quantità.
We have to do a comparision with these two
products to decide which to buy in bulk.

la conoscenza – knowledge, awareness, experience, skill
La conoscenza è il potere e l'entusiasmo accende l'interruttore.
Knowledge is power and enthusiasm pulls the switch. – Steve Droke

la conseguenza – consequence, result, outcome, effect
La sagezza consiste nell'anticipazione delle consequenze.
Wisdom consists in the anticipation of consequences. – Norm Cousins

il consiglio – advice, council, board, senate
È sempre saggio ascoltare un consiglio.
È spesso pericoloso seguirlo.
It's always wise to listen to advice. It's often
dangerous to follow it. – Charles Régismanset

il contatto – contact, communication
La chiave di un uomo si trova negli altri: è il contatto
con il prossimo quello che ci illumina su noi stessi.
*The key to a man is found in others: it's human
contact that lights us up. – Paul Claudel*

il conto – bill, check
Vorrei pagare il conto subito, per favore.
I'd like to pay the bill right away, please.

il controllo – control, inspection, checkup
"Chi controlla il passato controlla il futuro.
Chi controlla il presente controlla il passato."
*"He who controls the past controls the future.
He who controls the present controls the past." – 1984*

il coraggio – courage, bravery, guts, nerve
"Il tuo cuore è libero, abbi il coraggio di seguirlo."
"Your heart is free, have the courage to follow it." – Braveheart, 1995

il corpo – body
La sagezza è per l'anima ciò che la salute è per il corpo.
Wisdom is for the soul what health is for the body. – La Rochefoucauld

la corrente – current, stream, flow, power
Non dimenticate mai che solo i
pesci morti nuotano con la corrente.
*Don't ever forget that only dead fish swim with
the current. – Malcolm Muggeridge*

la corsa – race, run, ride
La vita non è una corsa ma un tiro al bersaglio: non è il risparmio
del tempo che conta, bensì la capacità di trovare un centro.
*Life is not so much a race but a target: it's not saving time that
counts, rather the capacity to find a center. – Susanna Tamaro*

il corso – course, class, avenue, line, track, path
Poca importanza ha la sorte per il saggio, perché le cose più grandi e
importanti sono governate dalla ragione, e così continueranno ad essere per
tutto il corso del tempo.
*Fate has little importance for the sage, because the greatest and most important
things are governed by reason, and thus they will continue to be for all
the course of time. – Epicurus*

271

la cosa – thing, matter, object
Più cambia, più è la stessa cosa.
The more things change, the more they stay the same. – Anon
Le cose più preziose della vita non sono quelle che si comprano col denaro.
The most precious things in life are not those you get for money. – Einstein

la coscienza - conscience
La coscienza è la presenza di Dio nell'uomo.
Conscience is the presence of God in man. – Swedenborg

il costo – cost, price
Non esiste una qualità che non abbia un costo.
Più bella e rara la qualità, più alto il costo.
There is no quality without cost. The more beautiful
and rare the quality, the higher the cost. – Andrea De Carlo

la costruzione – construction
Il sogno è una costruzione dell'intelligenza, cui il
costruttore assiste senza sapere come andrà a finire.
A dream is a construction of intelligence, where the builder
assists, not knowing how it will turn out. – Cesare Pavese

la creatività – creativity
La creatività è il permesso che dai a te stesso per
fare sbagli. L'arte è nel sapere quali tenere.
Creativity is allowing yourself to make mistakes.
Art is knowing which ones to keep. – Scott Adams

la crisi – crisis, fit, attack, seizure
Mio marito sta avendo una crisi di mezza età
e vuole un divorzio ed una Maserati…
My husband is having a mid-life crisis,
and wants a divorce and a Maserati…

la cucina – kitchen, cuisine
C'è tanto da fare in cucina; si deve progettare, preparare, tagliare,
mescolare, cucinare e poi pulire. Non si finisce mai...
There's so much to do in the kitchen; you've got to plan, prepare, cut,
mix, cook and then clean up. It never ends...

la cultura – culture, cultivation, civilization, refinement, education

Una ricca biblioteca può servire
a mascherare una cultura povera.
*A rich library can serve to conceal a poor
culture. – Alessandro Morandotti*

il cuore – heart

Sorridi, è la chiave che è adatta
alla serratura di ogni cuore.
*Smile, it's the key that fits the lock of
every heart. – Anthony D'Angelo*

la cura – care, treatment, cure

La vita è una malattia alleviata ogni circa seidici ore
dal sonno. Certo questo è solo un palliativo: la cura è la morte.
*Life is a malady alleviated about every sixteen hour by sleep. Of course
this is only a palliative; the cure is death. – Nicholas de Chamfort*

la danza – dance

La danza è una poesia in cui ogni parola è un movimento.
Dance is poetry in which every word is movement. – Mata Hari

la decisione – decision

Le decisioni giuste vengono dall'esperienza,
l'esperienza viene dalle decisioni sbagliate.
*Good decisions come from experience,
experience comes from bad decisions. – Anon*

il denaro – money

Il denaro è un buon servitore ma un cattivo padrone.
Money is a good servant but a bad master. – Proverbio

il dente – tooth

L'amore ha i denti; i denti mordono; i morsi non guariscono mai.
Love has teeth, the teeth bite; the bites never heal. – James Joyce

il desiderio – desire, hope, wish, yearning

Il comportamento umano scorre da tre fonti principali:
il desiderio, l'emozione e la conoscenza.
*Human behavior flows from three main sources:
desire, emotion, and knowledge. – Plato*

il destino – destiny, fate, chance, luck
Chi crede nel destino giustifica l'inerzia.
He who believes in fate justifies inertia. – Cicero

la difesa – defense
L'umorismo è semplicemente un'altra difesa contro l'universo.
Humor is just another defense against the universe. – Mel Brooks

la differenza – difference
Se pensi di essere troppo piccolo per fare
la differenza, prova a dormire con una zanzara.
If you think you're too small to make a difference,
try sleeping with a mosquito. – Dalai Lama

la difficoltà – difficulty
Le difficoltà fanno più forti i coraggiosi piuttosto che ostacolarli.
Difficulties embolden rather than impede the brave. – Proverbio

la dimensione – dimension, size
La dimensione del tuo successo
si misura con la forza del tuo desiderio.
The size of your success is measured by
the strength of your desire. – Robert Kiyosaki

il Dio – God
Dio, se chiude una porta, apre un portone.
If God closes a door, he opens a big door. – Proverbio

il direttore – director, head, leader, manager
Il nuovo direttore di vendita ha una filosofia
totalmente diversa del suo predecessore.
The new head of sales has a totally different
philosophy than his predecessor.

la direzione – direction
Qui in campangna, ci sono vigne in
ogni direzione; nord, sud, est ed ovest.
Here in the country, there are vineyards in
every direction: north, south, east and west.

il diritto – right, entitlement, law
La libertà è il diritto di fare ciò che le leggi permettono.
Liberty is the right to do what the laws permit. – Montesquieu

il discorso – conversation, discussion, speech, lecture, discourse,

La gente perdona a un uomo tutto, tranne un noioso discorso.
Men will forgive a man everything except bad prose. – Churchill

la distanza – distance, gap, length, stretch

La distanza non conta; è il primo passo quello che conta.
The distance doesn't matter; it's the first step that counts.
– Marie de Vichy-Champron

il dolore – pain

La felicità è un beneficio al corpo, ma è il
dolore quello che svilluppa le facoltà dello spirito.
Happiness is a benefit to the body, but pain is what
develops the powers of the spirit. – Marcel Proust

la domanda – question, inquiry, claim, demand

A volte non c'è miglior risposta di una domanda.
At times there's no better response than
a question. – Giovanni Soriano

la donna – woman, lady

Le donne sono soltanto
macchine per produrre i bambini.
Women are nothing but machines for
producing children. – Napolean

il dottore – doctor, general title of respect for a professional

Il mio dottore mi ha dato sei mesi di vita, ma quando
ho detto che non potevo pagare, me ne ha dati altri sei.
My doctor gave me six months to live, but when I said that I
couldn't pay, he gave me another six. – Milton Berle

il dovere – duty, obligation

La salute è il primo dovere della vita.
Health is the first duty of life. – Oscar Wilde

il dubbio – doubt, question

Il dubbio è il lievito della conoscenza.
Doubt is the yeast of knowledge. – Alessandro Morandotti

l'educazione – education, upbringing
L'educazione è il pane dell'anima.
Education is the bread of the soul. – Proverbio
L'educazione è il grande motore dello sviluppo personale.
*Education is the great engine of personal
development. – Nelson Mandela*

l'effetto – result, effect, consequence, outcome
Un insegnante ha effetto sull'eternità; non
può mai dire dove termina la sua influenza.
*A teacher affects eternity; he can never tell
where his influence stops. – Henry Adams*

l'elemento – element, component, ingredient
Il film era divertente perché aveva un elemento
comico e anche un elemento di sorpresa.
*The film was fun because it had a comic
element and also an element of surprise.*

l'energia – energy
Quando non c'è energia non c'è colore, non c'è forma, non c'è vita.
*When there's no energy, there's no color, there's no form,
there's no life. – Caravaggio*

l'entusiasmo – enthusiasm
L'entusiamo è il potere che sostiene tutte le grandi azioni.
Enthusiasm is the power that sustains all great action. – Anon

l'erba – grass, herb
È soltanto un lavoro. L'erba cresce, gli uccelli volano,
le onde battono la sabbia. Io picchio la gente.
*It's just a job. Grass grows, birds fly, waves pound
the sand. I beat people up. – Muhammad Ali*

l'errore – error, mistake
Lei ha fatto un errore fatale
quando ha mandato un SMS mentre guidava...
She made a fatal error when she sent a text while driving...

l'esame – exam, test
Il vero esame morale dell'umanità, l'esame fondamentale è il suo rapporto con
coloro che sono alla sua mercé: gli animali. E qui sta il fondamentale
fallimento dell'uomo, tanto fondamentale che da esso derivano tutti gli altri.
*The true moral test of humanity, the fundamental test is its relationship with those
who are at its mery: animals. And here is the fundamental flaw of man, so
fundamental that all others stem from this. – Milan Kundera*

l'esempio – example
I giovani hanno più bisogno di esempi che di critiche.
Children need more examples than critics. – Joseph Joubert

l'esperienza – experience
La sapienza è figlia dell'esperienza.
Wisdom is the daughter of experience. – Leonardo da Vinci

l'espressione – expression, term, pronunciation, look
Il silenzio è la più perfetta espressione del disprezzo.
Silence is the most perfect expression of disdain. – GB Shaw

l'età – age, period, epoch
Un diplomato è colui che ricorda sempre
il compleanno di una donna e mai la sua età.
*A diplomat is someone who always remembers a
woman's birthday but never her age. – Robert Frost*

la fabbrica – factory, mill, industrial plant
Alla fabbrica di scarpe, fabbricano scarpe da ginnastica,
da corsa, con lacci, con tacchi, sandali e stivali.
*At the shoe factory, they manufacture gym shoes, running
shoes, tie-up shoes, high-heels, sandals and boots.*

la faccia – face
La più divertente superficie della
terra è quella della faccia umana.
*The most entertaining surface on earth
is the human face. – Georg Lichtenberg*

il fallimento – failure
Tentare è il primo passo verso il fallimento.
Trying is the first step towards failure. – Homer Simpson

la fame – hunger
Come la fame rende gustosi i cibi,
così la stanchezza rende beati i sonni.
*Just as hunger renders food tasty,
so does fatigue bless sleep. – Anon*

la famiglia – family
La moglie è la chiave della famiglia.
The wife is the key to the family. – Proverbio
Avere una famiglia è come avere una pista
da bowling installata nel tuo cervello.
*Having a family is like having a bowling alley
installed in your head. – Martin Mull*

la fantasia – imagination
La fantasia umana è immensamente più povera della realtà.
*The human imagination is immensely poorer
than reality. – Cesare Pavese*

la fatica – effort, strain, fatigue
Una piccola fatica ne risparmia spesso una grande.
A bit of effort often saves much effort.
Chi fatica in giovinezza, gode i frutti in vecchiezza.
He who works hard in youth, enjoys the fruits in old age. – Proverbi

il fatto – fact
Se i fatti e la teoria non concordano, cambia i fatti.
If the facts don't fit the theory, change the facts. – Einstein

la fede – faith, hope, trust
Anche durante i tempi più brutti, la sua fede non vacillava mai.
Even during the worst of times, her faith never waivered.

la felicità – happiness, joy
Uno dei grandi segreti della felicità è
moderare i desideri e amare ciò che già si possiede.
*One of the great secrets of happiness is moderating
desires and loving what you have. – Emillie du Châtelet*
Esercitare liberamente il proprio ingegno, ecco la felicità.
Freely exercising one's own ingenuity, that is happiness. – Aristotle
La vera felicità costa poco; se è cara, non è di buona qualità.
*True happiness costs little, if it's expensive, it is of poor quality.
– Francois de Chataubrand*

la festa – party, feast, holiday
La vecchiaia è il periodo in cui
i compleanni non sono più delle feste.
*Old age is the time when birthdays
are no longer parties. – Robert Sabatier*

278

la figlia – daughter

Mia figlia pensa che io sia una ficcanaso.
Almeno così ho letto sul suo diario.
My daughter thinks that I'm a busybody. At least
that's what I read in her diary. – Jenny Abrams

il figlio – son

Avevo una ragazza e dovevamo sposarci, ma c'era un conflitto religioso.
Lei era atea e io agnostico. Non sapevamo quale religione educare i figli.
I had a girlfriend and we were supposed to get married, but there was a
religious conflict. She was atheist and I was agnostic. We didn't know
what religion to raise the kids. – Antonio Ricci

la figura – figure, character, shape, impression

Ti prego di fare una bella figura e dimentica questo disaccordo pubblico.
I'm asking you to make a good impression and
forget this public disagreement.

il film – film

Adoro vedere qualsiasi tipo di film – azione, giallo, avventura,
drammatico, musicale, biografico, fantascienza, fantastico,
storico, commedia, guerra, animazione, erotico o documentario.
I adore seeing any type of film – action, thriller, adventure,
drama, musical, biography, science fiction, fantasy,
history, comedy, war, animation, erotic or documentary.

il filo – thread, yarn, wire, strand

Oggigiorno usiamo una varietà di filo. Solo per cominciare,
c'è ago e filo, filo interdentale, filo elettrico, filo metallico,
filo tensione, filo del telefono e filo spinato.
Nowadays we use a variety of threads and wire. Just for starters,
there's needle and thread, dental floss, electric wire, metal wire,
live wire, telephone cord and barbed wire.

il fine – purpose, conclusion, intent, aim

Il fine giustifica i mezzi. *The end justifies the means.*
– paraphrase of Machiavelli

la fine – end

Le persone affascinate dall'idea del progresso non intuiscono che
ogni passo in avanti è nello stesso tempo un passo verso la fine.
People who are fascinated with the idea of progress don't understand that every
step forward is at the same time a step towards the end. –Milan Kundera

la finestra – window
Gli occhi sono le finestre dell'anima.

The eyes are the windows of the soul. – Georges Rodenbach

il fiore – flower
Se le regali dei cioccolatini, è a dieta. Se le regali dei fiori, è allergica.

*If the gift is chocolates, she's on a diet. If the gift is
flowers, she's allergic. – Arthur Bloch*

il fiume – river
L'Italia ha numerosi fiumi, tra cui c'è
il fiume Po, che è il più lungo in Italia.

*Italy has numerous rivers, among which,
is the river Po, which is the longest in Italy.*

la foglia – leaf
È autunno, e ci sono foglie cadenti di ogni tipo e di
bellissimi colori d'oro, arancione, rosso, e marrone.

*It's autumn, and there are falling leaves of every type with
beautiful colors of gold, orange, red and brown.*

il fondo – bottom, end, fund
In fondo alla strada, gira a sinistra, poi a destra,
poi c'è un incrocio. La chiesa è all'angolo.

*At the end of the street, turn left, then right, then
there's an intersection. The church is on the corner.*

la forma – form, shape
È stato detto che la democrazia è la peggior forma
di governo, eccezione fatta per tutte quelle altre
forme che si sono sperimentate finora.

*It has been said that democracy is the worst form of
government, except all those others that have been
tried from time to time. – Winston Churchill*

la fortuna – luck, fate, chance, success
La fortuna, la sorte ed il destino non valgono un quattrino.

Luck, fate and destiny aren't worth a dime. – Proverbio

la forza – force, strength, effort, power
La forza senza intelligenza crolla sotto il suo stesso peso.

*Force without intelligence collapses under
its own weight. – Horace*

la frase – sentence, phrase
La frase chiave di un paragrafo deve esprimere
il concetto fondamentale che sarà sviluppato.
*The topic sentence of a paragraph should express
the main concept to be developed.*

il fratello – brother
Il Grande Fratello ti sta guardando.
Big Brother is watching you. – George Orwell

la fretta – hurry, rush, haste
Quelli che impiegano male il loro tempo sono
i primi a lamentarsi che passi troppo in fretta.
*Those who employ their time poorly are the first to complain
that time passes too quickly. – Jean de La Bruyère*

la frutta – fruit
il frutto – fruit, product, offspring, yield, result, revenue
La frutta non cade lontano dall'albero.
The fruit doesn't fall far from the tree. – Proverbio
La pazienza è amara, ma il suo frutto è dolce.
Patience is bitter, but its fruit is sweet. – Rousseau

la funzione – function, feature, capacity, role
La funzione implicita di una macchina del tempo è
di viaggiare nel passato e nel futuro.
*The implicit function of a time machine is
to travel into the past and the future.*

il fuoco – fire
Il bambino non è un vaso da riempire,
ma un fuoco da accendere.
*A child is not a vase to be filled, but a
fire to be lit. – Francois Rablais*

il futuro – future
Per la maggioranza di noi, il passato è
un rimpianto, il futuro un esperimento.
*For the majority of us, the past is a regret,
the future an experiment. – Mark Twain*

il gatto – cat, feline
Dio fece il gatto perché l'uomo potesse
avere il piacere di coccolare la tigre.
God made the cat in order that man could have the
pleasure of caressing the tiger. – Fernand Mery

il genitore – parent
Quand'ero piccolo i miei genitori
traslocavano spesso, ma io li trovavo sempre.
When I was young my parents moved often,
but I always found them. – Rodney Dangerfield

la gente – people
Se vuoi essere vicino a Dio, stai più vicino alla gente.
To be closer to God, be closer to people. – Kahlil Gibran

il giardino – garden
Coltivare il giardino ci macchia le mani, ma ci pulisce la mente.
Tending a garden soils your hands, but it cleans
your mind. – Ramòn Eder

il gioco – game, match, bet
Si può negare, se si vuole, quasi ogni astrazione: giustizia,
bellezza, verità, divinità. Si può negare la serietà, ma non il gioco.
You can deny, if you want, almost any abstaction: justice, beauty,
truth, divinity. You can deny the gravity, but not a game. – Edward Hall

la gioia – joy, delight, happiness
La gioia non è nelle cose, è in noi.
Joy is not in things, it is in us. – Richard Wagner

il giornale – newspaper, journal
La pubblicità contiene le uniche verità affidabili di un giornale.
The advertisements contain the only reliable truth
in a newspaper. – Thomas Jefferson

il giorno – day
"Dopotutto, domani è un alto giorno!"
"After all, tomorrow is another day!" – Gone With The Wind, 1939

il giovane – youth, young man, adolescent
Oggigiorno i giovani credono che il denaro sia
tutto, e quando sono grandi ne hanno la certezza.
Nowadays, young people imagine that money is everything,
and when they grow older, they are certain of it. – Oscar Wilde

il giro – turn, tour, circle, drive, ride, trip
La vita è come la doccia: un giro
sbagliato e sei nell'acqua bollente.
Life is like a shower: one wrong turn and
you're in hot water. – Martin Short

il giugno – June
30 giorni ha novembre, con aprile, giugno e settembre.
Di 28 ce n'è uno, tutti gli altri ne han 31.
30 days has November, with April, June and September.
Of 28, there is one, all the others have 31.

la giustizia – justice, equity, law
La giustizia senza forza è impotente;
la forza senza la giustizia è tirannia.
Justice without force is impotent;
force without justice is tyranny.
– Blaise Pascal

il governo – government
Un governo è un male necessario.
Government is a necessary evil. – Honoré de Balzac
Un governo d'onesti è come un bordello di vergini.
An honest government is like a bordello
full of virgins. – Roberto Gervaso

il grado – grade, degree, level, step, rank, point
Non hai veramente capito qualcosa fino a quando
non sei in grado di spiegarlo a tua nonna.
You do not really understand something unless you
can explain it to your grandmother. – Albert Einstein

il gruppo – group, bunch, cluster
L'uomo mediocre aumenta il proprio valore facendo
parte di un gruppo; l'uomo superiore lo sminuisce.
The mediocre man augments his value being part of a group;
the superior man diminishes it. – Gustave Le Bon

la guerra – war
Se le donne governassero il mondo, non avremmo
le guerre, solo trattative molto intense ogni 28 giorni.
If women ran the world, we wouldn't have wars, just
intense negotiations every 28 days. – Robin Williams

il gusto – taste, flavor

Il peggior nemico della creatività è il buon gusto.
The worst enemy of creativity is good taste. – Picasso

l'idea – idea, thought

Tutte le idee che hanno enormi
conseguenze sono sempre idee semplici.
*All ideas that have enormous consequences
are always simple ideas. – Tolstoy*

l'importanza – importance, relevance, significance

La cosa più importante della vita è non essere morto.
*The most important thing about life is to
not be dead. – Ramón de la Serna*

l'industria – industry, trade, factory, mill

L'industria cinematografica
è un'industria chiave per la zona di Los Angeles.
The film industry is a key industry for the Los Angeles area.

l'inizio – beginning, start

L'inizio dell'amore è spesso simultaneo. Non
così la fine: da ciò nascono le tragedie.
*The beginning stage of love is often simultaneous. Not so with
the end: therein is born the tragedy. – Alessandro Morandotti*

l'intenzione – intention, purpose, aim

L'inferno è lastricato di buone intenzioni.
Hell is paved with good intentions. – Samuel Johnson

l'interesse – interest, concern, attention, involvement

Fa il tuo vero interesse e farai l'interesse di tutti.
*Follow your true interest and you will
interest others. - Carlo Dossi*

l'inverno – winter

Le quattro stagioni dell'anno sono:
l'inverno, la primavera, l'estate e l'autunno.
*The four seasons of the year are:
winter, spring, summer and autumn.*

l'isola – island

Sicilia e Sardegna sono le due isole più grandi d'Italia.
Sicily and Sardegna are the two largest islands of Italy.
Nessun uomo è un isola.
No man is an island. – John Donne

l'istante – instant, moment

Vivere significa nascere ad ogni istante. La morte
subentra quando il processo della nascita cessa.
*Living means being born continuously. Death creeps
in when the process of birth stops. – Erich Fromm*

l'istituto – institute

Dopo aver finito l'istituto navale, mio fratello
ha studiato in un istituto tecnologico.
*After having finished at the naval college, my brother
studied at a technological institute.*

il lato – side

"Rabbia, paura, aggressione: il Lato Scuro della Forza sono loro!"
*"Anger, fear, aggression: the Dark Side of the Force they are!"
– Yoda, Star Wars, Episode V*

il latte – milk

Adoro il latte, così tanto che lo bevo in qualsiasi modo;
latte intero, latte scremato, latte al cioccolato,
latte al malto, latte bianco, latte in polvere o latte con ghiaccio.
*I adore milk, so much so that I drink it in any manner;
whole milk, skimmed milk, chocolate milk,
malted milk, white milk, powdered milk or iced milk.*

il lavoro – work, job

Il lavoro d'equipe è essenziale. Ti
permette di dare la colpa a qualcun altro.
*Team work is essential. It permits you
to blame someone else. – Arthur Bloch*

la legge – law, regulation, rule

In una società incivile, c'è un'assenza di legge,
oppure, la legge della giungla.
*In an uncivil society, there is an absence of law,
or rather, the law of the jungle.*

la lettera – letter, character

La bellezza è la migliore lettera di raccomandazione.
Beauty is the best letter of recomendation. – Aristotle

il letto – bed

La sventura costringe l'uomo a far
la conoscenza di ben strani compagni di letto.
*Misery acquaints a man with strange
bedfellows. – William Shakespeare*

la libertà – liberty, freedom

Ogni individuo ha diritto alla vita, alla
libertà e alla sicurezza della propria persona.
Everyone has the right to life, liberty and security of person.
– U.N. General Assembly

il libro – book

I libri sono l'alimento della giovinezza e la gioia della vecchiaia.
Books are the nourishment of youth and the joy of old age. – Cicero

il limite – limit, edge, boundary

La felicità sta nel conoscere i propri limiti e nell'amarli.
Happiness is knowing one's own limits and
loving them. – Romain Rolland

la linea – line, route, course, connection

Ha bevuto un po' troppo ieri sera e aveva alcuni problemi per
camminare in linea retta di fronte al poliziotto.
He had a bit too much to drink last night and had some
problems walking a straight line in front of the cop.

la lingua – language, speech, tongue

La lingua è la veste del pensiero.
Language is the dress of thought. – Samuel Johnson

la lotta – battle, fight, struggle

La vita è, di fatto, una lotta
Life is, in fact, a battle. – Henry James
Certe persone vivono in lotta con altre, con sé stesse, con la vita.
Certain people live in battle with others, with
themselves, with life. – Paulo Coelho

la luce – light

La mente umana è la luce dell'Universo.
E le sue emozioni gli danno significato.
The human mind is the light of the Universe.
And its emotions give it significance. – Mario Vassalle

la luna – moon

La luna è l'anima, è il nostro modo di vivere le emozioni,
i desideri, i sogni. La terra è la realtà, il luogo in cui lottare.
The moon is the soul, it's our way of living emotions, desires,
dreams. The earth is reality, the place to fight. – Romano Battaglia

il luogo – place, spot, location, site
La nostra meta non è mai un luogo, ma
piuttosto un nuovo modo di vedere le cose.
*One's destination is never a place, but rather a
new way of looking at things. – Henry Miller*

la macchina – car, machine, appliance
La nostra macchina è una vecchia Cinquecento, una Fiat classica.
Our car is an old 500, a classic Fiat.
Mio padre ha un negozio e vende tutti tipi di elettrodomestici:
macchine da caffè, macchine per la pasta, macchine da scrivere,
macchine da cucire, macchine fotografiche, macchine da presa, ecc.
*My father has a store and sells all types of home appliances:
coffee machines, pasta makers, typewriters,
sewing machines, cameras, movie cameras, etc.*

la madre – mother
Le madri dimenticano volentieri che il cordone
ombelicale viene tagliato al momento del parto.
*Mothers happily forget that the umbilical cord was
cut at the moment of birth. –Vera Caspar*

il maestro – teacher, master
L'abitudine è in tutte le cose il miglior maestro.
Practice is, in all things, the best teacher. – Pliny the Elder

la malattia – disease, malady, illness
La malattia, cronica e degenerativa, ti dà pure qualcosa: sai distinguere ciò
che è importante da ciò che non lo è, sei più sensibile al dolore del mondo,
più "intelligente". Ma non è un grand'affare.
*Disease, chronic and degenerative, really does teach you something: you know how
to distinguish between what is and isn't important, you're more sensitive to world
suffering, you are more "intelligent." But it's not a lot of fun. – Cesarina Vighy*

la mamma – mom, mommy, mother
Tutto vorrebbero salvare il pianeta. Nessuno
vorrebbe aiutare la mamma a lavare i piatti.
*Everybody would like to save the planet. Nobody
wants to help mom wash the dishes. – PJ O'Rourke*

la maniera - manner, way, fashion
L'unica maniera per ritrovare un oggetto
smarrito è comprarne uno nuovo.
*The only way to find an lost object
it to buy a new one. – Arthur Bloch*

287

la mano – hand
La mano è il vero organo della civiltà,
l'iniziatore dell'evoluzione umana.
The hand is the true organ of civilization,
the initiator of human evolution. – Ernst Fischer

il mare – sea
Il mare è l'origine della vita, la gioia, la completezza. Il mare ha lunghe
braccia protettive che ti possono ricevere sempre. Il mare è un fratello che
dà molto senza ricevere niente.
The sea is the origin of life, the joy, completeness. The sea has long protective
arms that will always welcome you. The sea is a brother that gives much
without receiving anything. – Romano Battaglia

il marito – husband
È molto difficile far felice il proprio marito;
è molto più facile far felice il marito di un'altra.
It's very difficult to please one's own husband; it's much
easier to please someone else's husband. – Zsa Zsa Gabor

la massa – mass, lump, bunch, heap
Se l'obbedienza è il risultato dell'istinto delle
masse, la rivolta è quello della loro riflessione.
If obedience is the result of the instinct of the masses,
revolt is that of their reflection. – Honoré de Balzac

il materiale – material, equipment, stuff
Il vizio e la virtù sono per un artista materiali di un'arte.
Vice and virtue are to the artist materials for art. – Oscar Wilde

il matrimonio – matrimony, marriage
Il matrimonio è la causa principale del divorzio.
Marriage is the chief cause of divorce. – Groucho Marx

la mattina, il mattino – morning
Il mattino ha l'oro in bocca.
The morning has gold in its mouth.
The early bird catches the worm. – Proverbio

il medico – medical doctor, physician
I medici hanno fatto tutto quello che hanno
potuto, ma nonostante ciò sono ancora vivo...
The doctors did everything they could, but
I'm still alive anyway... – Anon

la memoria – memory
Ci sono tre sintomi della vecchiaia: perdita della
memoria... e mi sono dimenticato gli altri due.
There are three symptoms of old age: loss of memory...
and I forget the other two. – Red Skelton

il meglio – best
Sono facilmente soddisfatto con il meglio del meglio.
I'm easily satified with the very best. –Winston Churchill

la mente – mind, brain
È la mente che fa sani o malati, che
rende tristi o felici, ricchi o poveri.
It is the mind that makes a man healthy or sick, that makes
him sad or happy, rich or poor. – Edmond Spencer
La fortuna favorisce la mente preparata.
Luck favors the prepared mind. – Louis Pasteur

il mercato – market
Compriamo la frutta e la verdura ogni giorno nel mercato in piazza.
We buy fruit and veggies every day at the market in the square.
Ha comprato droga sul mercato nero.
He bought drugs on the black market.

il merito – merit, credit, worth
Il mondo ricompensa più spesso
le apparenze del merito che il merito stesso.
The world more often rewards the appearance of worth
than worth itself. – François de La Rochefoucauld

il mese – month
Passiamo i primi 12 mesi della vita dei nostri figli ad insegnare loro a
camminare e a parlare, e i seguenti 12 anni a dire loro di sedersi e tacere.
We spend the first 12 months of the life of our kids teaching them to walk and talk,
and the following 12 years telling them to sit down and be quiet. – Phyllis Diller

la metà – half
La prima metà della vita è rovinata dai
genitori, e la seconda metà dai figli.
The first half of life is ruined by parents,
and the second half by kids. – Clarence Darrow

il mezzo – center, half, medium, way, means, midst
Nel mezzo delle difficoltà nascono le opportunità.
In the midst of difficulty, opportunity is born. – Einstein

il minimo – minimum

Un giornale dev'essere il massimo
d'informazione, e il minimo di commento.
*A newspaper should be the maximum of information,
and the minimum of comment. – Richard Cobden*

il minuto – minute, moment

In un minuto c'è il tempo per decisioni e
scelte che il minuto successivo rovescerà.
*In a minute there is time for decisions and
revisions which a minute will reverse. – TS Eliot*

la misura – measure, size, dimension

La misura del talento non è ciò che vuoi ma ciò che puoi. L'ambizione
indica solo il carattere dell'uomo, il sigillo del maestro è l'esecuzione.
*The measure of talent is not what you want but what you can do. Ambition
indicates only the character of man, the seal of the master is the execution.
– Henri Frédéric Amiel*

il modo – way, manner, fashion, style, mode

La cocaina è il modo che usa Dio
per dirti che stai facendo troppi soldi.
*Cocaine is God's way of telling you that you're
making too much money. – Robin Williams*

la moglie – wife

Non parlo con mia moglie da anni.
Non la volevo interrompere.
*I haven't spoken to my wife in years. I didn't
want to interrupt her. – Rodney Dangerfield*

il momento – moment

Non aspettare il momento giusto. Crealo.
Don't wait for the right moment. Create it. – Anon

il mondo – world, earth

L'amore fa girare il mondo.
Love makes the world go round. – Anon

la montagna – mountain

Quanto monotona sarebbe
la faccia della terra senza le montagne.
*How monotonous the face of Earth would be without
its mountains. – Immanuel Kant*

il monte – mountain
La regione, Piemonte, nel nordovest d'Italia, è così
chiamata perchè vuol dire, "al piede della montagna."
*The region Piedmont, in the northwest of Italy, is so
called because it means "at the foot of the mountain."*

la morte – death
La cronaca della mia morte
era una vera e propria esagerazione.
*The reports of my death have been
greatly exaggerated. – Mark Twain*

il motivo – motive, reason
Non c'è nessun altro motivo, nessuna ragione specifica perchè qualcuno
debba scalare una montagna, se non la passione individuale, l'orgoglio,
l'entusiasmo per la natura.
*There is no other motive, no other specific reason why someone should scale a
mountain, other than individual passion, pride and enthusiasm for nature.
– Reinhold Messner*

il movimento – movement, motion, traffic
La grazia è bellezza in movimento.
Grace is beauty in motion. – Gotthold Lessing

la musica – music
Lei ascolta una grande varietà di musica: la musica di coro,
di chiesa, classica, strumentale, etnica, sacra,
vecchia, moderna, melodica, ritmica ed elettronica.
*She listens to a great variety of music: choral,
church, classical, instrumental, ethnic, sacred,
old, modern, melodic, rhythmic, and electronic music.*

la natura – nature, character
Amo la natura, però non voglio nessuna parte di lei su di me.
I love nature, I just don't want to get any of it on me. – Woody Allen

la nazione – nation, country
Un uomo di Stato è un politico che dona sé stesso al servizio della nazione.
Un politico è un uomo di Stato che pone la nazione al suo servizio.
*A man of state is a politician who gives himself to the service of his country. A
politician is a man of state who puts the nation at his service. – Georges Pompidou*

la necessità – necessity
La necessità è la madre dell'invenzione.
Necessity is the mother of invention. – Proverbio

la noia – boredom

Il lavoro allontana da noi tre grandi mali: la noia, il vizio e il bisogno.
Work removes from us three evils: boredom, vice and need. – Voltaire

il nome – name, noun

É il 90% dei politici che rovinano
il buon nome di tutto l'altro 10%.
*It is the 90% of politicians that give the
the other 10% a bad name. – Henry Kissinger*

il nord – north

Milano è un comodo punto centrale per noi. Milano è, più o meno,
a nord di Genova, ad est di Torino, a sud di Como, e ad ovest di Verona.
*Milan is a convenient central point for us. Milan is, roughly speaking,
north of Genoa, east of Turin, south of Como and west of Verona.*

la notizia – news

Le cattive notizie sempre giungono al momento sbagliato.
Bad news always arrives at the wrong moment. – Marco Oliverio

la notte – night

Non prendere mai, sotto nessuna circostanza, una pillola
per dormire e un lassativo durante la stessa notte.
*Never, under any circumstances, take a sleeping pill
and a laxative on the same night. – Dave Barry*

il numero – number

Qual'è il tuo numero di telefono e il tuo indirizzo email?
What's your telephone number and email address?

l'occasione – opportunity, occasion, chance circumstance, bargain, situation, possibility

L'arte di vivere, in practica, è l'arte di
crearsi le occasioni giuste e di saperle sfruttare.
*The art of living, in essence, is the art of creating the right
circumstances for oneself and of knowing how to
enjoy them. – Giovanni Soriano*

l'occhio – eye

Occhio per occhio, e il mondo diventa cieco.
Eye for an eye, and the world becomes blind. – Gandhi

l'odore – odor, smell

I due odori più buoni e più santi son quelli del
pane caldo e della terra bagnato dalla pioggia.
*The two most blessed smells are that of hot bread
and the earth wet of rain. – Ardengo Soffici*

l'offerta – offer

"Gli farò un'offerta che non potrà rifiutare." – Il Padrino, 1972
"I'll make him an offer that he can't refuse." – The Godfather, 1972

l'oggetto – object, item, article, subject

Un oggetto cadrà sempre in modo
da produrre il maggior danno possibile.
*An object will always fall in such a way to produce the
maximum damage possible. – Arthur Bloch*

l'onore – honor

Chi apprezza il denaro più del proprio
onore è indegno dell'uno e dell'altro.
*He who appreciates money more than his own
honor is unworthy of either. – Axel Oxenstierna*

l'opera – work, activity, opera, opus

Un'opera è un posto dove un uomo viene
pugnalato e, invece di morire, canta.
*An opera is a job where a man gets beat up
and instead of dying, sings. – Leopold Fechner*

l'operazione – operation (general and medical)

L'alcol è un anestetico che permette
di sopportare l'operazione della vita.
*Alcohol is the anesthesia by which we endure
the operation of life. – George Bernard Shaw*

l'opinione – opinion

L'opinione pubblica per molte persone è solo
una scusa per non averne una propria.
*Public opinion for many people is just an excuse
to not have one of one's own. – Anatole France*

l'ora – hour

Anche un orologio fermo segna l'ora giusta due volte al giorno.
Even a stopped watch shows the right time twice a day. – Hermann Hesse

293

l'ordine – order
L'ordine è la prima legge del cielo.
Order is the first law of Heaven. – Alexander Pope

l'orecchio – ear
Il silenzio è per le orecchie ciò che la notte è per gli occhi.
Silence is for the ears what the night is for the eyes. – Edmond Jabès

la pace – peace
La pace non è assenza di guerra: è una virtù, uno stato d'animo, una
disposizione alla benevolenza, alla fiducia, alla giustizia.
*Peace is not the absence of war: it is a virtue, a mood, a disposition
toward benevolence, trust and justice. – Baruch Spinoza*

il padre – father   il papà – dad, daddy
Non è difficile diventar padre;
essere un padre, questo è difficile.
*It's not difficult to become a father; being a father,
that's the difficult part. – Wilhelm Busch*

il padrone – owner, master, boss, proprietor
Il padrone del negozio ha deciso
di vendere il suo commercio e andare in pensione.
The owner of the store has decided to sell his business and retire.

il paese – country, village
L'Italia è un Paese che è conosciuto per un alto livello di cultura.
Italy is a country that is known for a high level of culture.
L'Italia è piena di piccoli paesi incantevoli.
Italy is full of charming little villages.

la pagina – page
Il mondo è un libro, e quelli che non viaggiano
ne leggono solo una pagina.
*The world is a book, and those who don't travel
read only one page. – Agostino d'Ippona*

il palazzo – building, palace
La strada dell'eccesso conduce al palazzo della saggezza.
The road of excess leads to the palace of wisdom. – William Blake

il pane – bread
I sapori semplici danno lo stesso piacere dei più raffinati; l'acqua
e un pezzo di pane fanno il piacere più pieno a chi ne manca.
*Simple flavors are as pleasurable as the most refined; water
and a piece of bread satisfy those in need. – Epicurus*

la parola – word
C'è sempre tempo per lanciare una
parola, ma non sempre per riprenderla.
*There is always time to cast a word, but not always
time to take it back. – Baltasar Gracian*

la parte – part
Se non sei parte della soluzione, allora sei parte del problema.
*If you're not part of the solution, then you're part of the problem.
– Charles Rosner*

la partita – game
Il talento ti fa vincere una partita, ma l'intelligenza e
il lavoro di squadra ti fanno vincere un campionato.
*Talent wins games, but teamwork and intelligence
win championships. – Michael Jordan*

il partito – political party
I partiti di oggi sono soprattutto
macchine di potere e di clientela.
*Today's political parties are above all machines
of power and clientele. – Enrico Berlinguer*
Quel che più spaventa nei partiti non è quello che
dicono, è quello che trascurano o si rifiutano di dire.
*What is scary about political parties is not what they say, but
what is disregarded or what they refuse to say. – Louis Blanc*

la passione – passion, fondness, weakness, hobby
In ogni attività la passione toglie gran parte della difficoltà.
*In every activity, passion removes a great
part of the difficulty. – Erasmus*

il passo – step, footstep, pace, action
Questo è un piccolo passo per un uomo,
un grande passo per l'umanità.
*This is one small step for a man, one giant
leap for mankind. – Neil Armstrong*

la patria – country, homeland, homeland
La famiglia è la patria del cuore.
Family is the heart's homeland. – Giuseppe Mazzini

la paura – fear

Mia sorella è un caso mentale. Ha paura del buio, dell'altitudine, del fuoco,
dell'acqua profonda, del sangue, delle malattie incurabili, dei cani,
dei pesci, degli squali, dei serpenti, dei topi dei ragni e della seta.
My sister's a mental case. She's afraid of the dark, heights, fire,
deep water, blood, incurable diseases, dogs,
fish, sharks, snakes, mice, spiders and silk.
L'unica cosa di cui aver paura è la paura.
The only thing we have to fear is fear itself. – FDR

la pazienza – patience

Non c'è strada troppo lunga per chi cammina lentamente e senza fretta,
non ci sono mete troppo lontane per chi si prepara ad esse con la pazienza.
There's no street too long for he who walks slowly and without hurry, there's no
goal too far for he who prepares for it with patience. – Jean de La Bruyère

il peggio – worst

Sono pronto al peggio ma spero per il meglio.
I am prepared for the worst but hope
for the best. – Benjamin Disraeli

la pena – pain, sorrow, punishment, pity, anguish, suffering
vale la pena – to be worth, worthwhile

Soltanto una vita vissuta per gli altri è
una vita che vale la pena vivere.
Only a life lived for others is a life
worthwhile. – Albert Einstein

il pensiero – thought

Il pensiero è l'anima della vita.
Thought is the soul of life. – Gustave Flaubert
I grandi pensieri vengono dal cuore.
Great thoughts come from the heart. – Luc de Vauvenargues

il pericolo – danger

Non importa morire presto o tardi, ma morire bene o male;
morire bene significa sfuggire al pericolo di vivere male.
It matters not whether you die early or late, but whether you die well or
badly; dying well means fleeing the danger of living badly. – Seneca

il periodo – period, sentence, term, era, cycle, age

La gioventù, la maturità e la vecchiaia sono tre periodi della vita che
potremmo ribattezzare "rivoluzione, riflessione e televisione".
Youth, maturity, and old age are three periods of life that we could rebaptise,
"revolution, reflection and television." – Luciano De Crescenzo

la persona – person

È assurdo dividere le persone in buone e cattive.
Le persone si dividono in simpatiche e noiose.
It is absurd to divide people into good or bad.
People are either charming or tedious. – Oscar Wilde

il peso – weight

Lei ha perso peso dopo aver iniziato a sollevare pesi
She lost weight after having started to lift weights.

il pezzo – piece

Ruba un pezzo di legno e ti chiamano ladro;
ruba un regno e ti chiamano duca.
Rob a piece of wood and I call you a thief; rob a
kingdom and I call you a duke. – Chuang Tzu

il piacere – pleasure, delight, enjoyment

Non ho mai ucciso un uomo, ma ho
letto molti necrologi con grande piacere.
I have never killed a man, but I have read many
obituaries with great pleasure. – Clarence Darrow

il piano – plan, story,
piano, the musical instrument

Abbiamo un piano per mettere il piano al terzo piano.
Installiamo un ascensore nell'edificio.
We have a plan for putting the piano on the third floor.
We're installing an elevator.

la pianta – plant

Per me la natura è, non lo so, i ragni, le cimici... il pesce grosso che mangia
il piccolo, e le piante che mangiano piante... e gli animali che mangiano... è
un enorme ristorante, così la vedo.
To me nature is, I don't know, spiders and bugs... the big fish eating little
fish, and plants eating plants, and animals eating... It's like an enormous
restaurant, that's the way I see it. – Woody Allen

la piazza – plaza, public square

Internet sta diventando la piazza
del villaggio globale del domani.
The internet is becoming the town square for
the global village of tomorrow. – Bill Gates

il piede – foot
È meglio morire in piedi che vivere in ginocchio.
It's better to die standing than live on
bended knee. – Emiliano Zapata

la pietra – stone, rock
La virtù è simile a una pietra preziosa,
bellissima se montata semplicemente.
Virtue is similar to a precious stone, beautiful
if mounted simply. – Francis Bacon

la poesia – poetry, poem
Poesia è un modo di prendere la vita alla gola.
Poetry is a way of taking life by the throat. – Robert Frost

la politica – politics, policy
La politica è una questione troppo seria da lasciare ai politici.
Politics is much too serious a thing to be left to the politicians. – Charles de Gaulle

la polizia – police
Capisce che l'amore è finito quando hai detto che saresti arrivato per le
sette e arrivi alle nove, e lui non ha ancora chiamato la polizia.
You know love is gone when you said you'd be there at seven, and you arrive at
nine, and he has not called the police yet. – Marlene Dietrich

il pomeriggio – the afternoon
Nel mattino un uomo cammina con il suo intero
corpo; nel pomeriggio, solo con le sue gambe.
In the morning a man walks with his whole body;
in the evening only with his legs. – Ralph Waldo Emerson

il ponte – bridge
Venezia ha 435 ponti, tra i quali il Ponte di Rialto
e il Ponte dei Sospiri, sono i più famosi.
Venice has 435 bridges, among which Rialto Bridge
and Bridge of Sighs, are the most famous.

il popolo – people, folks, populace, crowd, mob
Si può indurre il popolo a seguire una causa,
ma non far sì che la capisca.
You can induce a mob to follow a cause,
but not make them understand it. – Confucius

la porta – door

Il destino, quando apre una porta, ne chiude un'altra.
Dati certi passi avanti, non è possibile tornare indietro.
When destiny opens a door, it closes another. With certain
steps, it's not possible to turn back. – Victor Hugo

il porto – port, harbor, freight

I porti più attivi nel mondo sono nel Lontano Est:
Singapore, Shanghai e Hong Kong, In Europa, Rotterdam,
è il porto più attivo. Genova è il porto più attivo d'Italia.
The most active ports in the world are in the Far East:
Singapore, Shanghai and Hong Kong. In Europe, Rotterdam,
is the most active port. Genova is the most active port in Italy.

la posizione – position, status

I principi di giustizia sono quelli che persone razionali
sceglierebbero in una posizione iniziale di eguaglianza.
The principals of justice are those that rational people would
choose in an original position of equality. – John Rawls

la possibilità – possibility, chance, opportunity

L'autostima non sostituisce un tetto sulla testa o una pancia piena, ma
aumenta la possibilità che l'individuo trovi il modo di soddisfare queste
necessità.
Self-esteem is not a substitute for a roof over one's head or food in one's
stomach, but it increases the likelihood that one will find a way
to meet such needs. – Nathaniel Branden

il posto – place, post, job, site, seat

Questo posto è libero? *Is this seat free?*
Tutto a posto? *Is everything alright?*

la potenza – power, might, strength, potency

Il calcio è inscritto nei geni degli uomini e ciascuno dei suoi spermatozoi è
un calciatore in potenza che sogna di essere un giorno selezionato per
andare in finale.
Soccer is inscribed in the genes of men and each one of their sperm is a potential
soccer player who dreams of one day being selected to go to the finals.
– Vincent Roca

il potere – power

Il potere tende a corrompere e il potere
assoluto corrompe assolutamente.
Power tends to corrupt and absolute power
corrupts absolutely. – Lord Acton

il pranzo – lunch
Se la vita è un pranzo, le donne sono il dessert.
If life is lunch, women are the dessert. – Anon

la presenza – presence, appearance, attendance
Se volete sapere cosa si dice di voi in vostra assenza, ascoltate ciò che si
dice degli altri in vostra presenza.
*If you want to know what they say about you in your absence, listen to what they
say about others in your presence. – Jean-Benjamin de La Borde*

il presidente – president, speaker, chairman
Il presidente del consiglio di amministrazione
ci ha chiesto di organizzare una riunione.
*The board chairman has asked
us to organize a meeting.*

il prezzo – price, cost, value, rate
Se non c'è un prezzo da pagare, allora non ha un valore.
If there's no price to be paid, it is also not of value. – Einstein

il principio – beginning, start, principle, tenet
Al principio fu creato l'Universo. Questo fatto ha sconcertato non poche
persone ed è stato considerato dai più come una cattiva mossa.
*In the beginning the Universe was created. This has made a lot of people very
angry and been widely regarded as a bad move. – Douglas Adams*

il privilegio – privilege
Un popolo che apprezza i suoi privilegi più
dei sui principi presto perde entrambi.
*A people that values its privileges above
its principles soon loses both. – Eisenhower*

il problema – the problem
Un problema è una possibilità per fare del tuo meglio.
A problem is a chance for you to do your best. – Duke Ellington

il processo – trial, lawsuit, legal proceedings, case, process
Il giudice era corrotto e il processo diventava una parodia di giudizia.
The judge was corrupt, and the trial became a mockery of justice.

il prodotto – product
Oggi il consumatore è la vittima del produttore, che gli rovescia addosso
una massa di prodotti ai quali deve trovar posto nella sua anima.
*Today the consumer is the victim of the manufacturer, who dumps a
mass of products on him, which must find place in
his soul. – Mary McCarthy, paraphrase*

la produzione – production

Mio zio ha una caseificio per la produzione
di latte, burro e formaggio.
*My uncle has a dairy farm for the production
of milk, cream and cheese.*

il professore – professor, teacher

Il professore di matematica e
la professoressa di scienza si sono sposati.
The math teacher and the science teacher are married.

il proposito – goal, intention, aim, purpose
a proposito - by the way

Il mio proposito per questa settimana è di sistemare il mio ufficio.
My goal for this week is to organize my office.
A proposito, volevo dirti che ho visto Gemma ieri nel centro.
By the way, I meant to tell you that I saw Gemma yesterday downtown.

la proposta – proposal, suggestion, advice, proposition

Vorrei fare una proposta che terminiamo
questa riunione e andiamo all'enoteca all'angolo.
*I'd like to propose that we wrap up this meeting
and head to the wine bar on the corner.*

la prova – proof, test, experiment, evidence, attempt

La prova fondamentale del valore di un leader è che si lasci dietro, in altri
uomini, la convinzione e la volontà di proseguire la sua opera.
*The final test of a leader is that he leaves behind him in other men the
conviction and will to carry on. – Walter Lippmann*

il pubblico – public, audience

Il pubblico ha un'insaziabile curiosità di conoscere
tutto, tranne ciò che vale la pena conoscere.
*The public have an insatiable curiosity to know everything,
except what is worth knowing. – Oscar Wilde*

il punto – point, detail, period

L'occhio è il punto in cui si mescolano anima e corpo.
The eye is the point where the soul and the body mingle. – Christian Hebbel

il quadro – painting, picture, square

La prima virtù di un quadro è essere una festa per gli occhi.
*The first virtue of a painting is to be a feast
for the eyes. – Eugène Delacroix*

la qualità – quality
La qualità conta più della quantità.
Quality counts more than quanity.

la questione – question, issue,
problem, matter, subject, point
È tutta una questione di punti di vista, e spesso la sfortuna
non è che il segno di una falsa interpretazione della vita.
It's all a question of point of view, and often misfortune is only
a sign of a misinterpretion in life. – Henri de Motherlant

il ragazzo – boy, kid, boyfriend
Fra tutti gli animali, il ragazzo è il più indomabile.
Among all the animals, the boy is the most untamable. – Plato

la ragione – reason, cause
È meglio essere ottimisti ed avere torto
piuttosto che pessimisti ed avere ragione.
It's better to be an optimist and be wrong rather
than be a pessimist and be right. – Einstein

il rapporto – rapport, relationship, connection, report
Esiste un solo vero lusso, ed è quello dei rapporti umani.
There is only one true luxury, and it is that of human
relations. – Antoine de Saint-Exupéry

la realtà – reality, truth
La vita non è un problema
da risolvere, ma una realtà da sentire.
Life is not a problem to be solved, but a reality
to be experienced. – Soren Kierkegaard

la regione – region
Cercano funghi ogni autunno in una regione
remota della foresta con il loro cane.
They look for mushrooms every autumn
in a remote region of the forest with their dog.

la regola – rule
Non seguo il libro delle regole…
Mi faccio guidare dal cuore, non dalla testa.
I don't go by the rule book… I lead from
the heart, not the head. – Princess Diana

la relazione – relationship, connection

Una sana relazione amorosa è il modo più efficace di
superare l'abisso che divide gli esseri umani.
*A healthy, loving relationship is the most effective way
of overcoming the abyss that divides human
beings. – Abraham Maslow*

la religione – religion

Mia moglie mi ha convertito alla religione: non
credevo nell'inferno prima di sposarla.
*My wife converted me to religion: I didn't believe
in hell until I married her. – Hal Roach*

il resto – rest, remainder, residue,
change (regarding money, as in a tip)

L'ho incontrato ad una festa, e il resto è storia.
I met him at a party, and the rest is history.
Ho detto al cameriere di tenere il resto.
I told the waiter to keep the change.

la ricchezza – richness, wealth,
abundance, prosperity, opulence

La più grande ricchezza è nel bastare a sé stessi.
Self-sufficiency is the greatest of all wealth. – Epicurus

la ricerca – research

La scienza è dopotutto un'arte, una questione di
consumata abilità nel condurre la ricerca.
*Science is after all, an art, a question of consummate
ability in the conduct of research. – John Dewey*

ricordo – memory

I ricordi sono la chiave, non del passato, ma al futuro.
*Memories are the key, not to the past, but
to the future. – Corrie Ten Boom*

il rischio – risk

Quando rischi, forse perdi. Ma quando non
rischi, non hai l'opportunità di vincere.
*When you take a risk, you may lose. But when you don't take
a risk, you don't have an opportunity to win. – Anon*

il rispetto – respect, esteem

Il coraggio incute rispetto anche ai nemici.
Courage inspires respect even to enemies. – Alexandre Dumas

la risposta – response, reply, answer

Lo scienziato non è l'uomo che fornisce le vere
risposte; è quello che pone le vere domande.
The scientist is not the man who furnishes the real answers;
it is he who poses the real questions. – Claude Lévi-Strauss

il risultato – result, outcome, findings, conclusion

L'annuncio per perdere peso promette, "massimo
risultato col minimo sforzo!" Ma io non ci credo!
The weight loss ad promises, "maximum results
with minimum effort!" But I don't believe it!

il ritorno – return

Il viaggio perfetto è circolare. La gioia
della partenza, la gioia del ritorno.
The perfect trip is circular. The joy of
departure, the joy of returning. – Dino Basili

la rivoluzione - revolution

Quando la dittatura è un fatto, una rivoluzione diviene un diritto.
When dictatorship is a fact, revolution becomes a right. – Victor Hugo

la roba – stuff

Perchè non fanno l'intero aereo di
quella roba come la scatola nera?
Why don't they make the whole plane out of
that black box stuff? – Steven Wright

il sacrificio – sacrifice, cost

Nella donna tutto è sacrificio, nell'uomo tutto è dovere.
Sacrifice is of a woman, duty is of a man. – Libero Bovio

la sagezza – wisdom

La saggezza consiste non tanto nel vedere ma nel prevedere.
Wisdom consists not so much in seeing as in foreseeing. – Hosea Ballou

la sala – room, hall

Dopo essere stati tutto il giorno nella sala
conferenza, siamo andati nella sala da cocktail.
After being in the conference room all day long, we went to the cocktail lounge.

la salute – health

L'uomo passa la prima metà della vita a rovinarsi
la salute, e la seconda metà provando a guarirsi.
Man spends the first half of his life ruining his health,
and the second half trying to get better. – Anon

la scala – steps, staircase, scale, ladder
Prendiamo le scale invece della scala mobile.
Let's take the stairs instead of the escalator.
Lo scienzato è diventato molto sconvolto
quando ha guardato la scala Richter.
*The scientist became very upset
when he saw the Richter scale.*

la scelta – choice
La vita è la somma di tutte le nostre scelte.
Life is the sum of all our choices. – Albert Camus

la scena – scene, setting, episode,
stage, shot, sight, panorama
Gli inglesi hanno inventato il calcio, i francesi l'hanno
organizzato, gli italiani lo mettono in scena.
*The English invented soccer, the French organized it
and the Italians produced it. – Serge Uzzan*

la scienza – science
Prima studiava la scienza politica ma poi ha deciso di
combinarlo con una laurea nella scienza dell'informazione.
*First she studied Political Science but then she decided to
combine it with a degree in Computer Science.*

lo scopo – purpose, goal, aim
La donna per l'uomo è uno scopo,
l'uomo per la donna è un mezzo.
*For a man, a woman is a goal, for a woman,
a man is a means. – Alphonse Karr*

lo scrittore – writer
Questi scrittori scrivono vari generi: romanzi, novelle,
biografie, gialli, epiche, poesia, racconti, saggi e cronache.
*These writers write in various genres: novels, short stories,
biographies, mysteries, epic works, poetry, stories, essays and reports.*

la scuola – school
Ogni istruzione seria s'acquista
con la vita, non con la scuola.
*All serious instruction is acquired through
life, and not through school. – Tolstoy*

il secolo – century

Un secolo fa, la società era in piena trasformazione dinamica
e culturale, dovuta alla rivoluzione industriale.
A century ago, society was in the midst of dynamic and
cultural transformation, due to the Industrial Revolution.

il segno – sign, mark, symbol

Dubitare di se stesso è il primo segno dell'intelligenza.
Doubting oneself is the first sign of intelligence. – Ugo Ojetti

il senso – sense, feeling, meaning

Per avere molto buon senso bisogna essere fatti in modo che
la ragione predomini sul sentimento e l'esperienza sulla logica.
To have good common sense, reason must predominate over
sentiments and experience over logic. – Luc de Vauvenargues
Senso dell'umorismo vuol dire senso della proporzione.
A sense of humor means a sense of proportion. – Kahlil Gibran

il sentimento – feeling, sentiment, emotion

Il valore di un sentimento è la somma dei
sacrifici che si è disposti a fare per esso.
The value of a sentiment is the amount of sacrifice that
you are prepared to make for it. – John Galsworthy
I buoni sentimenti promuovono sempre ottimi affari.
Good feelings promote good business. – Leo Longanesi

la sera – evening, night

La bisessualità raddoppia immediatamente le tue
possibilità per un appuntamento al sabato sera.
Bisexuality immediately doubles your chances for
a date on Saturday night. – Woody Allen

la serie – series, set, sequence, succession, range

L'uomo non è altro che la serie delle sue azioni.
Man is none other than the series of his actions.
– Friedrich Hegel

il servizio – service, duty, operation, favor

La fabbrica non può guardare solo all'indice dei profitti. Deve distribuire
ricchezza, cultura, servizi, democrazia. Io penso la fabbrica per l'uomo, non
l'uomo per la fabbrica.
The factory can not only look at the profit index. It must distribute riches,
culture, services, democracy. I think of the factory for the man, not the
man for the factory. – Adriano Olivetti

306

il sesso - sex
Un intellettuale è una persona che ha
scoperto qualcosa di più interessante del sesso.
An intellectual is a person who has discovered
something more interesting than sex. – Edgar Wallace
L'amore è la risposta, ma mentre aspettate la
risposta, il sesso può suggerire delle ottime domande.
Love is the answer, but while you're waiting for the answer,
sex raises some pretty good questions. – Woody Allen

la settimana – week
Ho smesso di fumare. Vivrò una settimana
di più e in quella settimana pioverà a dirotto.
I quit smoking. I'll live a week longer and in that
week it will rain cats and dogs. – Woody Allen

lo sforzo – effort, exertion, strain, struggle, force
Lo sforzo continuo – non la forza o l'intelligenza –
è la chiave nell'aprire la nostra potenziale.
Continuous effort – not strength or intelligence –
is the key to unlocking our potential. – Winston Churchill

la sicurezza – security, safely
Ho un nevrosi classica e ciò
da molta sicurezza al mio analista.
I have a classic neurosis and that makes my
analyst feel very secure. – Marco Stefanon

la signora – Mrs., ma'am, lady, woman
C'è una signora nel nostro ufficio che conosce il primo ministro.
There's a woman in our office who knows the Prime Minister.

il signore – Mr., sir, man, gentleman, Lord
Si, Signore, lo porto subito al suo ufficio.
Yes, Sir, I'll bring it right away to your office.

la signorina – miss, young lady, unmarried woman
La signorina mi ha spiegato come arrivare al nostro albergo.
The young lady explained to me how to get to our hotel.

il silenzio – silence, quiet
Niente rafforza l'autorità quanto il silenzio.
Nothing strengthens authority so much as
silence. – Leonardo da Vinci

il sistema – system, method, process
Ogni volta che ti arrabbi, avveleni il tuo sistema.
Every time you get angry, you poison your
own system. – Alfred Montapert

la situazione – situation
Non ci sono situazioni disperate, ci sono
soltanto persone disperate.
There are no desperate situations, there are only
desperate people. – Heinz Guderian

la società – society, company, corporation,
association, partnership, guild, club
La società italiana è una parte essenziale e integrale
della economia e cultura europea.
Italian society is an essential and integral part
of European economy and culture.
Lei fa parte di un società di signore che lavorano a maglia.
She's part of a group of women who knit.

il sogno – dream
La speranza è un sogno ad occhi aperti.
Hope is a waking dream. – Aristotle

il sole – sun
Un pasto senza vino è come un giorno senza sole.
A meal without wine is like a day without sunshine. – Savarin

la soluzione – soluzione
Le soluzioni non sono la risposta.
Solutions are not the answer. – Richard Nixon

il sonno – sleep
Ieri sera ho dormito malissimo. Avevo il sonno inquieto,
disturbato, leggero e due incubi in seguito. È strano
perchè di solito ho il sonno profondo e sereno.
Last night I slept very poorly. My sleep was restless,
agitated, light and full of nightmares. It's strange,
because usually I sleep deeply and peacefully.

la sorella – sister
Ho una sorella maggiore che è sposata e una
sorella minore che frequenta il liceo.
I have an older sister who is married and a
younger sister who attends high school.

il sorriso – smile

Povero quel viso dove non c'è sorriso.
Poor is the face where there is no smile. – Proverbio

la spalla – shoulder

Il suo gatto è morto e ha perso il lavoro, tutto nello stesso giorno.
Ha proprio bisogno di una spalla su cui piangere.
Her cat died and she lost her job, all on the same day.
She really needs a shoulder to cry on.

lo spazio – space

Quello che l'arte offre è lo spazio – una specie
di spazio per far respirare lo spirito.
What art offers is space – a certain breathing
room for the spirit. – John Updike

lo specchio – mirror

Il volto è lo specchio dell'anima.
The face is the mirror of the soul. – Cicero

la specie – sort, kind, variety, type, manner, species

Ci sono due specie di sciocchi: quelli che non dubitano
di niente e quelli che dubitano di tutto.
There are two kinds of fools: those who doubt
nothing and those who doubt everything. – C.J. de Ligne

la speranza – hope

Il ponte fra la disperazione e la speranza è una buona dormita.
The bridge between desperation and hope is a good night's sleep. – Anon
Finche c'è vita c'è speranza.
While there's life, there's hope.
– Proverbi

la spesa – grocery shopping, expense, investment, shopping

Dico sempre che fare le spese è
più economico che uno psichiatra.
I always say that shopping is cheaper than a
psychiatrist. – Tammy Faye Bakker

lo spettacolo – show, performance, spectacle, sight

La gente è il più grande spettacolo del mondo. E non si paga il biglietto.
People are the greatest show on earth.
And you do not pay the ticket. – Charles Bukowski

lo spirito – spirit, wit, sense of humor, personality, ghost

I due fratelli non potrebbero essere più diversi: Marco è
un spirito libero e Tommaso è sempre stressato.
*The two brothers couldn't be more different; Mark's
a free spirit and Thomas is always stressed.*

la stagione – season

La gioventù non è una stagione della vita, è uno stato mentale.
Youth is not a season of life, it's a mental state. – Mateo Alemán

la stampa – press, print, engraving

La stampa è per eccellenza lo
strumento democratico della libertà.
*The press is the chief democratic instrument
of freedom. – Alexis de Tocqueville*

la stanza – room, stanza

Una stanza senza libri è come un corpo senz'anima.
A room without books is like a body without a soul. – Cicero

lo stato – state, condition, status, shape, country

Niente provoca più danno in uno Stato del
fatto che i furbi passino per saggi.
*Nothing provokes more damage to a state as
when the sly pass for sages. – Francis Bacon*

la stazione – station

Dopo l'incidente, hanno preso la mia macchina
alla stazione del servizio per ripararla.
*After the accident, they took my car
to the service station to repair it.*

la strada – street, road

Tutte le strade portano a Roma.
All roads lead to Roma. – Proverbio

la storia – story, history

Secondo la storia che tu mi dici, non hai fatto niente.
Ma c'è evidenza al contrario…
*According to your story, you did nothing.
But there's evidence to the contrary…*
La storia è la maestra della vita.
History is life's teacher. – Proverbio

lo strumento – instrument, tool, utensil
Come professore di musica, aveva una conoscenza
di strumenti musicali: strumenti a corda,
strumenti di percussione, strumenti ad aria
e gli ottoni.
*As a music professor, he had familiarity
with musical instruments: string instruments,
percussion, woodwinds and brass instruments.*

lo studio – study, report, research, office
Quando vado all'università, la biologia sarà il mio campo di studio.
When I go to college, biology will be my field of study.
Lui è avvocato e lavora in uno studio in centro.
He's an attorney and works in an office downtown.

il successo – success
L'azione è la chiave fondamentale a tutto il successo.
Action is the foundational key to all success. – Picasso

lo sviluppo – development, progress, growth, expansion
C'è una sola libertà: quella del proprio necessario sviluppo.
*There is only one freedom: that of our own necessary
development. – Giovanni Papini*

il talento – talent
Il talento è solo la voglia di fare qualcosa.
Tutto il resto è sudore, traspirazione e disciplina.
*Talent is only the desire to do something. All the rest is
sweat, perspiration and discipline. – Jacques Brel*

la tavola, il tavolo – table, board
A tavola! *To the table!/Dinnertime!*
Dobbiamo ancora comprare molti mobili per la nuova casa:
un divano, poltrone, un tavolo da pranzo, un tavolo da cucina,
alcuni tavoli da angolo e sedie.
*We still need to buy a lot of furniture for the new house:
a couch, armchairs, a dining table, a kitchen table,
some corner tables and chairs.*

il teatro – theater
Il teatro unisce tante discipline creative in uno spettacolo:
la storia, il dialogo, la musica, la danza, i costumi, l'azione e lo scenario.
*The theater united so many creative disciplines into one show:
the story, dialogue, music, dance, costumes, action and scenery.*
Il vecchio teatro è stato rinnovato ed adesso è un teatro moderno di 4 sale.
The old theatre was renovated and now is a modern theatre of 4 cinemas.

il tempo – time, weather
Il tempo è denaro. - *Time is money.*
Il tempo è la cosa più preziosa che un uomo può spendere.
Time is the most precious thing that a man can spend. – Teofrasto

il termine – term, boundary, limit, conclusion, ending, final stage, period, deadline
Trovo quest'articolo difficile da leggere a causa di tutti i termini tecnici.
I find this article hard to read because of all the technical terms.
Quando si invecchia, la memoria a breve termine diminuisce.
When we age, short-term memory diminishes.

la testa – head, brain, mind
Dire molte parole e comunicare pochi pensieri è dovunque segno infallibile
di mediocrità; invece segno di testa eccellente è il saper rinchiudere molti
pensieri in poche parole.
*To say many words and communicate few thoughts is an unfallible sign of
mediocrity; on the other hand, knowing how to encapsulate many thoughts in
few words is a sign of an excellent mind. – Arthur Schopenhauer*

il tipo – kind, sort, type, model, fellow, guy
C'è un solo tipo di successo: quello di
fare della propria vita ciò che si desidera.
*There is only one kind of success: that of making one's life
what one desires. – atttributed to Henry David Thoreau*

il tono – tone, shade, quality, pitch, tint
La parola comunica il pensiero, il tono le emozioni.
*Words communicate thought, tone communicates
emotions. – Ezra Pound*

il tratto – trait, feature, course
Secondo me, ha molti tratti di personalità irritante:
è accusativo, aggressivo, impaziente, insistente, maleducato,
ossessionato, pretenzioso, sospettoso. In tutto, è intollerabile!
*In my opinion, he has many irritating personality traits:
he's accusative, aggressive, impatient, insistent, ill-bred,
obsessive, pretentious and suspicious. All in all, he's intolerable!*

il treno – train
Quella luce che vedi alla fine della galleria è
un treno che viene nella tua direzione.
*That light that you see at the end of the tunnel
is an on-coming train. – Murphy's Law*

la tristezza – sadness
Buon umore è la salute dell'anima, la tristezza il suo veleno.
Good humor is the health of the soul, sadness
its poison. – Lord Chesterfield

l'ufficiale – official, officer
I cattivi ufficiali sono eletti dai
buoni cittadini che non votano.
Bad officials are elected by good citizens
who do not vote. – George Jean Nathan

l'ufficio – office, department, agency
Il cervello è un organo favoloso. Comincia a lavorare dal momento
in cui ti svegli la mattina e non smette fino a quando entri in ufficio.
The mind is a fabulous organ. It starts to work the moment you wake up in the
morning and doesn't stop until you get in the office. – Robert Frost

l'umanità – humanity
L'umanità è una sola famiglia.
Humanity is one single family. – Gandhi

l'umorismo – humor
L'umorismo, che splendido modo per
neutralizzare la realtà quando essa ci cade addosso.
Humor, what a splendid way of neutralizing reality
when it falls on top of you. – Marc Levy. paraphrase

l'uomo – man
Il desiderio è l'essenza dell'uomo.
Desire is the essence of man. – Spinoza

l'uso – use, usage, purpose
La felicità non dipende da quello che ci manca, ma
dal buon uso che facciamo di quello che abbiamo.
Happiness doesn't depend upon what we lack, but on the
good use of what we do with what we have. – Thomas Hardy

l'università – university, college
Dopo aver finito il liceo, lui ha scelto
di studiare ad un'università all'estero.
After finishing high school, he chose
to study at a university overseas.

il valore – value, amount, price, merit, validity, valor, courage

I dolori, le delusioni e la malinconia non sono fatti per renderci
scontenti e toglierci valore e dignità, ma per maturarci.
*Suffering, disappointments and melancholy are there not to vex us or deprive
us of our dignity, but to mature and transfigure us. – Hermann Hesse*

la verità – truth, reality

Ama la verità ma perdona l'errore.
Love truth but pardon error. – Voltaire

la via – street, way, path, chance

La via dell'eccesso conduce al palazzo della saggezza.
The path of excess leads to the palace of wisdom. – William Blake

il viaggio – trip, travel, journey

Sono appena tornato da un viaggio di piacere.
Ho accompagnato mia suocera all'aeroporto.
*I just returned from a pleasure trip.   I took my
mother-in-law to the airport. – Milton Berle*

la villa – villa, residence, mansion

La vera felicità sta nelle piccole cose: una piccolo
villa, un piccolo yacht, una piccola fortuna.
*Real happiness is found in the little things: a small
villa, a little yacht, a small fortune. – Anonimo*

il vino – wine

Il vino è la poesia in una bottiglia.
Wine is poetry in a bottle. – Clifton Fadiman

la visita – visit, tour, inspection, examination

Abito sempre nel mio sogno e di tanto in tanto
faccio una visita alla realtà.
*I always live in my dream and from time to time
I make a visit to reality. – Ingmar Bergan*

la vista – view

La più diffusa malattia degli occhi è l'amore a prima vista.
The most common eye disease is love at first sight. – Gino Cervi

314

la vita – life

Nella vita, lieti o tristi, siamo tutti dei turisti.
In life, happy or sad, we are all tourists. – Proverbio
Meglio aggiungere vita ai giorni che non giorni alla vita.
Better to add life to the days than days to life.
– Rita Levi-Montalcini

la voce – voice

Presta a tutti il tuo orecchio, a pochi la tua voce.
Give every man thy ear, but few thy voice. – Shakespeare

la voglia – desire, wish, longing

Ottimo è quel maestro che, poco insegnando, fa
nascere nell'alunno una voglia grande d'imparare.
*Great is the teacher who, teaching a little, sparks in
the student a great desire to learn.* – Arturo Graf

la volontà – will, wish, desire

L'intelletto deve governare la testa, il cuore e la volontà.
The intellect must govern the head, the heart and the will. – Anon

la volta – time, (as in one time, once)

Un passo alla volta. – *One step at a time.*

la zona – zone, area

Nella vita non bisogna mai rassegnarsi, arrendersi alla mediocrità, bensì
uscire da quella "zona grigia" in cui tutto è abitudine e rassegnazione
passiva.
*In life one must not yield or give into mediocrity, reject the "grey zone" where
all is habit and passive resignation. – Rita Levi-Montalcini*

MISCELLANEOUS ESSENTIAL VOCABULARY

ESSENZIALI PAROLE VARI

MISCELLANEOUS ESSENTIAL VOCABULARY ESSENZIALI PAROLE VARI

a – at, to, by
Vado a scuola alle otto domani mattina.
I'm going to school at eight o'clock tomorrow morning.

abbastanza – enough, quite, pretty much, fairly
Grazie, mamma, ho mangiato abbastanza!
Thanks, mom, I ate enough!
Il giornalista è abbastanza esperto in questo campo.
The journalist is pretty experienced in this field.

accanto – beside, next to
Il cane dorme accanto al gatto ogni notte.
The dog sleeps next to the cat every night.

accordo – accord, agreement, settlement   d'accordo – OK
Vuoi andare in piscina? – D'accordo!
Do you want to go to the pool? – OK!
Non sono mica d'accordo con la decisione del tribunale.
I'm not at all in agreement with the court decision.

adesso – now
Adesso sono pronto ad andare.
I'm ready to go now.

addirittura – even, still, directely, straight, "Really!" completely, absolutely,
Era molto arrabbiata con l'impiegato;
addirittura gli ha gridato.
*She was very angry with the employee;
she even yelled at him.*
Esco stasera con Franco! – Addirittura?!
I'm going out tonight with Frank. – Really?!

affatto – not at all, in no way, by no means
Non sono affatto abituato a questo nuovo quartiere.
I'm not at all used to this new neighborhood.

318

allora – so, then, thus
Allora, cos'altro c'è di nuovo? *So, what else is new?*
E allora, cosa è successo? *And then what happened?*

almeno – at least
Ci vuole almeno un'ora per guidare in città.
It takes at least an hour to drive to the city.

anche – also
Quest'acqua è per noi, ma anche per i nostri vicini.
This water is for us but also for our neighbors.

ancora – again, still, yet, more
Era fatto male; lo devo fare ancora.
It was done poorly, I have to do it again.
Lui è ancora qui? Deve partire adesso!
He's still here? He needs to leave now!
Non ho ancora parlato con il mio fidanzato.
I still haven't talked to my boyfriend.

anzi – as a matter of fact, more to the point, rather, on the contrary
Sciare è molto divertente, anzi, è la mia passione.
Skiing's great fun, as a matter of fact, it's my passion.

appena – just, as soon as, barely
Ero appena ritornata dal dottore quando
mamma mi ha telefonato con la brutta notizia.
*I had just returned from the doctor's office when
mom phoned me with the bad news.*

appunto – precisely
Tu credi che lui sia andato perchè
si era arrabbiato, vero? - Appunto.
You believe he left because he was angry, right? - Precisely.

assai – rather, very, plenty
Lei è assai cattiva; non ci lascia nemmeno usare il bagno!
She's very mean; she won't even let us use the bathroom!

attorno – around
C'è un giardino che va tutto attorno al parco.
There's a garden that goes all around the park.

avanti – forward, ahead, before
Abbiamo passato il pallone avanti e indietro tutto il pomeriggio.
We passed the ball back and forth all afternoon long.

bene – well
Mangia bene. Rimani in forma. Muori lo stesso...
Eat right. Stay fit. Die anyway..

certamente – certainly, sure
Vuole venire con noi alla festa stasera?   - Certamente!
Do you want to go with us to the party tonight? - Sure!

che – that, which, what, who, than
La studentessa non capisce che deve studiare di più.
The student doesn't understand that she needs to study more.

chi – who
Con chi parli? - Parlo con la mia ragazza/fidanzata.
Who are you talking to? - *I'm talking with my girlfriend.*

chissà – literally, "who knows?" "I wonder..."
maybe, perhaps, possibly
Chissà se c'è vita nello spazio?
Who knows if there's life in outer space?

ci – us, ourselves; each other
here, there, it
Ci conosciamo da venti anni.
We've known each other for 20 years.
Ci sono sempre problemi nell'ufficio.
There are always problems in the office.

ciò – this, that, what, it
Dimmi ciò che vuoi, e lo faccio.
Tell me what you want and I'll do it.

cioè – that is (to say,) namely, like, (often used
as a linguistic staller; as in the Valley Girl "like")
Mio zio, cioè il padre di Giuseppe, mio cugino, è andato a caccia.
My uncle, that is the father of Giuseppe, my cousin, went hunting.

come – how, like, as
Come sai tutta questa informazione?
How do you know all this information?
Il vaso di fiori è bello come un quadro.
The vase of flowers is as pretty as a picture.

completamente – completely
Mia zia è intelligente, ma purtroppo, è completamente pazza.
My aunt is intelligent, but unfortunately, she's completely crazy.

comunque – however, anyway, but
Siamo occupatissimi con la nuova casa,
comunque vogliamo vedervi lo stesso.
We're very busy with the new house,
however, we want to see you just the same.

con – with
Vado al negozio questo pomeriggio con mia sorella.
I'm going to the store this afternoon with my sister.

contro – against, versus
Quello che hai fatto era contro la legge, e tu lo sai!
What you did was against the law, and you know it!

cui – which
L'incidente è sucesso nello stesso momento
in cui io sono entrata nella camera.
The accident happened at the same moment
in which I entered the room.

da – from   da – since
Lei viene da Brescia. *She comes from Brescia.*
Lasciami dare la vera versione dei fatti.
Ho quarantasei anni e lo sono da alcuni anni.
Allow me to put the record straight. I am
forty-six and have been for some years past. – Erica Jong

davanti – in front of, before
La scrivania è davanti lo scaffale.
The desk is in front of the bookcase.

davvero – really, indeed, actually, quite
Mia sorella si sposerà un principe. – Davvero?!!
My sister is marrying a prince. – Really?!!

dentro – in, inside, into, within

Il gatto è dentro casa, ma il cane invece è fuori casa.

The cat is inside the house, but the dog,
on the other hand, is out of the house.

di – of, about, by

L'imitazione è la più sincera forma di adulazione.

Imitation is the sincerest form of flattery.

dietro – behind, back, after, at the rear

Dietro ad ogni uomo di successo, c'è una donna, e dietro di lei, sua moglie.

Behind every successful man, there's a woman, and behind her, his wife.

domani – tomorrow

Domani dobbiamo riportare i libri alla biblioteca.

Tomorrow we have to return the books to the library.

dopo – after

Siamo molto occupati qui; c'è sempre una cosa dopo l'altra.

We're very busy here; it's always one thing after another.

dove – where

Chissà dove e quando andiamo in vacanza quest'anno...

Who knows where and when we'll go on vacation this year.

dunque – then, therefore, thus, so

Devo lavorare fino a tardi stasera, dunque, mio marito prepara la cena.

I have to work late tonight, so my husband's preparing dinner.

durante – during, while

Mia nonna è nata durante la seconda guerra mondiale.

My grandmother was born during the Second World War.

e – and

Signora, prendo due melanzane e quattro pomodori oggi.

Ma'am, I'll take two eggplants and four tomatoes today.

ecco – here

Dov'è la mia borsa? Oh, eccola! *Where's my purse? Oh, here it is!*

egli – he
(generally used in literature and Southern Italy)

Egli non scrive ancora bene, ma sta migliorando.

He doesn't write well yet, but he's improving.

entro – in, within, by, inside

Non parlare così forte! Lei è entro il raggio di ascolto.
Don't talk so loud! She's within hearing range.

eppure – and yet, still, nevertheless

Gli ho spiegato la situazione tre volte, eppure non mi capisce.
I explained the situation three times to him,
and yet he still doesn't understand.

essa – her, it
(said of animals and inanimate objects,
used in literature more than everyday speech)

La mia gatta ha appena dato alla luce. Essa dorme adesso serenamente.
My cat just gave birth. She's sleeping peacefully now.

esso – he, it (of animals, things)

Ferro è un cane molto affettuoso.
Esso ci segue intorno alla casa e dorme con noi.
Ferro is a very affectionate dog.
He follows us around the house and sleeps with us.

finalmente – finally

Ho finalmente perso peso! Ci è voluto
un sacco di tempo per farlo.
I finally lost the weight! It took me a long while.

finchè – until, while

Resterò con te finchè arrivino i tuoi genitori.
I'll stay with you until your parents arrive.

fin, fino a – until

Vivrò in questa casa fino a che muoio, Dio volendo.
I'll live in this house till I die, God willing.

forse – maybe, perhaps

Forse questo odore viene dall'immondizia.
Maybe this odor is coming from the garbage.

fronte – in front of, facing, before

Siamo impotenti di fronte alla forza della natura.
We are powerless facing the forces of nature. – Anon

fra – within
Ti vedo fra mezz'ora nel ristorante.
I'll see you within half an hour in the restaurant.

fuori – outside
Tutti i ragazzi giocano fuori oggi perchè fa tanto bello.
All the kids are playing outside today because it's so nice out.

già – already
Lo spettacolo è già cominciato. *The show has already started.*

giù – down, below, downstairs
Non possiamo andare giù nella cantina mentre c'è acqua sul pavimento.
We can't go down in the basement while there's water on the floor.

grazie – thanks
Grazie di tutto il tuo aiuto, amico mio.
Thanks for all you help, my friend.

ieri – yesterday
Ieri ho portato mio figlio all'aeroporto.
Yesterday I took my son to the airport.

il – the
Il libro spiega tutto di questo argomento.
The book explains everything on this subject.

in – in
Ti dico questo in segreto, non lo dire a nesunno!
I'm telling you this in secret; don't tell anyone!

infatti – in fact, indeed, as a matter of fact
Siete andati in chiesa stamattina?   - Si, infatti.
Did you guys go to church this morning? - Yes, indeed.

inoltre – moreover, besides, what's more, furthermore, also, plus
Voglio inoltre dirvi che il vostro aiuto era
un grande conforto alla mia famiglia.
*I also want to tell you that your help was
a great comfort to my family.*

insieme – together
I ragazzi giocano insieme tutta l'estate.
The kids play together all summer long.

insomma – in summary, so, all in all, therefore, by and large, all things considered
Siamo stanchi della sua sciocchezza, insomma, io lo butto via!
We're tired of his nonsense, that's it, I'm kicking him out!

intanto – at the same time, in the meanwhile
Ti parlo domani, ma intanto ti auguro una buona notte.
I'll talk to you tomorrow, but in the
meantime, I wish you a good night.

intorno – around
La luna orbita intorno alla Terra, e la Terra orbita intorno al sole.
The moon orbits around the Earth, and Earth orbits around the sun.

invece – instead, rather
Devo studiare in biblioteca stasera invece di uscire con gli amici.
I have to study at the library tonight instead of going out with friends.

io – I
Io conosco quella donna da tanti anni.
I've know that woman for many years.

la – the
La sede principale della Fiat si trova a Torino.
The Fiat headquarters are found in Turin.

là – there
Metti la ricetta là, sul tavolo, per favore.
Put the recipe there, on the table, please.

lei – she
Lei è la mia sorella più giovane.   *She's my youngest sister.*

li – them
Parlo con i miei genitori ogni settimana e li vedo ogni fine settimana.
I speak with my parents every week and I see them every weekend.

lì – there
Arrivo lì verso mezzogiorno,
aspettami di fronte alla stazione, va bene?
I'll arrive there around noon,
wait for me in front of the station, OK?

lo – the, it
Lo studente vicino allo specchio si lava la faccia.
The student is by the mirror is washing her face.
Dov'è il prezzo? Non lo vedo.
Where's the price? I don't see it.

lontano – far
Se vuoi viaggiare lontano, viaggia leggero.
Togli via tutta la gelosia, l'ira, l'egoismo e la paura.
If you want to travel far, travel light.
Take off all the jealousy, anger, selfishness and fear. – Anon

loro – they, them
Loro pagano sempre con la carta di credito,
invece noi paghiamo sempre in contante.
They always pay with the credit card, whereas
we on the other hand, always pay with cash.

lui – him
L'origine del problema comincia con lui.
The origin of the problem starts with him.

lungo – long, along
È una lunga passeggiata fino alla stazione.
It's a long walk to the station.

ma – but
Ho sete ma non c'è niente da bere.
I'm thirsty but there's nothing to drink.

mai – never, ever
Mai dire mai!   *Never say never!*
Non si sa mai… *You never know…*

magari – maybe, perhaps
Voi andate a Singapore in vacanza quest'anno? –- Magari!
Are you going to Singapore on vacation this year? – Maybe!/I hope so!

male – badly, illness, evil
Mia figlia si sente male oggi, così,
non va a scuola, rimane a casa.
My daughter isn't feeling well today,
so she's not going to school, she's staying home.

meglio – better

È meglio aver amato e perduto che non aver mai amato.
It is better to have loved and lost than
never to have loved at all. – Tennyson

meno – less

Più sai, e meno sai.
The more you know, the less you know.

mentre – while

Faccio la spesa mentre mio marito fa un sonnelino.
I do the shopping while my husband takes a nap.

mi – me, to me

Mi puoi dire la verità, non la dirò a nessuno.
You can tell me the truth, I'll tell no one.

naturalmente – naturally, of course

Ci vediamo ancora? – Ma, naturalmente.
Will we see each other again? – But of course.

ne – some, of him/her/it/them, about, any
about it, some, of him, of her, of it, of them
né – neither, nor

Che me ne frega? What do I care (about it)?
Né questo né quello funziona per me. Devo trovarne un altro.
Neither this nor that one works for me. I have to find another one.

neanche – not even, neither

Non mi piace la nuova scuola. Sono
qui da un mese e non ho neanche un'amica.
I don't like the new school. I've been
here a month and I don't even have one friend.

nemmeno – not even

Non l'ho visto da molto tempo.
Non posso nemmeno ricordare come si chiama.
I haven't see him in a long time. I can't even remember his name.

neppure – not even

Non so cucinare. Non posso neppure bollire l'acqua...
I don't know how to cook. I can't even boil water...

niente – nothing
Quello non ha niente da fare con i fatti.
That has nothing to do with the facts.

no – no
No, non puoi giocare fuori; è buio.
No, you can't play outside; it's dark.

noi – we
Noi prendiamo sempre un caffé dopo il dolce.
We always have a coffee after dessert.

non – not
Le cose non sono mai così terribili da non poter peggiorare.
Things are never so terrible that they can't
get worse. – Antonio Fogazzaro

nulla – nothing
Si annoia durante l'estate, non fa nulla eccetto guardare la tv.
He's bored during the summer, he doesn't do anything except watch TV.

o – or
Non so se voglio il tè o il caffè stamattina...
I don't know if I want tea or coffee this morning...

oggi – today
Ieri è storia, domani è mistero e oggi è un dono.
Per questo si chiama il presente.
Yesterday is history, tomorrow is a mystery,
and today is a gift. That's why it's called the present.

ognuno – each, every, everyone
Ognuno di noi ha l'obbligo di tenere la casa in ordine.
Each one of us has an obligation to keep the house in order.

oltre – beyond
L'entusiasmo rilascia la voglia di portarti oltre gli ostacoli
e aggiunge il significato a tutto quello che fai.
Enthusiasm releases the drive to carry you over obstacles
and adds significance to all you do. – Norman Vincent Peale

oppure – or, otherwise, or else
Vieni con noi, oppure resti a casa?
Are you coming with us, or staying at home?

ora – hour, now
Che ora è? What time is it?
Devi rispondere ora a quella lettera.
You need to respond to that letter now.

ormai, oramai – now, by now, at this point
È troppo tardi per cambiare idea. Ormai è deciso.
It's too late to change your mind. It's already decided.

per – for
La democrazia è il governo del popolo, dal popolo e per il popolo.
Democracy is the government of the people, by the
people and for the people. – Abe Lincoln

perchè – because, why
Perchè vai fuori adesso? - Perchè il tempo è bellissimo!
Why are you going outside now? - Because it's beautiful out!

perfino – even
Lei è antipatica a tutti, perfino alle suore.
She's unpleasant to everyone, even to the nuns.

però – but, however
Questo vestito è bellissimo, però, è molto caro.
This dress is beautiful, but it's very expensive.

piuttosto – rather, quite, pretty (much)
Mio fratello è piuttosto povero; spesso non può pagare l'affitto.
My brother is pretty poor, he often can't pay the rent.

poco – little
Sarà sempre uno schiavo chi non sa vivere con poco.
He will always be a slave who knows not how
to live with little. – Quinto Orazio Flacco

poiché – since, as
Poiché non ti senti bene, restiamo a casa
stasera e guardiamo la tivù, va bene?
Since you're not feeling well, let's stay home
tonight and watch TV, OK?

presto – soon, quickly, early
Devo arrivare molto presto di mattina.
I need to arrive very early in the morning.

prima - before, earlier, first

Tocca a me; io vado prima di te. *It's my turn; I go before you.*
È la prima volta che faccio la conoscenza di tua sorella.
It's the first time that I'm meeting your sister.

probabilmente – probably

Probabilmente andiamo in Toscana per un paio di giorni.
We'll probably go to Tuscany for a few days.

pure – too, also, so, even, although
is also a word of encouragment

Venite pure alla festa con noi stasera!
"Please/absolutely/do come/just do it/go ahead,"
come to the party with us tonight!

qua – here

Dove sei stato tutto il giorno? – Oh, qua e là...
Where were you all day long?   - Oh, here and there....

qualcosa – something

Ho qualcosa interessante di dirti.   Infatti, è un segreto.
I have something interesting to tell you.
As a matter of fact, it's a secret.

qualcuno – someone

Qualcuno mi ha chiamato, ma non so chi...
Someone called me, but I don't know who...

quasi – almost

Ho quasi finito di leggere il libro.
I have almost finished reading the book.

qui – here

Ti incontro qui dopo la riunione.
I'll meet you here after the meeting.

quindi – so, therefore

Il mio fidanzato è stanco morto, quindi non esce stasera.
My boyfriend is dead tired, so he's not going out tonight.

se – if, whether
her, him, it, herself, himself, itself
Se non ti trovo dopo scuola, ti vedo più tardi a cena.
If I don't find you after school, I'll see you later at dinner.
Dominare gli esseri umani è forza, dominare se stessi è potere.
To dominate human beings is force, to dominate oneself is power. –Anon

secondo – second, according to, depending on
Questa è la seconda volta che ti vedo oggi!
This is the second time that I've seen you today!
Cucino sempre questa pasta secondo la ricetta della mamma.
I always cook this pasta according to my mom's recipe.
Secondo me, lui è molto capace.
In my opinion, he's very capable.

senza – without
Questi poveri sono senza i beni fondamentali.
The poor people are without basic goods.

si – the "impersonal you" one, man, you, we, people
reflexive pronoun - oneself, himself,
herself, itself, yourself, themselves,
Si vive una volta sola.
You only live once.
Dopo che si sveglia, si fa la doccia e si veste.
After waking up, she takes a shower and dresses.

sì – yes
Vieni con noi? - Sì, assolutamente.
Are you coming with us? - Yes, absolutely.

solo – only, sole
Solo due cose sono infinite, l'uinverso e la studipità umana,
e non sono sicura della prima.
*Only two things are infinite, the universe and human stupidity,
and I'm not sure about the former. – Albert Einstein*

soltanto – only, merely, just
Ha soltanto un po' di soldi in tasca.
He has only a little bit of money in his pocket.

sopra – on top, above, over, upstairs, aloft

Mentre piangevo, babbo mi confortava
con il braccio sopra la spalla.
While I was crying, dad comforted me
with his arm over my shoulder.

soprattutto – overall, especially, mainly, chiefly, most importantly

Voglio ringraziare la mia famiglia, e soprattutto
mia mamma per il sostegno morale.
I want to thank my family, and especially
my mother for the moral support.

sotto – under

Ho trovato il mio portafoglio sotto il giornale.
I found my wallet under the newspaper.

spesso – often, frequently

Andiamo spesso in palestra nel pomeriggio.
We go often to the gym in the afternoon.

stamattina – this morning

Stamattina ho visto un uccello morto a terra di fronte casa mia.
This morning I saw a dead bird on the ground in front of my house.

stasera – this evening

Loro devono partire stasera per l'aeroporto.
They have to leave this evening for the airport.

su – on, upon, over, above, upstairs

La solidità del matrimonio poggia
sull'elasticità delle parti.
The solidity of marriage rests upon the elastisity
of the parts. – Alessandro Morandotti

subito – quickly, immediately

Venite subito a tavola, ho fame!
Come quickly to the table, I'm hungry!

tardi – late

Non arrivo mai puntualmente; faccio sempre tardi!
I never arrive on time; I'm always late!

tra – between, in, among

Tra due mali scelgo sempre quello che non ho mai provato.
Between two evils, I always choose the one
I never tried before. – Mae West

tu – you (informal)

Tu devi cominciare a fare i compiti.
You need to start to do your homework.

tuttavia – yet, still, however, but, anyway, even so, despite, nevertheless

Lui è intelligente e capace, tuttavia,
dopo un anno non trova lavoro.
He's intelligent and capable, however,
after a year he still hasn't found work.

un – a, an, one

Roma non fu costruita in un giorno.
Rome wasn't built in a day. – Proverbio

uno – one

Uno, due, tre, via!
One, two, three, go!
Uno per tutti e tutti per uno!
One for all and all for one!

veramente – really, truly

Questa lezione era veramente difficile, ti dico la verità!
This lesson was really difficult, I tell you the truth!

veloce – quick, fast (think velocity)

Te ne sei mai accorto che chiunque guida più lento di te è
un idiota, e chiunque guida più veloce di te è un maniaco?
Have you ever noticed that anybody driving slower than you is
an idiot, and anyone driving faster is a maniac?

verso – towards

Per arrivare dalla nonna
devo guidare verso nord.
To get to my grandmother's I have to
drive towards the north.

voi – you plural
Voi conoscete tutti?
Do you know everyone?

volentieri – gladly, willingly
Vieni con noi a cena stasera? - Si, volentieri!
Will you come to dinner with us tonight? - Yes, gladly!

vi – you (plural), yourselves, each other
Vi auguro buona fortuna.
I wish you good luck.

RESOURCES

RESOURCES

Given today's technology, the opportunities to improve your Italian are seemingly endless and growing month by month. Following are many ideas, but this list is by no means exhaustive.

APPS

There are thousands of Italian apps for smartphones and tablets, and new Italian apps are being added monthly. Some suggestions follow, but the lists are subjective, tailored to individual tastes and just the tip of the iceberg. Explore and you will find your own apps. If you don't have a smartphone or tablet, computer versions of most of these exist.

APPS - ITALIAN LANGUAGE

There many different types of apps available at the App Store to help you master Italian, and within each category many excellent apps to choose from. Research and find what suits you, but here are some suggestions:

Italian Language – general help with grammar and vocabulary
Italian Verb Conjugator – extensive verb conjugation lists
Italian Word of the Day – receive daily vocabulary builders
Italian Translator – translates for you when you're clueless
Italian Dictionary – to have an essential reference on you all day long

Obviously, a good dictionary is essential for the serious linguist. Having a smartphone with Italian dictionaries and a thesaurus in my pocket at all times has been a game-changer for me. Consequently, I am much more connected to the language, and anytime I wonder how to say a word, I look it up immediately, instead of waiting to check my dictionary at home and probably forgetting... I have 4 different such apps on my smartphone that I refer to constantly throughout the day, and they are among my most valuable apps. Many Italian dictionary apps are available, but these are personal favorites:

Word Pair Italian - Vocabulary words and phrases, loads quickly.
Word Reference Italian – Vocab, phrases and sentences, verb conjugator.
Facile Italiano – Italian only. For the more advanced linguist.
Sinonimi e Contrari - An Italian thesaurus, excellent
for vocabulary expansion.

APPS - MISCELLANEOUS

A wealth of Italian apps is available through the App Store. Type specific words in Italian, regarding your interests or hobbies to see what's available. For instance, if you love animals, type in specifics like, *gatti*, *cani*, or more generally, *animali*. If you like soccer, type *calcio*. If you like the sciences, type *biologia, chimica*, etc.

There are history apps, (*Oggi nella Storia*), joke and humor apps (type *barzellette* or *umorismo*) game apps (type *giochi*, and find apps such as *Ruota della Fortuna - Wheel of Fortuna)*, wine apps *(vino)* audio books *(audiolibri)* and various versions of the Bible apps *(La Bibbia,)* etc.

Regarding travel, there are specific travel apps that come in handy. Major cities such as Milano, Torino, Firenze and Roma have informative apps about their towns.   Train schedule apps *(Info Treni)* and specific subway map apps are available. *Guida delle Città*, on the other hand, covers a multitude of global cities.

News of the Weird type apps are good language boosters. *Curiosone* and *Curiosità* both have brief story lines (1-2 paragraphs) that are amusing and workable.

There are many proverb apps that offer inspiration, wisdom and in the meantime, will challenge your Italian. Type *proverbi, frase famosi, citazioni*, or *aforismi* at the App Store.

If you're a news junkie, there's a wealth to choose from. Type *giornali*, *quotidiano* or *notizia* at the App Store. Type *rivista* and you'll see a selection of dozens of Italian magazines apps.

If food's your thing, type *ricette* or *cibo* to see recipe or food apps. Given the Italian culture's love affair with food, as you can imagine, there are hundreds of apps in this category.

BIKE AND WALKING VACATIONS

Thinking of a bike tour of Italy? There may be no better way to take in authentic Italy than by bike. It's an excellent way to see Italy up close; see charming towns and drop dead beautiful landscapes melt into each other. See people as the Italians see people, and at a lovely pace. Or if you prefer, many bike operators also offer walking vacations. Nature, excitement and exercise; a perfect vacation. And if you're green, at the end of the day, you can feel totally good about yourself... Here are some comments from friends who have used these tour companies.

BACKROADS.COM
For the serious athlete and partyer; hard drivers,
hard drinkers, stay up late, keep up or die…

BUTTERFIELDANDROBINSON.COM
"Luxury active travel," for perhaps the more "seasoned" biker. Serious
biking, but refreshments every 30 clicks, cocktails at the countess's house
and they'll fluff your pillow at night. Serious cultural integration after a
long day's ride.

GREAT EXPLORATIONS.COM
Terrific adventure travel and a great experience. Challenging biking,
excellent guides and accommodating hotels for a decent price.

VBT.COM
Vermont Bicycle Tours has plenty of biking and other activities, in and
around the small towns where you see the real Italy. VBT uses local
residents as guides, and the accommodations are four-star quality.
Well organized and great fun.

BLOGS AND WEBSITES
Here's a limited example of the many blogs and websites dedicated to Italian
language and culture.

BECOMINGITALIAN.COM
Dianne Hales is the author of a wonderful book about the
Italian language called La Bella Lingua. This is her blog.

BILLANDSUZY.COM
Join Bill and Suzy's Excellent Adventure as they eat, drink and dolce
vita their way through Italy. It's the next best thing to being there.

STUDENTESSAMATTA.COM
A blog written in Italian by an avowed Italophile American;
she discusses Italian language, culture and current events. Check
out the side bar of her blog; it lists a blog roll of numerous
blogs about Italy, some in English, some in Italian.

ITALIAN.ABOUT.COM
An Italian language and culture website.
Various language levels.

ITALIANLANGUAGEGUIDE.COM
All about the Italian Language.

ITALIANLANGUAGERESOURCES.COM
Use podcasts, streaming media and other audio/visual resources to improve listening comprehension and grow your vocabulary.

LIVEMOCHA.COM
Online language community. Learn a language and connect with native speakers for instructive help.

ITALIANNOTEBOOK.COM
Italian travel site. Daily emails of cultural gems and curiosities by local area experts.

ITALIAN.YABLA.COM
Improve your comprehension. Has an extensive online video library with speed-controlled listening exercises.

RAI.TV
Offers a selection of programs, clips and podcasts from the Rai networks.

BOOK DISTRIBUTORS

ADLERSFOREIGNBOOKS.COM
Huge selection of Italian, French, Spanish and German books

AMAZON.IT
Italian books, audio books and music

EMONSAUDIOLIBRI.IT
Audio books

FELTRINELLI.IT
Italian books, music, DVDs

SCHOENHOFS.COM
Schoenhof's Foreign Books, Cambridge, MA (617) 547-8855
Perhaps the best foreign language bookstores in the U.S;
most have closed. If you get to Boston, stop by.

BOOKS - LANGUAGE

Beyond the obvious Italian text and trade books found on store shelves, here are two gems that might be overlooked.

LA BELLA LINGUA by DIANNE HALES

La Bella Lingua is a tribute to the Italian language and culture. If you're an Italian Culture Vulture, this is your must-read. It's a captivating, informative book that celebrates the joys, not only of the Italian language, but also of Italian culture, cuisine, literature and history. Written by an unabashed Italophile, it offers a terrific overview of the Italian experience.

USING ITALIAN SYNONYMS
by MOSS AND MOTTA

A unique reference book for the voracious vocabulary hound.

BOOKS - LIVING ABROAD

LIVING AND WORKING IN ITALY
by GRAEME CHESTERS

LIVING, STUDYING AND WORKING IN ITALY
by MONICA LARNIER

BOOKS - TRAVEL NARRATIVES

If you can't travel to Italy any time soon, travel narratives will enable you to travel there vicariously. They're a blast to read, are culturally enlightening and will really make you feel like you're in Italy. Listed below are a few favorites, but many more exist:

UNDER THE TUSCAN SUN by FRANCES MAYES

Caveat Emptor, if you're thinking about buying property in Italy, read this book. Takes place in Tuscany.

TOO MUCH TUSCAN SUN by DARIO CASTAGNO

I couldn't put this down; endlessly entertaining, it's a guilty pleasure. Focus is on the Siena region in Tuscany.

THE RELUCTANT TUSCAN by PHIL DORAN

Again, if you're considering buying property in Italy, very wise council would suggest that you read this first. Tuscany region.

THE STONE BOUDOIR by THERESA MAGGIO

A lovely travel narrative written by an Italian-American, the writer escorts you through the history and culture of rural Sicily.

EAT, PRAY, LOVE by ELIZABETH GILBERT

You saw the movie, right? Gilbert's storytelling is ripe with visual and atmospheric detail. Regarding the Italian portion, focus is primarily in Rome.

COURSES IN U.S.

Most major metropolitan areas have language schools or institutes, and Italian is one of the more popular languages offered. Also, most major universities offer inexpensive, non-degree Italian classes. Check your local university for Italian classes in their Continuing or Extended Education programs.

COURSES IN ITALY

Italy is a major world economy, a leading global tourist destination, a cultural mecca and has the concept of *la dolce vita/the good life* down cold. Studying there would be a very smart move on your part... Courses are offered all over Italy. Decide what region is of interest to you, do your homework on the internet and *go!* For more information, see pages 29-30.

CULINARY VACATION

If you enjoy eating and drinking exquisite, authentic, locally grown food and nectar of the Gods, cooking and learning about Italian food and wine together in a convivial group atmosphere, then this is your next vacation. There are dozens of programs throughout Italy's 20 regions. This particular program, *Ecco La Cucina,* has been thoroughly tested and approved by friends:

ECCOLACUCINA.COM

USA phone 972-342-8308, marystipopotter@yahoo.com
Italian phone 011-39-338-774-5487, ginastipo@yahoo.com

DICTIONARIES

A good dictionary is an essential tool for the linguist. There are the handy paperback dictionaries for everyday, and the heavy-duty, hard-bound dictionaries ("six pounders") for when you need to research something in depth. There are "visual dictionaries" with thousands of objects photographed and labeled, as well as special interest dictionaries (medical, business, technological, film, etc.)

Nowadays, you have the option of using a hard copy or online dictionary. The various online dictionaries available on smartphones and tablets are invaluable and frankly, more convenient and easier to handle. It's a game-changer to have a dictionary on you at all times that enables you reference words at any moment. When mastering a language, you never stop learning vocabulary.

If you're looking for an Italian - English/English - Italian dictionary, spend some time comparing them to find one that you'll really treasure. Choose a baseline word and compare that word in the various dictionaries. Some dictionaries have grammar supplements, which is helpful.

If you're a serious linguist, consider buying a heavy-duty, reference dictionary. Consider the hard-bound or the on-line version, Hazan-Garzanti's Il Nuovo Dizionario or an equivalent, if you're dedicated to Italian language and culture; you'll use it throughout your life. These are available both as online apps or as books. I have found the e-versions infinitely more convenient than the actual books due to the books' weight and cumbersomeness.

Also consider getting an Italian-only dictionary, (what would be the Italian equivalent of our Webster's; an Italian dictionary for Italians.) Hazan-Garzanti, Zanichelli and il Sabatini Coletti are reputable reference dictionaries.

FILM

Italy has a rich cinematic history, and its importance is not to be overlooked, boasting world class directors (Federico Fellini, Vittorio Da Sica, Luchino Visconti) and globally recognized actors (Marcello Mastroianni, Sophia Loren, Claudia Cardinale, Roberto Benigni.) Italian cinema spans from the Avant-garde to the ultra-serious Neo-Classical period to Sword and Sandal epics to Spaghetti Westerns and beyond.

Both Netflix and Blockbuster have numerous Italian DVDs to rent and live-stream. Here are some popular classics and favorites:

FILM – COMEDIES

Amarcord
Big Deal on Madonna Street
Ciao Professore!
Divorce, Italian Style
Johnny Stecchino
Mediterraneo
Mid-August Lunch
Pane e Tulipani
Il Postino
Salt of Life
Seven Beauties
Swept Away

FILM - DRAMA AND CLASSICS

The Bicycle Thief
Cinema Paradiso
La Dolce Vita
8 ½
Gomorra
The Leopard
Life Is Beautiful
Malena
Ossessione
Rome, Open City
La Strada
I Vitelloni

LANGUAGE GROUPS

Google Italian Language Groups, Italian Meetup Groups, and Italian Conversation Tables in your area to see what's available.

MUSIC

Listening to music daily is an amazingly fun and effective way to boost vocabulary and absorb the language. The enjoyment factor of music enhances and facilitates the learning process big-time. Find the lyrics online in Italian. You can translate the song from Italian to English yourself, or if you dweeb out, you can often find the translation online.

Opera: Verdi, Puccini, Rossini, Donizetti and Bellini.
Rock and Pop: Claudio Baglioni, Lucio Dalla, Gianluca Grignani, Marcella Bella, Nek, Gino Paoli, Laura Pausini, Renato Zero and Zucchero, to name a few.

ITUNES

Download a huge variety of songs for about a dollar a pop. Language absorbtion by way of music may be both the funnest and the easiest way to learn a language. Reinforce grammar, vocabulary, get down and boogie.

YOUTUBE

Watch a huge variety of musical artists in action. Some of the songs show the lyrics on or below the screen, so that you can read the lyrics while you listen to them, thus using two modalities simultaneously. Totally tubular, dude.

NEWSPAPERS

Reading the newspaper is one of life's great pleasures, and that may go double for reading in Italian while improving your language skills. But unless you're some sort of linguistic flagellant, don't scare yourself off by trying to read difficult articles on Italian politics right away. Stick to lighter fare. There are short articles that are easy to piece together, especially if you're familiar with the subject matter. Check out the various sections of the paper such as AMBIENTE/Environment, BENESSERE/Wellbeing, CASA/Home, CUCINA/Kitchen, CULTURA/Culture, DONNA/ Woman, SCIENZA/Science, TECHNOLOGIA/Technology, VIAGGI/Travel, etc. If you're a sports fan, learn about the different soccer teams and follow the Italian soccer season.

The video articles in the above sections are a terrific tool for comprehension and often have the text printed underneath, for your listening and reading pleasure. The photo gallery articles are short, light and perfect for beginners, with lots of contextual information.

Some leading Italian newspapers are Corriere della Sera, La Stampa and La Repubblica. If you're particularly interested in a specific region of Italy, check out that region's paper. Visit http://www.ciao-italy.com/categories-/newspapers.htm for a complete listing of Italian newspapers. Ciao-Italy also has a list of Italian magazines, as well as a subscription site.

RADIO

ITALIA.FM

ITALIANSINFONIA.COM.STATIONS.HTM

RADIO.RAI

RADIO RAI offers three main channels plus a variety of secondary channels. RAI also has a wealth of podcasts, which are are a terrific linguistic aid, as you can listen to them repeatedly and comprehend more each time. If you need to work on comprehension, RADIO RAI is a gift. It's a free app on your smartphone.

TELEVISION

RAI television provides a wealth of fun content. Watch Italian movies, news, game shows and sitcoms. The more you watch, the more you'll understand. Give it a couple months and notice how your comprehension improves.

TRANSPORTATION

When planning your trip, reserve a private car and driver to take you around Italy in comfort and style. They'll pick you up at the airport, and take you anywhere you'd like to go, in style...

SPRINTCARSERVICE

www.sprintcarservice.com
enzosmntn@gmail.com
Enzo Sementini
US phone 610-952-2423
Italy 011-39-06-97271-973

YOUTUBE

YouTube is not only a terrific music tool, but an all around comprehension booster. Explore your interests visually, while your linguistic savvy improves. Language comprehension is facilitated by the visual cues. Educate yourself on any number of topics: cuisine, travel, music, exercise, science, alternative medicine or self-help. Just plug a key word in Italian and explore the world, Italian-style.

VILLAS/ALTERNATE ACCOMODATIONS

Whether you prefer a quaint Italian farmhouse or a stunning historic villa, you can creatively plan a vacation that you'll never forget.

AGRITURISMI.IT
AGRITURISMO.COM
AGRITURISMO.NET

Agritourism allows you to stay in charming rural settings and interact with the locals. Stay at a farm and experience authentic Italy. Consider this option if you're interested in an extended, economical stay to work on language. Many Italians stay at agriturismi lodgings, so there's a wealth to choose from across Italy. Many more sites exist beyond the above, so if you like the idea of a vacation in the countryside, do some research and find your treasure.

GOITALYHOMES.COM

PARKERVILLAS.COM

VRBO.COM

WIKIPEDIA

It cannot be stressed enough what a cool language tool Wikipedia is. Explore your intellectual passions in this free, online encyclopedia while improving your Italian. Educate yourself on politics, history, art, trends, media, famous people, culture, etc., while reinforcing grammar and vocabulary. The articles are offered in a couple dozen languages, including, *la bella lingua*.

BIBLIOGRAPHY

BOOKS

McKeane, Rossana. Italian Vocabulary Handbook.
Singapore: Berlitz Publishing, 1994.

Feinler-Torriani, Luciana and Gunter H. Klemm. Mastering Italian
Vocabulary, A Thematic Approach. USA: Barron's
Educational Series, 1995.

Marengo, Silvio Riolfo, et al. Il Nuovo Dizionario Italiano Garzanti.
Italy: Garzanti Editore, 1984.

Caselli, Lucia Incerti, et al. Il Nuovo Dizionario Italiano Hazon Garzanti,
Inglese-Italiano, Italiano-Inglese. Italy: Garzanti Editore s.p.a., 1990.

Ragazzini, Giuseppe. Il Ragazzini, Dizionario Inglese Italiano Italiano
Inglese. Bologna: Zanichelli Editore, 2008.

Rakas, Frank G. Talking Business in Italian. USA: Barron's
Educational Series, 1987.

INTERNET SITES AND APPS

Aformarismo. www.aformarismo.com

Brainy Quote. www.brainyquote.com

Rizzo, Leonardo. Frasi Famose. Leosoft, 2010.

Glossary of Musical Terms,
www.classicalworks.com/html/glossary.html

Le 1000 Parole Più Usate In Italiano.
http://telelinea.free.fr/italien/1000_parole.html

Oracle ThinkQuest library.thinkquest.org/15413/

Wikipedia. Wikipedia Foundation, 2012.

Kellogg, Michael. <u>Word Reference Italian.</u>
WordReference.com LLC, 2012.

Dung, Ha. <u>Word Pair English–Italian Translation.</u>
DYSoftware, 2010.

INDEX

ACKNOWLEDGEMENTS

First off, deepest genuflections and special thanks to Jeanne Pettenati, Joan Fitting Scott, Marie Francis, Rita Mangone, Gemma Furlan, Carlotta Vallaro and Alberto Cardini, my editors stateside and in the Motherland. *Siete tutti carissimi!*

Jeanne Pettenati, mia carissima amica, cosa ti posso dire? Sei proprio un tesoro mandato dal cielo.

Joan Fitting Scott, ehi, ragazza, sei proprio pazza! Intelligentissima, piena di vita e troppo divertente. È una gioia conoscerti!

Rita Mangone, carissima amica mia, ti ringrazio dal cuore per l'aiuto che mi hai dato. È un grande piacere conoscervi; tu, Paolo e Pietro (monello!)

Alberto Cardini, Carlotta Vallaro e Pietro (birichino!) Grazie carissimi amici, per la vostra generosità. Quanto mi mancate...

Karina Castro, I simply could not have written this book without you! You are among the most caring, faithful and patient people on the planet. It has been scientifically proven that *YOU ARE THE BEST!*

Daisy Castro, tu est un trésor! Tu est comme le soleil quand tu entres dans une pièce; je m'amuse tellement avec toi! Merci pour tout ce que tu as fait avec Sierra, cela m'a laissé le temps d'écrire mon livre!

Julie Knox Battle, my photographer *e bellissima amica mia,* I am so lucky to be the recipient of your incredible talent, skill and style. *Grazie!*

Bill McKinney, Esquire Extraordinaire, thank you for encouraging me to get this published; it meant a lot! And many, many thanks, for your esteemed legal council.

Jan Ballard, my most excellent Graphic Designer, thanks for revamping my cover and typeface into something that will allow me to be seen in public, and hopefully with Italian flair!

Additional thanks go to Claudio Cirulli and family, Rosemary Rector, Janie Frank, Alan Levy, Guy Manning, and my rockin' students. And most of all, to Paul, Ben and Sierra with greatest love.

ABOUT THE AUTHOR
SUSAN ELIZABETH NUS

Forced to move to Europe as a child, Susan went, kicking and screaming.
Turned out she liked the place pretty well, after all, and hasn't been the
same since. Fascinated with the European cultural scene and all
those funny languages, she got a Bachelor's in Spanish from
GWU and a Master's in Italian from Catholic University in
Washington D.C. She has been privileged to live and
work in various parts of Europe and roam
throughout Europe extensively.

She lives in Ft. Worth, Texas with her first husband,
two offspring, three felines and a fish called Dante.
She adores traveling, books and languages.
Having taught Spanish, French and
Italian, Italian remains her
wildest passion.

She welcomes your comments and cognates at
italian.fluency@att.net

3108486R00189

Printed in Great Britain
by Amazon.co.uk, Ltd.,
Marston Gate.